THE MALE

ALFRED ALLAN LEWIS. THE MALE is the eleventh book to be published by Mr. Lewis during the last ten years. In researching this book, he has consulted with and interviewed experts in many fields pertaining to it as well as a cross section of males of all ages and from almost every conceivable walk of life.

Among Mr. Lewis' other books are: *Man of the World, Three Out of Four Wives,* and *Miss Elizabeth Arden.* He previously had successful careers as a playwright, television scenarist, publicist, and actor.

THE MALE
His Body, His Sex

Alfred Allan Lewis

with

Dr. Eli Bauman and Dr. Fred Klein

Anchor Press/Doubleday
Garden City, New York
1978

The Anchor Press edition is the first publication of *The Male* in book form.
It is published simultaneously in hard and paper covers.

Anchor Press edition: 1978

ISBN: 0-385-11121-5
Library of Congress Catalog Card Number 77–11368

"The Best Exercise For You" © 1977
by The New York Times Company.
Reprinted by permission.

CONTENTS

INTRODUCTION

When I first thought about writing this book, I began to ask myself questions I'd never really asked before, neither of myself nor of anybody else—questions about my body and my sexuality. I was astonished by my ignorance.

The sum of my knowledge about the male body, its structure and functioning, was the fact that I had one. It worked very satisfactorily for me, performing most of the tasks that were required of it and without too much difficulty. It never seriously bothered me, and consequently, I never seriously bothered about it.

All that I knew about my sexuality was that, in the main, I enjoyed it. On those few occasions when it failed me, I could choose from a vast assortment of easy rationales that allayed any guilts or doubts. It was always her fault or his fault or their fault; my mother, my father, my sexual partner, the people in the next room. I can't recall ever thinking that I alone was responsible for my own orgasm or lack of one. If I ever did, I pushed the thought to the back of my mind, where it got lost in a sea of trivia. Through the years, my ignorance had guaranteed a very pleasant degree of bliss.

I began to ask around and found that most of the men I knew were in the same position. If they'd had a specific physical ailment or sexual problem, they knew about that. You'll find some of their responses scattered throughout this book. But the extraordinary thing was that most of us had never investigated the whole of ourselves. We couldn't even remember most of the facts we had learned in school. We accepted traditional roles and attitudes. There was an indefinable suspicion that to ask questions about ourselves was somehow effete, an admission of ignorance that led to a lessening of self-esteem. Yet, most of us could see that the conscious act of not asking was making us an endangered species.

If my friends were of no help, I had to go it alone. The time had come to review my relationship to myself, starting with the early years.

By the time I was ten or eleven, I had gone through the entire range of childhood diseases: chicken pox, scarlet fever, mumps, two varieties of measles. But I'd never really known or asked the significance of any of them. They came and went without making any lasting impression on me.

I'd had my share of colds and sore throats and had done some malingering, when I'd wanted to play hookey to go to a movie or ball game or just stay home and listen to the radio (I am of a pretelevision generation). There were a good number of scrapes, bruises, cuts, falls, with the tears that followed them. But it was not until I was in my twenties that I broke a bone, and that was only in the small toe of my left foot.

From my mother, I'd had all of the clichéd admonitions about my well-being:

"Bundle up, you'll catch a cold."
"Don't get overheated, you'll get sick."
"Eat the vegetables, they're good for you."
"Don't eat so much candy, it's bad for you."

There were never any explanations of why these things were so, and I nodded and proceeded to do exactly as I pleased. I was never told anything about the mechanics of this body that was being so carefully protected. Whatever questions I had, and they were few enough, were evaded with catch-all homilies. My mother was adept at spotting an illness and prescribing for it, which was more than could be said for my father, but I think she had only the haziest notion of what might have caused it, of preventions and the deeper physical implications of it.

As I grew older, the childhood questions faded, never to be replaced by more adult ones. I was an average man blessed with good health and a strong body that gave me so little trouble that it could be ignored. Except for a tonsillectomy at the age of three, I'd never had any surgery and consequently listened with something less than complete attentiveness when other people discussed their symptoms and operations. What I didn't know certainly did not seem to be hurting me.

While writing this book, it was repeatedly brought home to me that I was treating my body with far less concern than I accorded any other machine that I owned.

I've never had influenza and have gone through winter after winter without bothering about flu shots. Asian flu was like beriberi, a cause of national concern only to the Chinese. My teeth are strong, and those regular checkups are ignored until my vanity tells me that they need a professional cleaning. Complete medical examinations are disregarded for years on end, or until somebody badgers me into going for one. I occasionally drink too much and, until recently, always smoked too much. I sometimes overeat for long periods, which are followed by crash diets only when I can no longer get my trousers to button around my waist. Exercise has become a sometime thing indulged in only when it is convenient. In other words, I am exactly like most of the men I know. I do not believe in the statistics on male mortality and illness, because I have not yet become one. Even as I catalogue these things, my greatest worry is that I might sound as if I'm boasting, and that some vengeful God will punish me for having an excess of pride.

I wonder if my disregard might not be based on some sort of atavistic belief in the strength and robustness of the masculine body. Could it be the original source of male chauvinism? Do I really believe that men die earlier *only* because we work harder and under greater stress than women? Have I convinced myself that sitting at a desk and writing a book is harder labor and creates more inner tension than a woman experiences running a household and raising children? If that's the case, why do I seem to know more elderly female writers than male writers? We have to look elsewhere for an answer to the question of comparative longevity.

The male body is physically stronger and more robust, but the female body has a greater capacity for endurance and more resiliency. There are already indications of this in the prenatal stage. Although there are many more male fetuses conceived than female fetuses, the rate of male stillbirths exceeds that of female stillbirths at every stage of pregnancy: the ratio is 2 to 1 at midpregnancy and 1½ to 1 in the ninth month.

Perhaps it is because only the fittest of male embryos survive that we are larger and more robust from birth. The average newborn male is slightly less than one-half pound heavier than his female counterpart. We are apt to be born more quickly and to be of normal size even in cases of early births. Judged by weight, premature babies are likely to be female.

Men are obviously not puny, nor do we have delicate constitutions. I wonder if our accelerated decline and demise might not be based upon ignorance, a lack of concern and knowledge about our bodies. With respect to enlightenment in this area, the female is naturally in a more fortunate position. Motherhood is a great teacher about the body. Giving birth to and rearing children make her sensitive to the development of the body and to the things that can go wrong with it, because she is responsible for a young body and life other than her own. Men have no comparable experience. This does not imply that a mother may not be equally dismissive of her own illnesses when they interfere with her duties. But that dismissal is not rooted in ignorance; more likely, it is negligence. She shares with her husband the delusion that she does not have the time to be ill.

With respect to knowledge about her sexuality, a woman is also more fortunate than a man. Menstruation begins somewhere around her twelfth year. This radical change forces a girl to begin to question the workings of her own body. Fortunately, there has been a sexual revolution, and there are very few contemporary mothers who will not discuss the causes and full implications of what is happening to her daughter.

The majority of boys begin to be aware of their erections much earlier. Until puberty, they are more likely to be sources of fascination than embarrassment. If they ask any questions, they are usually told that it's normal and not to worry about it. The only thing I can recall being told was to call it a penis rather than the names I'd learned from the older boys.

In my youth, there was little sex education in the schools, and hygiene was generally confined to clean fingernails, teeth, and ears. Until I was twelve or thirteen, I believed that babies were made by urinating into the vagina, which was why women's stomachs got so large during pregnancy. Most of us picked up whatever information we had by listening to other boys or from "dirty" books. We thought that the illustrations in a sex hygiene manual were pretty hot stuff. None of us asked any questions, because it implied that we hadn't "scored," and most of us did a great deal of lying or exaggerating about our prowess. It came as no surprise to us that Kinsey had found that the male reached his sexual peak so early in life. We were jaded by innocence. If we had any sexual creed, it was that intercourse conferred instant enlightenment on all things pertaining to the subject.

Despite the greater availability of sexual experience, I can't help wondering if the contemporary teenager is any more enlightened than I was at his age. Free access to pornography has given many adolescents dangerous illusions about staying power, speed and quantity of orgasms, even dimensions of genitalia distorted by camera angles. One feels some apprehension over what this can do to the sexual attitudes of the inexperienced. For some, sex and the drug culture have become inextricably enmeshed. For others, the warped has become the norm. There are those who are in the throes of traumatic conflict between their genuine religious convictions and the sexual permissiveness of their generation.

Surveys indicate that sex education courses do not furnish the adolescent boy with the information he seeks. Depending on the hang-ups of the instructor, they tend to hover between the puritanical and the prurient, generally settling on a safe middle course of lessons in the mechanics of reproduction and in the need for proper contraception and hygiene. The information simply does not answer his more pressing questions.

With the help of Drs. Eli Bauman and Fred Klein, I have learned a great deal about the workings of my body and the subtle convolutions of my sexual attitudes. I think that my enlightenment may lead to a longer and more fulfilled life. What I now know allays my fears in many areas in which those fears were groundless and makes me want to change other things where a lack of concern was detrimental to my future well-being.

This book will serve us men as an introduction to ourselves. Its aim is to help us to help ourselves to be happier, healthier, and wiser about the fundamentals of our lives.

I am grateful to all of the men who've allowed me to quote their frank observations of their own experiences. Some brought the problems that we have tried to solve; others gave us solutions that we might not otherwise have found.

All of my respondents proved that men and women are alike in possession of strong streaks of curiosity and intuition. With a little self-knowledge, curiosity can become enlightenment and intuition can become perception.

HIS BODY

1

THE ACT OF PROCREATION

Any discussion of physiology and sexuality must start with a discussion of procreation, for it is in that act that the two are most meaningfully joined. One of the anomalies of life is that, of all the body's major functions, it is only sex that is unnecessary to its existence. We cannot go on living without eating, sleeping, breathing, excreting, but we can live without sex. The majority of us would agree that it would not be much of a life, but it would not be an end of life. There are men and women who have never experienced an orgasm, let alone contributed to propagation, without any lessening of their life spans.

Although the individual can exist without it, sexual intercourse is essential to the continuation of the human species. How fortunate we are as a race that it is such a pleasure that most of us cannot get enough of it. We'll reserve exploration of the joys and variations of sex for later. For the moment, let's concentrate on its reproductive function. We all know what stimulates an orgasm; we know the ecstasy of it and the occasional complications and guilts. But most of us are much more knowledgeable about the mechanics of contraception than we are about the intricacies of reproduction.

"Did you take the pill?"

"Do I have to wear a condom?"

"Are you wearing a diaphragm or coil?"

"Is it your time of month?"

"Can I come in you?"

We're all fairly sure that we know how to make a baby, but what most of us really know is what act makes a baby. Even those of us who've been taught tend to disregard the actual mechanics. We're far more concerned with the rapture of ejaculation and the pride of fatherhood than in what came between the two and preceded both.

THE ANATOMY OF REPRODUCTION

A group of us fathers got together and decided that we'd take turns taking all the kids on an outing one Saturday a month. For my turn, I chose the Museum of Natural History. Kids always get a big bang out of the dinosaurs. Almost the first thing we saw in the museum was a plastic model of a woman's reproductive organs. Before I could hustle them by, the kids were all over it, their eyes wide open with curiosity. Now, they were only nine or ten years old. I began to wonder how they would take it. How much would they understand? Would they think it was dirty? Would they really know what they were looking at? Most of all, I was worrying about what I would answer if one of them should ask a question. Sure enough, one of them did. Before I could formulate a response, this little fellow—he couldn't have been more than nine —cries out that he knows. My first reaction was—little smart ass. And then I felt very relieved. I was off the hook. So I told him to explain to the others. Well, he had it all down pat. There were times when I had to look at the legend to make sure. Because I didn't know as much of the technicalities as he did. And I've got three children. Then I felt enormously proud of him. And the way the others were listening. These kids were something else. I could remember going to an art museum with my class when I was about their age. We came into a gallery filled with these huge Rubens nudes. I was trying to hold back the giggles so hard that I almost peed in my pants. The teacher was very earnest and, when she asked what we saw when we looked at the paintings, it was too much for me. Laughing my head off at how clever I was, I blurted out: "titties and ass."

The paired female sex organs are called the ovaries, and at birth they contain several hundred thousand immature ova (the female sex cells), each surrounded by clusters of cells called follicles. Only 375 ova will mature during a woman's span of fertility from puberty to menopause.

The Fallopian tubes lead from the ovaries to the uterus (or womb). Once every twenty-eight days, a mature ovum will be released by its follicles and drop into a Fallopian tube to await fertilization. This usually alternates each month from one ovary and tube to the other.

Sperm is manufactured in the two male testes at the phenomenal rate of ten to thirty billion a month. Sperm can only be manufactured at about 95 degrees Fahrenheit, which is slightly lower than body temperature. For this reason, the testes are externally suspended in the scrotum just below and behind the penis. The left testis is generally a little lower and larger than the right. If it isn't, it is no cause for alarm. Like the penis, the size of the scrotum normally has nothing to do with its proper functioning.

The young spermatozoa take over two months to mature. During the incubation, they are stored in the epididymis, twenty feet of tightly coiled tubes adjacent to the testes, where they remain even after they are fully developed until released in an orgasm, or until they disintegrate and return to the testes.

In each ejaculation, between 78,000,000 and 787,000,000 sperm are released into a woman's vagina. Obviously, the higher the sperm count, the greater the possibility of pregnancy. But fertility has been known to happen even when the sperm count is below the minimum average. It only takes one sperm to do the job.

In its desire for reproduction, the male body is obviously profligate as well as pleasurable. The semen released in orgasm surges into the vagina. Some of the sperm remains in the uterus; some enters the resting Fallopian tube; the remainder enters the Fallopian tube containing the waiting ovum. Despite their vast number, none of the sperm may make contact, for there is no chemical attraction between the ovum and them. Call it hit-and-miss, blunder, lucky (or unlucky) accident, predestination, act of God, fate, or what you will, there is no biological reason why they do or do not stumble upon each other.

In the beginning, there are many sperm involved in the attack on the ovum, all excreting an enzyme that eats away the outer surface until one sperm can enter. The moment this happens, the surface hardens again, excluding the other sperms.

For two or three days, the cell formed by the single sperm and ovum travels down the Fallopian tube, splitting many times along the way. By the time it reaches the uterus, it is a hollow 100-cell ball of no determined sex. It is not until the ninth week of pregnancy that distinguishing sexual characteristics begin to develop. For over two months, there is no way of telling whether the fetus will become a male or female. But as we will see, the sex has already been determined by the composition of the sperm.

A LESSON IN GENETICS

A young woman came to consult me as a gynecologist. She was unmarried and unmistakably pregnant. I asked her what she planned to do and she told

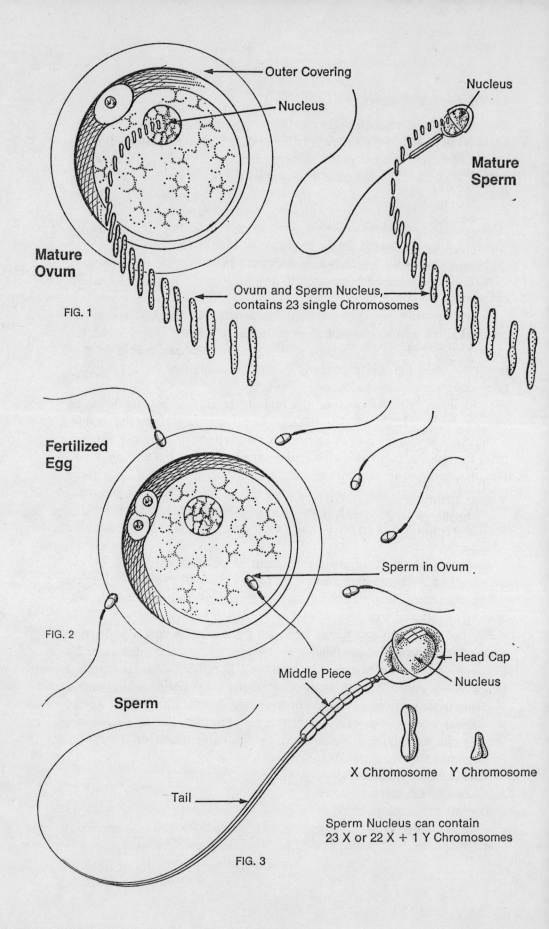

Outer Covering

Nucleus

Nucleus

Mature Sperm

Mature Ovum

FIG. 1

Ovum and Sperm Nucleus, contains 23 single Chromosomes

Fertilized Egg

FIG. 2

Sperm in Ovum

Middle Piece

Sperm

Head Cap

Nucleus

Tail

X Chromosome   Y Chromosome

Sperm Nucleus can contain 23 X or 22 X + 1 Y Chromosomes

FIG. 3

me not to worry. "I'll marry the father of my child as soon as I find out who he is." I was puzzled, and she explained that she was simultaneously having affairs with two young men. One was blond with blue eyes, and the other was dark with brown eyes. They both loved her and wanted to marry her. She would make her choice after the child was born. She said: "If my baby is fair, then the blond is the father, and I'll marry him. If it's dark, then it's the other one, and he's the one I'll marry." I could only marvel at the sophistication of this young person. And the ignorance. Did she really think that paternity could be proved by coloration? Or was she fooling herself and me? She seemed to know everything about modern life styles and nothing about old-fashioned biological facts of life. I suggested that, if she was determined to make her choice on the basis of which man had fathered her child, a blood test would be much more convincing evidence than the color of his hair. But that was out of the question, as neither knew of the other's existence, and each thought that he alone was her lover. I wondered what she would do if the child looked like her. Chestnut hair and gray eyes.

There are an infinite number of cells in the human body. Life begins with a cell and grows through its multiplication. Each cell contains twenty-three pairs of chromosomes, and each chromosome contains numberless genes, those mysterious entities that carry the basic factors of heredity and determine everything about us from our size to our coloration to our physical features to tendencies to certain diseases—even, it is thought, to our intelligence.

In the growth cells (those of which skin, bone, organs, etc. are composed), the chromosomes double up before the cell divides into two cells, each with twenty-three pairs of chromosomes containing the same genetic structure, properties, and capacities as the original cell. The cells of our bodies are constantly dying and being replaced—thus, growth continues as long as we live.

Reproductive, or sex, cells (the sperm and ovum) are different. The chromosomes do not double before they divide. The result is a cell with twenty-three *single* chromosomes. When the sperm enters or fertilizes the ovum, a new growth cell is created having the necessary twenty-three pairs of chromosomes—one of each pair coming from the male, and the other from the female. This is the beginning of a new life.

Each chromosome is represented by the symbol X. One might say that this stands for the unknown factors of heredity that it contains. The paired chromosomes then are XX. This is true of all twenty-three pairs in the life cell that will ultimately develop into a female child.

In the cell that will produce a male child, there is an exception in the twenty-third pairing. This exceptional chromosome (only one in a total of forty-six) that produces masculinity is called Y. Looking at it, Y is a fairly accurate symbolic representation of the male sex organs. In that male-producing cell, twenty-two pairs are XX and the twenty-third is XY.

The Y factor can only be transmitted from father to son. The female cell has only XX pairings and, when it splits to create an ovum, there can only be single X chromosomes. When the male cell splits, one sperm has all X chromosomes, and the other has the one Y chromosome. If the former fertilizes an ovum, the child will be a girl; if the latter does, it will be a boy. There is no way of predicting which sperm it will be; so, in the final analysis, our sex is a random thing.

Because the new life cell has chromosomes from both parents, it obviously carries the genes of both, which makes it possible for the resultant baby to have its father's nose and its mother's eyes. A child may even most strongly resemble one of its grandparents.

This resemblance is only a part of the wonder and mystery of genes. For all we know, they carry characteristics and traits that go back endless generations. Who can tell what else they may be carrying forward: instincts, fears, beliefs, patterns of human behavior from long-gone ages. It is possible that the sum of all that science has uncovered thus far is only the beginning of genetic knowledge. What we accept as a legacy of recorded history from the past may also be written in the essence of human life. We may yet prove to have a natural inheritance of riches beyond our present concepts.

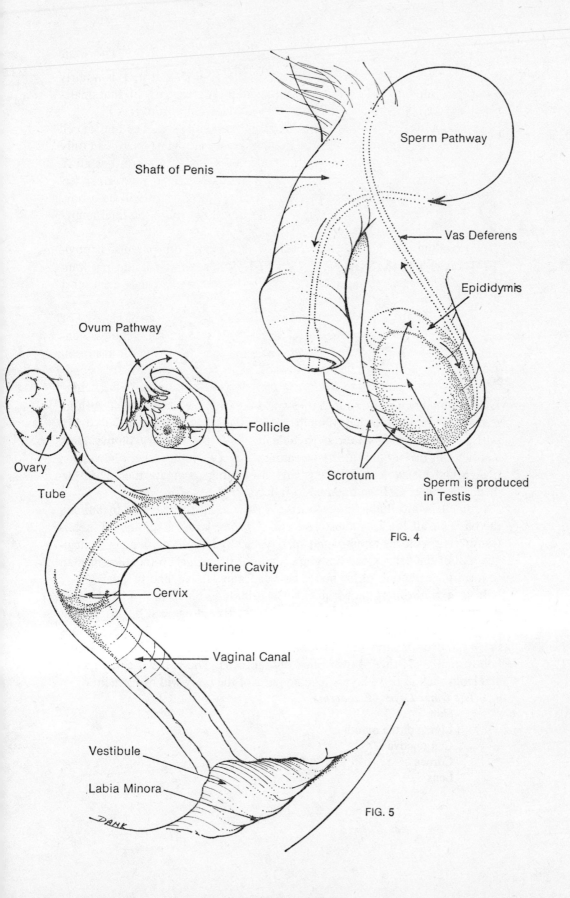

Sperm Pathway

Shaft of Penis

Vas Deferens

Epididymis

Ovum Pathway

Follicle

Ovary

Tube

Scrotum

Sperm is produced in Testis

Uterine Cavity

FIG. 4

Cervix

Vaginal Canal

Vestibule

Labia Minora

DANK

FIG. 5

2

THE ANATOMY AND SYSTEMS

Every human being comes into this world equipped with a body of such intricacy and perfection that, though science understands the workings of its parts, no scientist has ever been able to solve the mystery of the total. Throughout history and in the literature of every country, there have been benign and malevolent Frankensteins attempting to create their monster-men. They have all been doomed to failure.

From the unicellular ameba to the vastly sophisticated human animal, the basis of all life is a substance called *protoplasm:* a semiliquid, semi-transparent, colorless compound of oxygen, hydrogen, carbon, and nitrogen. All of the cells of the body are made of it and group together in man to form the essentials of his body: bones, organs, tissue, and blood.

It is extraordinary how quickly a primitive blueprint of that body develops in the protoplasmic embryo. The fertilized egg cell begins to split almost immediately after conception. As we've said, by the time it has made the two- or three-day journey to the uterus, it has shaped itself into a hollow ball consisting of over one hundred cells. The ball has three layers, and from each of these layers specific parts of the body will be formed:

The Outer Layer (Ectoderm)
    Skin
    Lining of the mouth
    Conjunctiva
    Cornea
    Lens

The Basic Systems

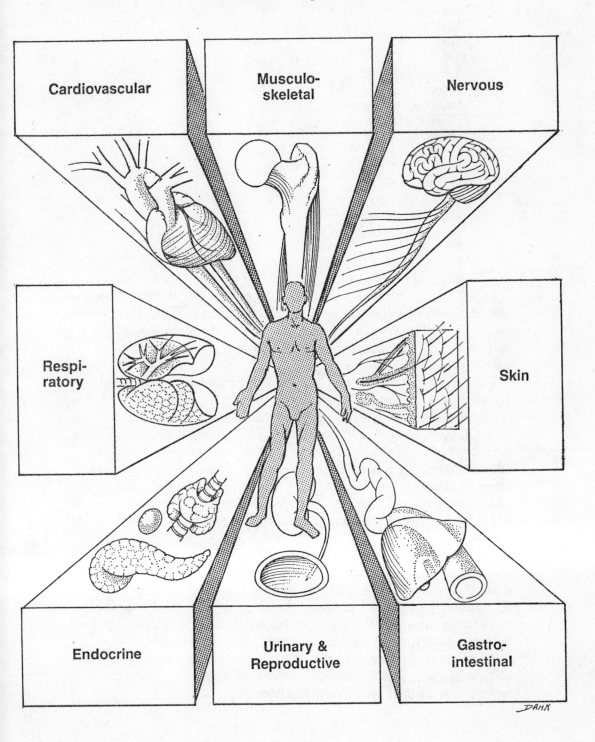

FIG. 6

The Middle Layer (*Mesoderm*)
  Brain
  Spinal cord
  Eye
  Sclera of eye
  Kidneys
  Reproductive organs
  Heart
  Uterus
  Cartilage
  Bone
  Skeletal muscle
  Outer wall of the gut
The Inner Layer (*Endoderm*)
  Inner wall of the gut
  Thyroid
  Liver
  Pancreas

By the time the infant is born, all of those parts that started to develop so soon after conception will have attained the form they will keep for the rest of his life. They will grow; their functions and capacities will expand; they will inevitably atrophy and decay. But the fundamentals will be unchanged from birth to death.

The physiognomy and color of man will differ from race to race and geographical area to area. Whether or not a man is pleasing to the eye is largely a question of esthetics and custom. In our society, thin is in. In others, it is the fat Buddha-like man who is considered beautiful and made the subject of adoration. Blue eyes can remind one person of friendly skies and another of icy waters. Beauty is indeed in the eye of the beholder. Shorn of considerations of masculine beauty or ugliness, the things that remain constant in all men of all races and cultures are the frames on which these externals are hung and the organs and life forces that reside within those frames.

The skeletal superstructure is made of bones: there are over two hundred in the body. Any damage to them will necessarily impede the movement of the outer parts. It may also damage the inner workings or organs by abrasion, puncture, or intrusion. As we grow older, the bones become more brittle and easier to break. The same fall that a child takes, with no harm to his body, can cripple an old man for the rest of his life.

All of the working parts of the body are grouped into eight remarkably efficient systems. For the purposes of examining man's physiology, it is easier to discuss these systems one at a time.

These systems are:

I. Skin
II. Musculoskeletal
III. Nervous
IV. Respiratory
V. Cardiovascular
VI. Gastrointestinal
VII. Urinary and Reproductive
VIII. Endocrine

3

THE SKIN SYSTEM

The skin is the membrane covering of the entire body. It is the largest of the systems, stretching some 20 square feet over the body of a man of average height and contributing 16 per cent of his total weight. Its color has been one of the greatest sources of hatred in the world, and its touch one of the most significant sources of love.

TOUCH

In his best-selling book *I'm O.K.—You're O.K.,* Dr. Thomas A. Harris said:

> The infant (at birth) is flooded with overwhelming, unpleasant stimulations, and the feelings resulting in the child are, according to Freud, the model for all later anxiety.
>
> Within moments the infant is introduced to a rescuer, another human being who picks him up, wraps him in warm coverings, supports him, and begins the comforting act of "stroking." This is the point of Psychological Birth. It is a reconciliation, a restatement of closeness. It turns on his will to live. Stroking, or repetitious bodily contact, is essential to his survival. Without it he will die, if not physically, then psychologically. Physical death from a condition known as marasmus once was a frequent occurrence in foundling homes

where there was a deprivation of this early stroking. There was no physical cause to explain these deaths except the absence of essential stimulation.

The extreme sensitivity of the skin is one of the essentials to the growth of a man. It is through stroking that he receives his first messages of love and security. With its stinging reaction of pain, the slap is one of the oldest means of teaching him a lesson (although it may not be the best one). Touching and being touched are fundamental for sexual arousal in most of us.

If a woman doesn't know how to use her hands, I don't want to shack up with her. I don't care how good she is with the rest of her body, I get a hard on from being caressed, and I don't mean only my penis. Touch me all over, and we're off to the races.

Most of the erogenous zones are located in the skin and, for many men, an erection starts with lightly stroking an arm or having sensitive fingertips glide gently over the face and neck. In some cases, stroking parts of the body, other than the genitalia, can even produce an orgasm.

PIGMENTATION

In addition to its contribution of color and touch, the skin serves the body in several other ways: protecting other tissues from injury, barring the entry of many foreign and harmful bodies, preventing the loss of water, regulating the temperature, assisting in excretion via perspiration, serving as a reservoir for food and water, acting as the origin of vitamin D.

The epidermis contains openings for the sweat glands and hair follicles. One of its most important functions is to protect the body from the on-slaughts of bacteria and ultraviolet rays. Infections, such as boils, sometimes originate in it, but generally, though the symptoms may appear on the epidermis, the actual disturbance is caused by some disorder beneath it or by some outside force such as a laceration or overexposure to sun or frost.

There are no blood vessels in the epidermis, but it does contain the various pigments that give us our coloration. The most important is the dark pigment, *melanin,* which provides a shield against the sun's ultraviolet rays. To put it another way, the epidermis gives us what is commonly called our complexions, while disturbances below determine its quality.

There are three basic ethnic types: Caucasoid, Mongoloid, and Negroid.

The Skin

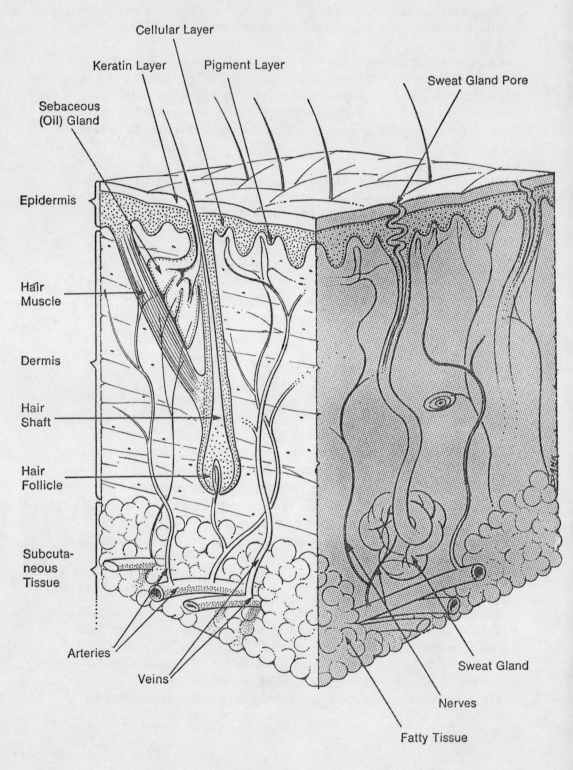

Cellular Layer

Keratin Layer

Pigment Layer

Sweat Gland Pore

Sebaceous
(Oil) Gland

Epidermis

Hair
Muscle

Dermis

Hair
Shaft

Hair
Follicle

Subcuta-
neous
Tissue

Arteries

Veins

Sweat Gland

Nerves

Fatty Tissue

FIG. 7

The colors of their skin have often been a cause of lethal prejudice in every part of the world. Although we tend to categorize them, respectively, as white, yellow, and black, the true colors run to much greater extremes and are apt to be the result of the body's defense against the dangers of climatic extremes. Geography, the location of racial origin, has more to do with color than does intermarriage.

Let us take a look at various examples of the Caucasoid, or "white" man. The pinkish-white Nordic type lives far from the dangers of direct ultraviolet rays and has relatively little melanin in his pigment. But the native of southern India is also a Caucasoid. He lives in the Tropic Zone, where the direct ultraviolet rays make a direct and relentless attack upon him. His skin is a dark brown, darker than the Negroid native to Temperate Zones, whose skin is sallow with a medium amount of melanin. It is the black Equatorial African whose body produces the highest quantity of melanin.

The greatest variation in pigment is probably found among the Mongoloids, or "yellow" men. We tend to think in terms of the Orientals, but the whitest of all men, the Eskimo, is also Mongoloid, as is the red American Indian and the brown Polynesian. The skin of the Mongoloid contains a large amount of *keratin,* a fibrous protein that acts as a shield against the reflected glare of the desert and snow that cover such large areas of the regions in which they are indigenous. Keratin is also the chemical base of epidermal growths: nails, claws, horns, and hair.

WARTS, MOLES, AND SKIN CANCER

I've always had a tendency to manufacture warts. I never paid much attention to them. I certainly never went to a doctor. They'd appear and, after a while, they'd disappear. This one persistent little bugger developed into a sore. At first, I thought I must've irritated it, and that it would heal and go away like all the others. But it didn't. Well, you know, I'd heard all that stuff about skin cancer. Hell, you can't live on this earth without hearing. So I decided I'd better go to a doctor. And a good thing I did too.

Melanoma is the form of skin cancer associated with melanin. If caught in the early stages, it is easily cured, but if ignored, it can be fatal. Metastasis starts, and it spreads to other parts of the body via the blood and lymph vessels.

Skin cancer first appears in one of two ways:

1. A small, nonhealing, indolent ulcer (break in the skin)
2. The enlargement and/or ulceration of an already existent wart or mole

A deeply pigmented mole can appear on any part of the body. It may resemble a wart or be no more than a discolored or deeply pigmented spot.

For some reason, these spots used to be called beauty marks and were considered very attractive. In the nineteen-twenties and -thirties, women would use eyebrow pencils to accentuate existing ones or to produce them artificially: in the eighteenth century, both sexes would paste on fancifully cut tiny black patches that simulated them.

Moles are immediately suspect. Most of them can and should be removed. The few that can't should be watched carefully for any signs of growth or ulceration.

A wart is caused by a virus. It is a horny knot that can develop anywhere on the body and will often disappear within a few months. Even if it is one of the ordinary now-you-see-it-now-you-don't variety, it can and should be removed by a physician. It's a painless procedure that can be done right in the examination room. Why take chances? At best, warts and moles are unattractive, and, at worst, they are dangerous.

For over twenty years my wife and I were sun worshipers. We couldn't get enough of it. If there was a nude beach nearby, so much the better. The result of this mania is very easy to tell. My wife looks like a prune, and I developed skin cancer.

The most common type of skin cancer is called *epithelioma*. It is caused by prolonged exposure of unprotected skin to the sun. While melanin generally provides effective protection for a dark or black skin, white people living in tropical climates or indulging in outdoor activities have a high propensity to skin cancer.

All skin cancer is easily detected in the early stages and is slow to develop. Consequently, most cases can be cured by surgery or radiation treatment before metastasis. This is not license to overindulge in sun bathing. Even if we're lucky enough to avoid skin cancer, there are many other dangers. There is always the possibility of sunstroke and heat prostration. A bad burn can lead to hospitalization or extreme discomfort for days, followed by irritating and unsightly peeling. In our youth-oriented world, we run the risk of looking old before our time, as the sun dehydrates our skin, causing a network of wrinkles all over our faces and bodies.

Until World War I, a pale skin was considered desirable by both sexes. We've since allowed the advertising propagandists for bathing suits, resorts, and sun creams to convince us that a tanned body is a sign of health and prosperity. A sunburn has become a status symbol, especially during the winter months, for it indicates the leisure and means to follow the sun south or to the ski resorts. We've been duped by allowing ourselves to be judged by the color of other people's profits. There is even a unisex line of sun-bronzing cosmetics. We can now paint on our tans and give the illusion of prosperity. Actually, these cosmetics are more beneficial than the real thing, for they usually contain moisturizers that are good for the skin combined with harmless coloring agents.

If a tan is too irresistible to do without, apply liberal layers of sun screens, oils, or creams. Expose yourself very gradually so that the melanin in your skin has a chance to build up a natural resistance to the harmful ultraviolet rays.

ALLERGIES AND SKIN DISEASES

Synthetic fabrics saved my life. I mean it. I'm allergic to wool. The minute I get near it, I break out in the damnedest rash you ever saw.

The skin is our greatest natural defense against foreign substances that can harm our bodies. As any environmentalist will tell you, there are certain chemicals that will always produce violent reactions in it. There are others to which only certain people have allergenic responses.

Among the most common substances causing skin irritations are: fabrics, foods, plants, chemicals, dyes, insecticides, and cosmetics. These allergic reactions sometimes take the form of a nettle rash (hives)—a series of smooth, raised, pinkish and itchy bumps. Another common response is eczema*—blisters which rupture, revealing the skin beneath, dry out, then flake off in scales. Antiallergenic medicine can help, but the only sure cure is to make certain not to come in contact with the irritating agent.†

I had eczema when I was a kid, but that's something kids can live with. But when psoriasis developed in my adolescence, it was like the end of the world. Who'd ever want to touch me? How could I ask a girl out on a date? What was I supposed to do—stand around and flake all over her?

The worst thing about psoriasis is what it does to the appearance of the skin, for it is not a serious disease. It usually first occurs somewhere between the ages of five and twenty-five and lasts a lifetime. It can appear on any part of the body but most often attacks the joints, legs, arms, and scalp, manifesting itself as blotches covered with flaking scales. On the scalp it is sometimes mistaken for dandruff.

Psoriasis most often appears in cold weather and abates during the

---

* In infants and young children, eczema is believed to be a nerve condition rather than an allergic reaction.
† When allergies attack the respiratory system, the results are far more serious—sometimes fatal, as the breathing apparatus contracts, causing asphyxiation.

warmer seasons. Although there is no cure, the condition can be alleviated by the application of crude coal tar and ultraviolet treatments.

Psoriasis is sometimes hereditary, but it is not contagious. The most damaging effects can be what it does to the psyche. The sufferer is always aware of disfigurement. He sometimes becomes ashamed of his body and fearful of entering relationships. He should make a sustained attempt to raise his own consciousness. His essence and his worth are not skin deep. Those who are truly attracted to him are not attracted to his surface. That sort of attraction remains on the surface even with the most physically perfect men. Those who love him see beyond the problems of his skin, or they do not love him and are not worthy of his love.

THE NAILS

The nails are thickened parts of the epidermis that protect the tips of the fingers and toes, are useful in self-defense, and are important to manual dexterity.

When I interview people for a job, the applicants with dirty or chewed-up nails get a very low priority. They're a turn-off to people they come in contact with. And they're a turn-off to me.

Good grooming and physical culture often come to an abrupt stop at the tips of the fingers. Broken, dirty, or gnawed nails can be a detriment to one's professional, social, and sexual life.

The brittle nail that breaks easily is often an indication of nutritional imbalance. Drinking more milk may completely clear up the problem. Curing oneself of nail biting takes greater effort. Although it is often symptomatic of a nervous person, it is a habit and, like all habits, can only be broken by an exercise in will power.

There is no excuse for dirty nails. It's simply a question of paying attention to grooming. Unfortunately, many men dismiss manicures as a symbol of either the effete or the Mafia. Actually, most of us can use one for health as well as hygiene. The hardening agent in polishes helps to protect these essential parts of our bodies.

ACNE

The dermis is directly under the epidermis. It contains all of the links to the rest of the body as well as the sweat glands, hair roots, and sebaceous glands, which are adjacent to the roots and secrete an oil, sebum, that prevents the hairs from drying up and breaking.

The sebum is secreted directly into the hair follicles and also acts as waterproofing and an antibacteriological agent. Its production accelerates at puberty as the body begins to produce *sexual hair* in the pubic area and armpits, as well as on the face, neck, back, and chest.

At first, my parents thought it was pimples, and that I was allergic to something. But is was acne. And it was hell.

Acne is an infection brought on by a disorder in the sebaceous glands and hair follicles. It usually occurs in adolescence and, though its cause is actually unknown, it might be an emotional reaction to the body changes or simply a defect in the regulation of the production of sebum. Pus-producing sores appear primarily on the face, neck, back, and chest. They leave scars when they heal, and the ravages remain after the disease has disappeared.

I can't see how I can win. The sun bathing helps my acne and makes me look better. But it may give me cancer. I don't know—the way I feel most of the time, when I look at this face of mine—I think, maybe, I'd rather have the cancer.

Little can be done to help the acne sufferer. There are no cures; the known medications only promote peeling, which unblocks some of the pores, releasing the pus. Diet does not help true acne, although it does clear up many adolescent rashes that are mistaken for it.

Ultraviolet rays are good for two reasons: the peeling action and the tan, which aids cosmetically by covering the scars. Extreme caution must be exercised in sun bathing, for all of the reasons already discussed and for another one: the newly opened enlarged pores can become clogged by lotions or creams. The safest ultraviolet treatments are those given under medical supervision.

The way my family was overreacting, you'd think I had smallpox. I wanted to say, "Relax, folks, I may not get laid much with acne, but it won't keep me out of law school."

Acne is a very sensitive condition for the young and can have grave psychological repercussions. The boy is already terribly self-conscious. His agony should not be intensified by too great a fuss within the family, but not making a big deal of it does not mean it should be ignored.

The parents should make an appointment for him to see a physician privately. When an adolescent male is taken to see a doctor, he may make a subconscious equation between adult medicine and pediatrics. He may feel reduced to the level of a child and, consequently, emasculated. It's never too early to start inculcating a young male with the idea that seeing a doctor is an adult action. He should be made secure in the knowledge that what transpires between a physician and him is personal and private. Proper handling during a male's formative years can eliminate part of the emasculation equation that he may later make with illness.

BLEMISHES

It often seems that all of the emotional confusions of puberty are written on the faces of the young in the form of skin disorders. Overnight, the freckle-faced kid seems to be replaced by the pimple-faced adolescent.

> I had a face as smooth as a baby's ass. Then, all of sudden, it looked like the Rocky Mountains. Somebody told me it came from masturbating. So I stopped. But the pimples didn't go away. In four years, I must have used enough calamine lotion to float a battleship.

What we call pimples can be any of a broad range of skin disorders or rashes. One thing that is certain is that masturbation has nothing to do with any of them. Before attempting any remedies, the sufferer should consult his doctor to try to discover the cause.

Skin blemishes are symptomatic of innumerable ailments. Among the most common are blocked pores. They usually do not happen in childhood but can become a recurring nuisance at any point after puberty. A minute plug clogs the pore. When it remains beneath the epidermis, it is a whitehead; when it rises to the surface and mingles with atmospheric dirt, it is a blackhead.

Whiteheads and blackheads can appear on any part of the face, neck, and shoulders, but they are most likely to be found on the forehead, nose, and across the cheekbones. A good way to discourage them is to wash the susceptible areas with warm water and a medicated soap. Those who suffer from them should eat plenty of fresh fruit and vegetables; avoid all greasy and fried foods; stick to lean meats, fish, and poultry that have been broiled, roasted, or, best of all, boiled.

The worst thing that one can do is to squeeze the whitehead or blackhead. Antiseptic cleansing and heat are the best remedies. If one is impatient with natural cures, there are extractors available that can usually remove the clog without damage to the skin. Any pressure or squeezing can leave a permanent pock in place of the removed clog.

A clogged pore can result in an ingrown hair in the shaved areas of the chin or neck. Do not remove it with a tweezer. Do not touch the infected area at all, or the infection is likely to spread. A doctor may be able to prescribe a medication. It is essential to follow the hygienic and dietary advice we've already given for clogged pores.

HAIR—GRAYING AND BALDING

The chief functions of hair are to protect and to regulate the temperature of the body. Scalp hair differs ethnically for the same reasons as skin pigmentation. Mongoloids have straight hair, which retains heat. Negroids have extremely curly or "kinky" hair which keeps the scalp cool by providing natural channels for the circulation of perspiration. Caucasoids have wavy hair with variations from nearly straight among Nordics to curly, often close to Negroid, among those from warmer climates such as the Mediterranean people.

In addition to sexual and scalp hair, every part of our bodies, except the palms and soles, is covered with a very fine, almost pigment-free body hair. This fuzz is often invisible to the eyes, but it is sensitive to touch.

I once knew a girl who could make me hot just by running her fingers over my body. She barely grazed my skin, but I got this absolutely sensational feeling.

The "touching" nerves are linked to the hair follicles. That's why we feel pain when the hairs are pulled or twisted. It's also why many of us experience a pleasure that can be erotic when we are merely very gently stroked.

I'd been with the same company for almost twenty-five years when they let me go. As far as they were concerned, I was over the hill. Christ, I wasn't even fifty. But it was the same wherever I went for a job interview. Oh, they couched it in meaningless expressions like, "You're overqualified," or, "You wouldn't be happy here." What they meant was I was too old. I lopped off a few years by ignoring my Army service, of which I'd always been rather proud. The gray flannel was retired to the attic, and a safari jacket became the uniform of the day. My gray hair turned brown overnight—with the help of Miss Clairol, of all things. At first, I felt like a damned fool. But when I got another job, that feeling left, and I told myself that I was only negotiating the system.

As one grows older, the loss of pigment in hair is a natural phenomenon. The manner in which this happens is hereditary and cannot be reversed except by artificial coloring. There's nothing wrong with dyeing your hair, if you think it will increase your professional chances or your personal attractiveness. It's best to have it done by a professional hair colorist. The do-it-yourself jobs are too often patently artificial and serve to accentuate the very thing you're trying to disguise.

When I first started to go bald, I panicked. I hated the whole idea. I tried a rug, but it made me nervous. I was aways afraid it was going to come off at the wrong time. Then I happened to see *Kojak* on television. What Barbra Streisand did for girls with lousy noses, Telly Sevalas did for me. I shaved my head, and suddenly I felt very sexy.

The three types of hair are constantly dying and being replaced by new hair. Naturally, it is the scalp hair that most concerns us and, with age, both sexes permanently lose a certain amount of it. What actually happens is that it dies and is replaced by the fine, almost invisible body hair. When this is due to emotional stress, disease, or malnutrition, the process can be reversed or halted by eliminating the cause. But the majority of men suffer from male-pattern baldness controlled by heredity factors in the male hormones. Despite the claims of medications, shampoos, and scalp-treatment centers, nothing can be done to reverse the process. The most that we can do is take care of what we have by careful grooming, shave it all off, or get the best wig that we can afford. Hair transplants are costly, painful, possibly harmful, and offer no guarantee of success. Hair weaving can destroy healthy hair and is constantly in need of expensive care.

There are three types of hair: dry, oily, and normal. A shampoo made for a particular type should be chosen and used one or more times a week, depending upon the degree of oiliness. There is no cure for dandruff, although certain medicated shampoos may slow the process of scaling. A hair dressing should be used that is consistent with the quality and texture of the hair. Sprays should be avoided. At best, they split hair; at worst, they completely destroy it.

LICE AND CRABS

In the town where I grew up, the movie house was called the Classic. But all of us kids renamed it the Itch. If you got so involved with the film that you scrunched down and leaned your head against the back of the seat, you were sure to come home with nits.

•

Listen, I honestly did pick up a case of crabs at the Turkish bath. But do you think my wife believed me? What a hassle!

Scalp and pubic hairs are subject to lice. In the scalp they're known by the name given to their eggs: "nits." In the pubic hair they're called "crabs" because of their crablike shape.

Crabs can be transmitted by unlaundered bed linen, towels, or undergarments that were used by somebody already infected with them, but they are most commonly transmitted through sexual contact.

Nits are contracted from somebody who already has them or from combs, brushes, hats, or towels used by them. People have also contracted them by leaning their heads against the backs of seats, especially fibrous ones, in public places.

Body lice cause extremely irritating and socially embarrassing itches. They can easily be exterminated by any number of painless remedies on sale without prescription at pharmacies. The application usually has to be repeated several times, because these insects are extremely tenacious. Simply keeping clean will not do the trick, for they, and their eggs, are impervious to regular soaps and shampoos.

Crabs and nits are not dangerous, but they're unpleasant and difficult to explain to one's sexual partner. At the first sign, the victim should delouse himself.

PERSPIRATION

Perspiration is necessary to the health of the body, and impolite only in regard to the offensive odor that may accompany it. There are those who think we Americans are too conscious of the aromatic part and accordingly have developed a multimillion-dollar deodorant industry. We won't quarrel with that one way or another except to wonder if those who think we're hypersensitive have ever gotten a good whiff of a Parisian cab driver or chambermaid.

Whether or not we like the odor, we have to sweat. One of the important functions of skin is to regulate the body temperature; another is to get rid of poisonous wastes. An essential part of excretion is carried out by the sweat (sudoriferous) glands. We shed about one-half pint of sweat a day.

Most of it is water, but it contains noxious chemicals dangerous to the system and sodium chloride, which accounts for its salty taste. A major portion evaporates on making contact with the air, but when the body gets too hot from exertion or when the outside air heats up, the sweat cannot evaporate as quickly and gathers on the skin.

The distasteful smell that we associate with sweat actually comes from the secretions of the apocrine glands, which become active after puberty. These glands are located in the armpits, genital, and perineal (between anus and scrotum) areas.

There are any number of deodorants on the market that retard the effects of the glands under the arms. There are also deodorants in many soaps and body powders. The problem with these products is that they often cause irritating rashes. Should this happen, stop using the product immediately and switch to another, making certain that it is made with a different chemical base.

Recently a number of deodorants (for both men and women) have been marketed that are specifically designed for the genital regions. They are of questionable value, and some may even be harmful. Daily washing of the area and changes of underwear should take care of the problem. Sometimes it is necessary to switch from jockey or bikini briefs to boxer shorts. If there is a sufficient problem to be conscious of it, tight trousers and underwear only aggravate it.

We live in our skin and are often judged by the look of it. We must take care of it. Any defects should be attended to immediately and professionally if necessary. We should protect it from extremes of climate and from harmful pollutants in the air. With healthy skin we'll look younger, feel stronger, and live longer.

4

THE MUSCULOSKELETAL SYSTEM

The weight of the average man should be distributed: 43 per cent in muscle, 14 per cent in bone, 29 per cent in organs, blood, skin, connective tissue, and 14 per cent in fat. As we can see, almost three-quarters of our weight is allotted to the musculoskeletal system.

We usually think of muscles in terms of those we can see and feel, the ones that adorn our bones and enable us to move, lift, pull, and push. There are others that are even more important to life. Indeed, a man can be completely paralyzed and live, so long as the involuntary muscles that control his organs are functioning.

There are three types of muscle tissue in the body:
1. Skeletal (or voluntary)
2. Smooth (or involuntary)
3. Cardiac (heart)

In a general way, the smooth muscles help all of the other systems to function and are responsible for such activities as breathing, digestion, and excretion. The cardiac muscles keep the heart beating and pumping blood through the body.

The skeletal muscles are the ones with which we are most consciously concerned. Not only are we more aware of their functions, but they are the ones that help to define the body's silhouette, the ones that give it an a esthetically or sensually pleasing shape. Many men consider them their most conspicuous embellishments (in some cases, accomplishments).

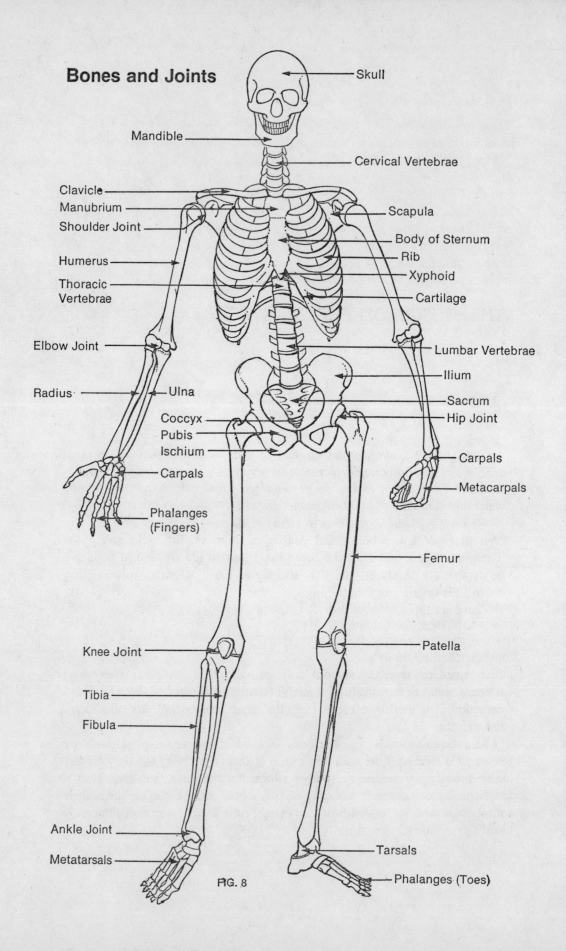

Bones and Joints

Skull

Mandible

Cervical Vertebrae

Clavicle

Manubrium

Shoulder Joint

Scapula

Body of Sternum

Humerus

Rib

Xyphoid

Thoracic Vertebrae

Cartilage

Elbow Joint

Lumbar Vertebrae

Ilium

Radius

Ulna

Sacrum

Coccyx

Hip Joint

Pubis

Ischium

Carpals

Carpals

Metacarpals

Phalanges (Fingers)

Femur

Knee Joint

Patella

Tibia

Fibula

Ankle Joint

Tarsals

Metatarsals

Phalanges (Toes)

FIG. 8

These are the ones that they build, flex, display—the muscles that provide an often deceptive measure of masculine beauty, strength, and health.

Many men spend a great deal of time, effort, and money on conditioning, toning, and building muscles. For some, physical culture has become a fettish. There are sections of gymnasiums that resemble ballet rehearsal halls without the bar. Mirrors line the walls of these brightly illuminated areas. Instead of tights, the men wear bikinis. They stand absorbed in the reflection of the lines of their bodies both in repose and when flexed. The muscles studied are exaggerated, often grotesque, lacking the grace and suppleness of those with which a dancer is equally involved.

I began lifting weights when I was a teenager. By the time I hit my twenties, I was Mr. Long Beach and then a runner-up for Mr. America. But like, you know, it's work. You gotta keep at it consistently. If you let down, you know, they turn against you, go to flesh. A lot of people think we're just dummies. Like, you know, I heard it all. Closet queens. There are a few. It's in all sports. Look at Dave Kopay. Narcissists. Well, sure, there's a little of that. Less than you'd think. You gotta like your body. Be proud of it. Want to keep it in shape. What's wrong with that? Pea brains with cocks to match. Bullshit. The guys around here, they're as well hung as anybody else. Better. And you can't pump iron and make it work for you, and be stupid too. Like, you gotta know a lot of things. You gotta know anatomy good. All the muscles and what to do—how to make them good. And nutrition. All the vitamins and minerals. What to eat. Like health foods and stuff like that. If you think it's just having the stamina to lift heavy weights, you're crazy.

There are over five hundred skeletal muscles in the body. When relaxed, they resemble soft rubber; but when contracted, or tensed for action, they are more like the hard surface of a handball. The more regularly they are tensed, the longer they will hold their hardened state even when relatively relaxed, thereby changing the definition of the body.

The muscles are grouped in bundles that are attached to the bones by tough, cordlike bits of connective tissue called tendons. *Tendonitis* is an inflammation of the tendons sometimes caused by bacteria. More often, it's the result of overexertion. In the pursuit of physical fitness, it's not a question of knowing one's own strength so much as knowing the limits of that strength.

The muscles of even the most sedentary scholar will increase fortyfold between his birth and the time he reaches full growth. "Muscle tone" is actually a partial contraction that keeps muscles in a state of preparation for use. Muscles may degenerate when idle for a period of time. The condition called *disuse atrophy* is associated with poor muscle tone and is a potential hazard to all retired weightlifters.

In addition to their primary mechanical functions, the muscles are the most important source of body heat. There is evidence of this in the manner in which the body becomes "overheated" when exerted. Muscles are not unlike engines. They operate on the consumption of energy-producing materials, and an adequate supply is necessary for maximum efficiency.

DESIGNING A PERSONAL PHYSICAL-FITNESS PROGRAM

Some sort of physical-fitness program is a necessity for all men, but it is wrong to think of it in terms of definition and dimension. Rare is the man whose frame is classically made. Most of us are either too short or too long in the waist, arms, or legs. Given these imperfect skeletal structures, muscles will not drape Adonis-like on them.

Strength, endurance, work capacity, flexibility: these must be our basic objectives. When we exercise our voluntary muscles, we are also exercising the involuntary muscles of the circulatory system, which links them to the rest of the body.

Our physical-fitness programs must relate to our lifestyles, professions, ages, and general state of health. A man who digs ditches for a living does not have the same needs as a man who works at a desk. A postman, making his rounds on foot, is not in the same category as a delivery man using a panel truck. A man with an overweight problem must follow a plan that will lessen his craving for food, as a lean man must follow one that will increase his appetite. The body of a man of fifty cannot stand the physical exertions that come easily to a man of twenty-five. There comes a time in all of our lives when gymnastics must give way to calisthenics, tennis to golf, jogging to walking.

The most important element in any physical-fitness program is discipline. Whether it's walking or weightlifting, it must be done on a regular schedule and at regular intervals. Weeks or months cannot be allowed to slip by before the sudden awakening to their loss.

Now that you mention it, no, I haven't had any exercise recently. I keep meaning to get over to the gym once or twice a week. But something always comes up. A business appointment. A dinner party. But I'm going down for a workout as soon as I leave here.

Sporadic exercise will not keep the muscles in shape. The unexpected strain might actually be detrimental to the general health. Certain hours of certain days of each week must be set aside for the program to be beneficial. The beginner, or the man who hasn't exercised for some time, must start well below what he thinks is his capacity; then, gradually, he should work up to it over a period of weeks or months and, as slowly, begin to increase it.

Keeping all of the factors of his life in mind, the exerciser should choose a form of exercise that he will enjoy. If it doesn't give him pleasure, he will not stay with it.

There are all kinds of new theories about running being good for the heart. They say we runners have fewer heart attacks. I don't know about that. It's also true that most of us don't smoke, that as a group we're fairly slim, and that we don't eat heavily before or after a run. As for me, the theories don't matter. I just enjoy running and the way it makes me feel about myself.

It's essential for the man who works out to know himself. If he has a strong competitive streak, his exercise should take the form of competitive sports. If he's gregarious, he should join an exercise class or team. If he's shy or embarrassed about his physique, he can savor the solitary pleasures of a long-distance runner or walker.

The New York *Times* asked five noted experts in physical fitness and cardiology to evaluate some of the more popular physical activities. They all advised that: (1) A sedentary person have a physical checkup before embarking on any exercise program. (2) Buildups should be gradual. (3) Overdoing is dangerous. (4) Regularity is essential.

Table I (page 30) summarizes their collective opinion:*

If a man really doesn't know where he is at, as far as a physical-fitness program is concerned, if he doesn't know a jog from a trot or a pushup from a situp, he should join an exercise class or go to a gym with a competent director who will help to work out the proper program for him. Short of that, there are many good exercise books available in paperback (e.g. *The Canadian Air Force Exercise Book* and *The American Air Force Exercise Book* featuring programs flexible enough to suit almost anybody. For those with an aversion to working up a sweat, there are isometrics and yoga, which accomplish good things with a minimum of moisture.

A little investigation will turn up the right physical-fitness program for

---

* *The New York Times,* March 27, 1977. The experts consulted were: Dr. Samuel M. Fox III, Director, Cardiology Exercise Laboratory, Georgetown University Hospital, Washington, D.C.; Dr. Henry Blackburn, Director, Laboratory of Physiological Hygiene, University of Minnesota School of Public Health; Dr. Ezra Amsterdam, University of California School of Medicine; Dr. Albert Oberman, Director, Division of Preventive Medicine, University of Alabama Medical Center, Birmingham; Dr. Robert J. Murphy, Columbus, Ohio, internist and head team physician of Ohio State University.

ACTIVITY	AGES SUITED FOR	CALORIES (expended per minute)	BENEFITS	CAVEATS
SKIING (cross-country)	Best for under 40 or younger, unless fit.	15-17	Probably the best conditioning exercise. Builds endurance. Promotes weight control. Injuries less common than in downhill skiing.	Preconditioning necessary. Exposure to cold and high altitudes hazardous for heart.
CALISTHENICS	All ages.	3-7	Enhances flexibility and muscle tone. Ideal for warmup and buildup before other programs.	Must be rigorously pursued to have conditioning effect. Be aware of special joint, orthopedic or muscle problems (e.g. deep knee bends are bad for persons with varicose veins and weak knees).
GOLF	All ages. Good for older persons and the less fit.	5, if you walk and carry your own clubs.	Relaxing.	Very little conditioning involved.
JOGGING	All ages if fit, under 40 best.	10-13	Excellent conditioner. Increases cardiac and lung capacity. Builds leg strength. Promotes weight control.	Hard on joints and ligaments. Have checkup if beginning 40 or over. Preconditioning necessary. Don't wear rubber or plastic sweatsuits. Don't overdo. Wear running shoes.
SWIMMING	All ages. Especially good for over 50.	9-11	Excellent conditioner. Exercises all muscles without trauma. Good for persons with orthopedic or muscle problems. Promotes weight control.	Should not swim alone. Heart patients need doctor's O.K.
WALKING	All ages.	5-7	Good all-round exercise for maintenance of heart and lung capacity and muscle tone. Excellent as a beginning exercise. Promotes weight control.	Very brisk pace (1 mile in 10-12 minutes) needed to have conditioning effect on heart.
TENNIS	All ages if fit, under 45 best.	7-9 (moderate game)	Good all-round physical activity. Good for body shaping, flexibility and balance. Good for strengthening arms. Promotes weight control.	Requires agility. Activity is sporadic. Conditioning depends on how vigorously one plays. May promote anxiety in players who worry about their game.

each of us. The important thing is to develop the discipline to keep at it until it becomes a part of our lives, a healthy habit that we wouldn't think of breaking.

ANEMIA, LEUKEMIA, AND HEMOPHILIA

Although bones have a hard structure, due to calcium deposits, they are made of living tissue well supplied with blood, lymph, and nerve cells. The external surfaces are tightly encased in a membrane (*periosteum*) that aids in natural growth and healing as well as serving as connective tissue to muscles and tendons.

The inner cavities of bones are made of marrow. The long bones of the extremities are filled with a yellow marrow consisting mainly of fatty tissue. Far more important is the red marrow of the other bones, for this is where blood is manufactured.

What we call *anemia* is actually one of a group of diseases relating to a reduction of red blood cells. There are many causes: hemorrhaging, infection, a nutritional deficiency in the food substances necessary to the manufacture of red blood cells, and an actual failure in the bone-marrow production of the cells. Another form, *pernicious anemia,* comes from a failure of the body to produce, store, or use a factor, found in the liver, necessary to the production of hemoglobin (one of the most important constituents of the blood cell responsible for, among other things, its color).

We've all heard the expression "He looks anemic." It refers to somebody who looks pale and wan. The word has come into the language as an adjective: "an anemic effort" or "an anemic portion," meaning small, feeble, bloodless, enervated. All of these qualities are symptoms of the disease. A physician should be consulted to find out the type of anemia it might be and what, if anything, can be done about it.

These same symptoms may also be the first signs of something far more serious: *leukemia,* a cancerous disease of the bone marrow. There are two types. *Acute leukemia* usually strikes the young and the old. It comes on suddenly and almost always leads to rapid death.

The onset of *chronic leukemia* is gradual, and twenty years may pass before the patient dies. There are many variations, but all of the chronic types are more common among men than women. Sometimes drugs and radiation can bring about a remission, but there is no known cure.

The earlier the leukemia is diagnosed, the more chances there are that some sort of remission may be possible. Because men are more susceptible to one form of leukemia, it is particularly important that we consult a physician the moment any of the symptoms occur. In addition to anemia, these include: difficulty in clotting after injuries; swollen feet and legs; enlarged spleen, liver, and/or lymph nodes; and high fevers.

There is one blood disease that might be called a male specialty: *hemophilia*. It is marked by uncontrollable bleeding even after slight wounds, and is caused by a deficiency in the X chromosome that determines sex. This chromosome also contains genes that govern the correct functioning of blood clotting and color vision. Color blindness is another defect that is almost exclusively found in males.

Both males and females can have X chromosomes carrying this deficient gene. When this faulty X chromosome is linked in procreation with a healthy X chromosome, the disease is not transmitted because the healthy one is dominant. Therefore, in women the defective chromosome is usually masked by a healthy one from the male. Women do not have hemophilia unless there is a weakness on both sides of the family. Thus far, there are only three recorded cases of female hemophiliacs.

But women do act as "carriers" of the disease and can transmit it to their sons just as they can transmit the carrier trait to their daughters. It is a matter of chance. The carriers can also have healthy children if they inherit the normal X chromosome. The odds are against this; only one child in four has a chance of escaping. A father cannot pass on the defective gene to his sons, because he only contributes his Y chromosome to them.

Hemophilia has been called the "royal disease" because of an impoverished German principality called Hesse whose ruling family had a gift for marrying its carrier daughters into all of the royal families of Europe. There was a threat to the English monarchy through the Battenberg (later Mountbatten) connection. By way of the Hapsburg dynasties, it made its way into German, Austrian, and Spanish royalty. Ultimately, a Hesse daughter, Alexandra, became the last tsarina of Russia. When she discovered that her son, the heir to the throne, had hemophilia, she came under the influence of a debauched Monk, Rasputin, who she believed might be able to cure him. The relationship was one of the things that turned the people against their rulers and indirectly contributed to the start of the revolution.

But the tsarina was wrong. No amount of faith in the world can cure hemophilia. The victims generally discover very early in life that they have it. The danger is not so much from external wounds. The missing clotting agent can be injected to stop the bleeding. Internal bleeding is the real menace. The hemophiliac can hemorrhage fatally without realizing what is happening to him. He must lead a very sheltered life and avoid anything that might accidentally bruise him in a way that would usually pass unnoticed by normal people.

FRACTURES

The bones become more brittle as we grow older, and the same sort of accident produces different results at different ages. We've all seen children fall and get up with no more serious mishap than a bruise. We've also seen or heard of old men stumbling no more seriously, yet breaking a leg. In the most literal sense, a man must watch his step as he ages.

> When I had my automobile accident, the car was a wreck, but I got out and walked away. The only thing I felt was a sort of vague discomfort across my chest. I thought that I'd probably bruised myself when I hit the steering wheel and forgot all about it. A few nights later, I got up startled. With a sharp pain. I swear—I heard a pop. Well, it seems I'd broken a rib and punctured a lung. It was miserable. And the weird thing is—I hadn't felt a thing.

The most common bone injury is the fracture. There are two types: simple and complex. In the former, the skin has not been pierced; in the latter, the skin has been broken, allowing bacteria to enter the wound and exposing the bone to infection.

Many breaks are easily discernible by the deformity that comes from them. There are other breaks that go unnoticed, for there is no visible sign of damage, and the pain is bearable. These breaks can be the most dangerous; a vital organ may be punctured. A complete examination is advisable after any serious accident, especially if there is lingering pain or swelling, no matter how slight it may seem. X-rays are often necessary to see the extent of the damage.

With fractures, or any other source of pain, allowances must be made for the individual *threshold of pain*. Most men have similar responses to (or thresholds of) pain. Given a specific stimulus of specific intensity, the degree of agony is predictable and might be called normal. However, for any of a number of physiological and/or psychological reasons, there can be extreme sensitivity or overreaction to pain. This is called a *low threshold of pain*. Conversely, a *high threshold of pain* is marked by a singular lack of response to the signals of distress (pain) unless they are overwhelming.

> I was always very proud of being able to take all kinds of pain. Made a big macho thing of it. Even when I actually did feel pain, I'd tell myself I had

to take it. Pretend that I was wounded on a battlefield and had to make it back to the lines alone. One day, I walked for about a mile with a nail going straight through my shoe into my foot. I didn't even know about it until I got home. The infection was so bad I had to keep off it for a couple of weeks. Now I look where I walk—examine how I feel. I can still take more pain than most people, but I no longer think it's one of my greatest assets.

Every man should learn about his own reactions to pain. We do ourselves a great disservice by not giving in to them. There is nothing about our bodies that we should ignore, and that certainly includes distress signals. Those with high thresholds of pain must be doubly careful. What seems like a manly display of courage can actually be a dangerous and losing game with crippling affliction.

TUMORS

I was slightly stoned when I got home. I didn't bother turning on the light and walked right into the bed. It wasn't much of a bang. Nothing really. The kind you normally don't even think about. But the goddam bone shattered. They found this thing growing right inside it. I was one of the lucky ones. Not like the Kennedy kid. It was benign. They were able to clean it out and do a bone graft.

Although tumors of the bone are rare, they are extremely dangerous and often fatal. A benign tumor usually takes the form of a cyst and is not detected until the weakened bone is fractured by some trivial accident. The cyst is scraped out and replaced by a bone graft.

There is a greater chance of recovery from a malignant tumor (*sarcoma*) if it is in the cavity of the bone. The sarcoma remains localized and does not involve other parts of the body with secondary growths. It often goes undetected until a large swelling appears covered by such a thin layer of bone tissue that the slightest pressure can fracture it. The treatment is complete removal of that part of the bone, even if it means amputation.

Cancer of the outer membrane of the bones (*periosteal sarcoma*) is almost always fatal. Because amputation generally does not stop it from spreading to other parts of the body, it has a higher rate of mortality than almost any other form of malignancy.

Although cancer may originate in the bones, it more often spreads to them from malignancies in other parts of the body. It is usually discovered too late to save the patient.

BACKACHE

I've always had a weak back. The minute anything went wrong, or I was overtired, it would hit me right there. Damp heat, dry heat, tranquilizers, ointments, sleeping on my back, sleeping on my stomach, sleeping in a fetal position—I've tried it all. Some people get headaches when things go wrong. I get backaches.

•

I wasn't doing anything strenuous. I sort of turned around suddenly. And I ended up in traction.

Aching backs probably cause more loss of productivity than all other ailments combined. People can be off the job for days, weeks, even months. When they return to work, the most inconsequential chores can be painful. They may find it impossible merely to sit at a desk for a full day.

We all understand the sudden pain in the back that results from a fall, twist, or injury. More insidious are the persistent and recurrent pains which sometimes originate with a sudden trauma but are likelier to have their sources in other problems. In order to understand the latter, we must know a little about the nature of the back.

The back is the weakest link in the skeletal chain that ultimately joins our toes to our heads. Yet, next to the brain, it is the most significant factor in the evolutionary process that has made man supreme in the animal world. It enables us to stand erect, and it acts as the support structure for our bodies, connecting head with pelvis as well as anchoring the rib cage so necessary for protection of the vital organs of lungs and heart. Its unique structure of vertebral bones is the primary source of our flexibility, enabling us to bend, twist, turn, push, pull, and carry.

The spinal column is often misnamed the backbone when, in fact, it is comprised of many linked bones. It provides protection for the spinal cord, which controls the nervous system by acting as the central channel of communication between the brain and all of the other parts of the body.

Despite its enormous contribution to our development, the back has not kept astride of the rest of the body in adapting to our upright stance. Many of us are born with postural defects; many more acquire faulty posture through indolence and lack of proper attention to the needs of that part of the body.

When I was a kid I slouched. My whole crowd slouched. It was our way of
looking tough. In those days nobody ever heard of walking tall. It was the
war that fixed my posture. Officers' Training. I can still hear those rugged
bastards. "Pull in that chin! More! I want to count the wrinkles in it. More!
Climb that wall with your back!" You stop slouching fast. I'm sixty. I can still
square my head, shoulders and butt against that wall and pull in my gut until
you can't slip a hand between it and the small of my back. My son always
says I walk as if I had an iron poker rammed up my asshole. Well, it's better
than the way his friends and he walk. They look as if they had daisies
rammed up theirs.

Bad posture, and the ensuing backaches, can be exacerbated by heed-
lessness of how we live in our environment. Most of us exist with daily oc-
cupational hazards that threaten to bring on chronic back conditions. They
can be corrected with a minimum of effort. If you're in a job that calls for
a great deal of bending and lifting, be sure that your knees bend with you.
There is a strain on the back from picking up something as light as a sheet
of paper with your knees straight.

A man who earns his living sitting at a desk should treat himself to a
good orthopedic chair, one that supports his back at all of the points of
strain. It's an excellent and deductible business expense. But even with the
best chair, he must train himself never to sit in a slumped position, because
this produces unrelenting strain on the lower back.

Too few automobiles and trucks feature seats that give the drivers adequate support for long hauls. If you do a lot of driving in your work, get a
good back support from an automotive supply store and make certain that
your back is positioned to avoid stress.

A proper mattress is as necessary to a good and pain-free day's work as
it is to a good night's rest. Somehow, many of us have gotten things
reversed in our minds. We think of soft, downy, yielding mattresses and
pillows as a symbol of ease and luxury, while firm beds are thought of as
back-breakers. When we're actually in one of those overly soft beds that
many hotels feature, the best thing we can do for our backs is send down
for a board to give some support to that bed.

In addition to postural attacks on the back, occupations offer subtler,
less physical reasons for severe back pain. Chief among these are: fatigue,
tension, anxiety, stress. They may be induced by external threats in our environment (physical danger, noxious chemicals, etc.), or they may come
from within (inability to cope, fear of failure, compulsiveness, etc.).
Whether self-induced or from outside ourselves, the distress can be intense.

The aching back is giving us danger signals. Relax, slow down, cut back. It's trying to brake our reactions before our reactions break us.†

Lumbago is the name for intense pain in the lower back often accompanied by muscle spasm. *Sciatica* is pain which radiates down along the sciatic nerve (buttock, back of thigh, calf, and foot). Until recently, the two were considered separate diseases in their own right. We now know that most cases, *not all,* are symptomatic of what is known in common parlance as a *slipped disc.* It is actually not a disc, nor does it slip. It is one of the intervertebral joints in the spine, and the "slip" is in reality a breakdown in its functioning.

Of all the backaches in the world, a damaged disc ranks very close to the most severe. It is very much a male specialty. Although it can be found in both sexes at any age, the bulk of the sufferers are men in their thirties and forties. We are speaking of the preponderance of cases, which are degenerative, and not of disc problems due to accidents. The latter obviously have no limitations of age or sex.

> For a long time, whenever I got tired or upset—or even lifted something in a bad way—the pain would start. I always thought it was just lumbago acting up again. I'd get into bed with a heating pad for a couple of days, and it would go away. Then, one day, it didn't go away. I bent over to pick something up and saw stars. I couldn't straighten up. I never knew there was such pain. It was the disc, all right. It had always been the disc, only I didn't know it. And I never had a doctor really check it out. I was put in traction for a week. It didn't help. I had to have a myelogram, not the world's pleasantest experience, and it confirmed the doctor's suspicions. A fusion was necessary. It was a long time before I could get out of bed. Even after that, I had to continue to do exercises. Once I let down for a while, and I began to experience some pain again. The exercises have become a way of life. I don't mind. They're also helping to keep the rest of me in shape.

Any type of recurrent backache, no matter how bearable, must be diagnosed immediately. If it is a disc problem, the sooner it is discovered, the more likely it is that it can be successfully treated without surgery.

Doctors sometimes jokingly ask: "What did we do before the slipped disc?" The ailment is very much a post-World War II phenomenon. This does not mean that it did not exist before the war, it simply means that it had not been isolated as a single malady rather than a series of interrelated ones.

On every level, the disc is a disability of our times. We live in an au-

† Other areas of the body particularly sensitive to the stress reactions are: the stomach, skin, and head.

tomated age. We do not exercise the muscles of the back as much as people did in earlier eras, who had to put their back into many of their activities in order to survive. Muscles atrophy from lack of use. At the same time, we've become more sedentary both at work and on holiday. Backs stiffen from being too long in one position.

We have to compensate by keeping limber. There are many simple exercises designed for just these purposes. Some derive from yoga, some are isometric, others are warmups. They can be found in any book of physical fitness and should be a part of our daily regime, especially if there has been any indication of sensitivity in the area of the back.

RHEUMATISM

There are inflammations that can disrupt the functioning of any of the joints of the body, including the discs. *Rheumatism* (or its synonym, *arthritis*) is the most common. There are two major varieties of it: *osteoarthritis* and *rheumatoid arthritis*.

Osteoarthritis exists to some degree in most people over sixty. It is often the result of the natural erosion of aging aggravated by exposure to cold and damp and by general ill-health, although an accident can also be a predisposing factor. X-ray diagnosis reveals permanent changes in the joints. However, it is usually not crippling unless it attacks the hip. Its main feature is pain, which can be relieved by physiotherapy and analgesics.

Rheumatoid arthritis attacks more women than men and generally starts in middle age. Although the disorder can be controlled by treatment and many sufferers do lead normal lives, early diagnosis is essential. It is a disease of attrition that can lead to permanent crippling and an invalided life of intense pain. At the first sign of swelling or pain in any of the joints, have a doctor x-ray the infected area. The results can be devastating if too much time is allowed to elapse.

GOUT

Gout is often considered the price exacted for the pleasures of the good life. In literature, and even history (we need only think of "gouty" old Ben Franklin), it is depicted as a disease that preys on those who lead rich sedentary lives consuming enormous quantities of juicy beefs, creamy cheeses, and expensive ports or sherries.

Some people enjoy thinking of gout as the retribution exacted from the rich for their indolent and self-indulgent lives. Unfortunately, there is no truth in the fable. The neediest welfare case can be victimized by gout. The only barrier it knows is one of sex, for it is another of those ailments that is prevalent in the male: 95 per cent of the sufferers are men.

Gout is a metabolic disorder of unknown origin in which uric acid is either overproduced or not properly eliminated in urine. The uric salts and crystals are deposited in the joints, causing an extremely painful inflammation. The most susceptible joints are those in the hands and feet, particularly in the big toe.

It usually doesn't attack men under forty-five, and the few women sufferers are all beyond menopause. In over three quarters of the cases there is a history of the disease in the family. These two facts lead to unproven theories that there might be some connection between gout and heredity and/or the production of sex hormones.

Attacks of gout often take place at night. There are drugs that will effectively relieve the pain. During primary treatment, a great deal of fluid should be consumed to flush the system and stimulate the kidneys. The chronic sufferer must forego alcohol completely, keep himself slightly underweight, and faithfully adhere to the diet prescribed by his physician.

All of the chronic diseases of the joints require a great deal of rest for alleviation of the pain. Sunlight (or ultraviolet treatments) is often efficacious. It is sometimes beneficial to remove the patient to a warm, dry climate. Depending upon the case, hydrotherapy or radiation may be considered as courses of treatment. Massage, limited exercise, and manual manipulations are often advised. One may have to submit to one form of treatment after another until the most advantageous one is found. Chemotherapy sometimes becomes a way of life. Ultimately, one may have to resort to surgery.

A man's body is a collection of movable parts. An attack on any one of them can be so devastating that it interferes with the normal functioning of all. It is essential for us to have early diagnosis and treatment of joint diseases, or we may ultimately lose our capacity for enjoying a professionally, socially, and sexually active life.

TENNIS ELBOW

In the last few years there has been a boom in tennis enthusiasts, so we will close this discussion with a few words about an affliction associated with the popular sport: *tennis elbow*. This is actually a form of *bursitis*.‡ The bursae are saclike structures located around the joints, muscles, ten-

‡ Other forms of bursitis are known as housemaid's knee and student's or miner's elbow.

dons, and bones. Their function is to reduce friction between the moving parts of the body, and bursitis is the extremely painful inflammation of these sacs. Sometimes, one can stoically endure it, and it will eventually go away. If tennis is your favorite pastime, however, there's no reason to put up with the sensitive elbow. Your physician knows how to alleviate, if not eliminate, the pain.

TEETH

The teeth are the final part of the musculoskeletal system. It can be safely assumed that everybody has heard about the necessity for taking care of them, for having regular dental checkups, for brushing at least twice a day and preferably after every meal. It is doubtful that anybody has not had or seen a demonstration of the correct up-and-down motion in brushing and massaging the gums.

It is also likely that many of us pay no attention to this valuable information. That's unfortunate. Unlike the dreaded "jaws" of the shark, which just keep sprouting set after set of teeth as the old ones decay or fall out, our permanent (or adult) teeth are the last ones we are going to grow naturally. We must certainly try to pay attention to all of the time-honored shibboleths about taking care of them. Although dentists make marvelous false teeth that work very well, nature makes still better real ones, and we should try to keep them healthy and with us for as long as possible.

5

THE NERVOUS SYSTEM

"He's a nervy son of a bitch."
  "My nerves are shot."
  "He's got nerves of steel."
  "I'm as nervous as a cat on a hot tin roof."

When we hear these lines, we think we know what they mean. But is our knowledge exact or merely a hazy comprehension of colloquialism? What are nerves? What is the nervous system?

Actually, the nervous system is divided into two parts: the central nervous system (brain and spinal cord) and the peripheral nervous system (the links to the nerves that exist in every part of our bodies). The essence of life can be broken down into stimulation and response, and the nervous system is our stimulus-response mechanism. It regulates and co-ordinates our responses to internal and external environmental conditions.

In addition to co-ordinating all of our physical activities, the nervous system is the center of memory, intelligence, and consciousness, enabling us to think, reason, and make judgments. It is also in charge of all of our emotional responses. Without it, we would feel neither pain nor pleasure. Our senses would cease to perceive, and we would not be able to distinguish between tastes, sights, sounds, smells, touches.

The brain is the center of these functions and also the center of the automatic functioning of all our organs. It has been justifiably called "the most complex mechanism in the world." If we draw an analogy between the body and a machine, the brain is the control center, and the nerves are the wires linking it to all the other parts. Via these wires, the brain receives and transmits countless messages every moment. It is responsible for everything from breathing, to the beat of the heart, to the circulation of the blood; from pangs of hunger, to the taste of food, to the digestion of it; from sensual arousal, to erection, to ejaculation; from the opening of a book to the comprehension of the words written in it.

NERVOUS DISTRESS SIGNALS

Everybody knew I was having a nervous breakdown except me. It's funny, if anything else had broken—an arm, a leg, anything—they'd have seen that I got treatment pronto. But not with the nerves. They were afraid to say anything to me, afraid of making it worse, afraid to face it themselves. They just tiptoed around my rage pretending it wasn't there. Until one day we couldn't pretend any more. I had what you might call an hysterical paralysis. There was nothing physically wrong with me. But I couldn't move.

A breakdown or blockage in the nerves can cause a dysfunction or paralysis in the part of the body that it connects with the brain. The damage can be temporary or permanent, seemingly inconsequential or terribly serious, or merely embarrassing. It can be anything from numbness in the small toe to paralysis of the whole foot; from a twitch in the eyelid to blindness; from no erection while in bed with an extremely desirable woman to a sudden, unconcealable hard on in a crowded bus.

There is almost no symptom that may befall us that cannot be traced as readily to the nervous system as it can to the part of the body in which it appears. This makes us subject to a dangerous temptation. We're apt to dismiss things with an airy: "It's nothing. Just nerves."

Even if it is "just nerves," it should be thoroughly investigated. The brain is sending out a distress signal. Something is wrong. Something is not functioning as smoothly as it should. We must look into it.

Modern medical technology has become the master sleuth of all times. There are machines to track down almost any mysterious ailment, and we should avail ourselves of them. A little time, money, and discomfort at the beginning can save a fortune in all three later.

Most of us would never dream of treating our automobiles the way we treat our bodies. The slightest knock in the family car, and it's off to the body shop. As family fathers, we should think about giving ourselves the same consideration. When the car is laid up, we become dependent on public transportation. When the man of the family is laid up, it can be public welfare, which is a good deal more uncomfortable. Many of the most debilitating ailments (nervous and otherwise) can be avoided by careful and early scrutiny.

Right after my stroke, I couldn't speak. You can hear, I still slur a little. And I couldn't move my right hand. But with physical therapy, I've almost regained full use of it. Believe me, when you think of what could've been, I was some lucky guy.

The nervous dysfunction may have its origin in the brain itself. A stroke is a vascular accident in a portion of the brain (we will discuss it more fully in a later section on the *cardiovascular system*). The damage will be manifested in the parts of the body that the stricken section of the brain controls. An injury or tumor can cause similar reactions.

I keep telling myself, What do I need it for? The tension's too much. The anxiety keeps building. If I don't give it up, I'm going to have a heart attack. But how do you give it up? You're used to making a certain amount a year. You can't live on less. Hell, half the time you can't even live on that.

STRESS

The most common disease of the nervous system is something many of us do not even think of as an illness. Call it stress, or strain, or anxiety. They all mean pretty much the same thing and, by any name, it is a disease of our times so common that many of us think of it as a normal condition of life. By definition, one might call it the strain or uneasiness of mind brought about by the internal resistance we offer to those external pressures that bear down upon us. There are times when the pressures themselves are internalized in that we bring them to bear upon ourselves. In addition to being internal or external, tension can be either permanent or temporary. There are four general types, and examples of them can be found in our professional lives.

Temporary external tension: I was racing to get to a meeting on time. The car went into a skid. I just managed to pull it out in time. As I came to a stop, my heart was beating a mile a minute.
Permanent external tension: The smell of those chemicals really gets to you. I

don't have breakfast any more. What's the use? I know I'm likely to lose it before lunch.

Temporary internal tension: When I found the mistake, I knew I'd cost the company a couple of grand. I didn't know what to do. I could feel that knot in my stomach growing tighter. Should I own up or wait and hope they wouldn't discover it? I was a mess.

Permanent internal tension: What do you do when you hit forty-five and realize it's all been a mistake? You've gone as far as you're going to go in your line. It's too late to change even if there was something else you could get into. You're what is known as "overqualified." You're stuck where you are, even though you know it's not for you.

In all forms of tension, the nerves are sending danger signals to the brain. The brain is alerting the organs that a greater effort is necessary to try to overcome the problem. The heart begins to beat faster. There is a shortness of breath. The muscles become rigid, may even go into spasm. The blood vessels constrict. Because the body needs greater supplies of fuel to combat this obstacle, adrenalin is pumped into the bloodstream, and the blood sugars are activated.

In cases of psychic threats, these responses are largely of a negative value. However, there are times when the same responses are a positive force, and that happens when the threat is real and physical. These automatic actions of the nervous system give us the extra energy necessary to defend ourselves when attacked or to race out of the way of some falling object.

The body reacts to both psychic and physical threats in the same way. It releases extra *juices.* When they are absorbed in a physical action, all is generally well: there is little danger of related psychosomatic illness or defect. This is also true once we are removed from the sources of temporary tension, no matter how severe (e.g. combat fatigue, involvements in disasters such as floods, fires, train wrecks).

NEUROSES

The noun *neurosis* and the adjective *neurotic* have entered everyday popular conversation. No cocktail party would be complete without them. A few years ago we might have dismissed people as "crazy" or "nuts"; now we agree that they're "neurotic." Any alien behavior is a symptom of neurosis. Some keep a close watch on their every action and word, fearful they may betray some form of neurosis. Others think that *eccentric* and *neurotic* are synonymous and that to be unneurotic is the same as being square or dull.

Neuroses are actually very common disorders stemming from an inability to handle unconscious emotional conflicts and distressing life situations. The consequent anxiety may be experienced as simple tension, or it may hide from us in disguises of obsessional thoughts, depressions, compulsive acts, physical complaints or symptoms without evidence of disease, or in the form of phobias. Who among us has not on occasion experienced one or another of these reactions? The common cure is to remove ourselves from the source or, more likely, adjust to it. "Well adjusted" simply means being able to adjust to neurosis-provoking situations in most instances— *but not in all instances.* Nobody is automatically or completely adjusted in all the stressful situations of his life. And how fortunate we are that this is true.

Fortunate? you may ask, and the response is a loud affirmative. Let us go back for a moment to the examples of temporary external tension. We cope with them by releasing extra "juices." This is actually a form of neurotic behavior in that we are not handling the disturbing situation in a natural way. As you can see, we would probably be in serious trouble if we did not react in an unnatural way. It is likely that this would indicate that the acceleration factor in our nervous systems was not working, which, in turn, would mean that we would be unable to function in a truly dangerous situation.

I got a slight case of food poisoning from eating bad fish. For months after, I'd break out in hives just from smelling fish that had been ordered by somebody else in a restaurant.

When abnormal reactions persist temporarily, even after removal from the original provocation, they are called *symptomatic neuroses.* More formidable than these, which have to do with reactions to removable external factors, are *character neuroses,* for they involve our total personalities and our ways of relating to others. Symptomatic and character neuroses rarely exist in the pure "textbook" form. They are constantly being modified by our internal visions and external situations.

Heredity plays almost no part in the formulation of neuroses, nor does the physical constitution with which we are born. Beauty no more confers happiness than ugliness does neurosis; a highly intelligent man is not automatically better adjusted than one with low or average intelligence (too often, it is the reverse); a man with a large penis is not necessarily less sexually frustrated than one with a small penis; thin may be in, but it is not naturally less neurotic than fat; a man of the physical stature of Charles De Gaulle does not have greater innate qualities of leadership than one with the statue of Napoleon. Helen Keller, born deaf, dumb, and blind, was one of the most admired women of her time, while Charlotte Corday, born with these faculties intact, was a crazed murderer.

What creates a neurosis is our interaction with the social, economic, and emotional environment in which we live. Love-hate relationships with our parents, sibling rivalries, unhappy marriages, conflicting loyalties, financial problems, unfulfilled ambitions, social or sexual rejection, religious guilts: these are far more influential in the formation of a neurotic than the length of his nose or penis.

Although there is often overlapping, and auxiliary symptoms appear, there are six general classifications of neurotic behavior: anxiety, phobia, conversion, dissociative reaction, obsessive-compulsive reaction, depressive reaction.

Deep down, I guess I was expecting the axe to fall for months before it actually did. I'd fly off the handle at the drop of a hat; get these palpitations every time I was called in by the boss. Talk about diarrhea, it was my favorite indoor sport.

Anxiety is a state of constant or sporadic tension which is often expressed in the form of apprehensiveness. This neurotic is expecting the worst to happen and, thus, generally precipitates it. At the time, he doesn't consciously know the source of his frustrations and cannot control the outcome. He finds himself inexplicably subject to fits of temper, agitation, sleeplessness, palpitations, shortness of breath. Although there is no reason for it that he can discern, he begins to fear that he is dying or going insane. In a crisis, it can be manifested in a nervous stomach, nausea, diarrhea, frequent urination.

I've always had claustrophobia. Well, maybe not always. But as long as I can remember. There's nothing I can do about it except avoid things that bring on the panic, like elevators or crowded buses or sitting in booths in restaurants. It's a limitation. But it's no big deal. I can live with it.

Phobias are also expressions of anxiety, only the fear has been displaced from the general unconscious idea to the conscious specific. Although phobias stem from the same subconscious aggressions and sexual frustrations as anxiety, they are localized on one external and symbolic fear, often not unrelated to its source. An adolescent becomes nauseous in all forms of transportation because he has oedipal feelings about his mother and doesn't want to leave home. A girl won't go out in the streets alone because she fears her frustrated longings for sexual abandon will cause her to be mistaken for a prostitute.

Some of the more common forms of phobias are: acrophobia (fear of high places), claustrophobia (fear of enclosed places), agoraphobia (fear of open places), fear of venereal disease and fear of impotence. The phobic man can control himself by avoiding the situation or thing that provokes the phobia. That, however, is control and not cure. It enables him to function, albeit incompletely. He can be set off again by an elevator, the view from a tall building, an open field, a sexual encounter. Dealing with the subconscious motivation is the only way to cure the conscious fear, and analysis has often been successful in this area.

> The doctors can tell me there's nothing wrong. But I'm the one who gets the terrible cramps. And don't tell me it's psychosomatic. It's real. My poor wife will vouch for that. She's had to take care of me. It's just that the medical profession doesn't know its ass from third base.

Conversion is turning the anxiety in upon oneself and converting it to a general hypochondria or attacks on specific parts of the body controlled by the central nervous system. Without any physical ailment, the person in this state can experience pain, numbness, lassitude, insomnia. He can become partially paralyzed, blind, deaf, subject to tics, tremors, fainting spells.

In addition to displacing anxiety with a seemingly real physical disability, the conversion reaction reaps the extra benefit of garnering sympathy generally reserved for the ill or handicapped. Everybody else may be anxious about him, but he is peaceful and very contented with his state. He no longer gets anxieties, he gives them.

His tranquillity is illusory. He is actually placing himself in physical jeopardy. Disuse over a long period of time can eventually bring about the physical changes that convert his imaginary ailment into a real one.

Psychosomatic disease is related to the conversion syndrome. The emotional distresses inflicted upon the body, the secretion of unabsorbed adrenalin and fatty acid may cause a real physical dysfunction. The most common examples of this are: stomach ulcers, colitis, back and joint aches, vascular hypertension (high blood pressure), high cholesterol, skin rashes, allergies, and asthma.

Many physicians and psychologists prefer to treat the asthma or ulcer. They think it is wiser to ease the patient's physical suffering than to tamper with the balance of his life by attempting to uproot some deep frustration or depression.

I know I have a violent temper. But I think I'm healthier than people who keep it all bottled up inside. At least I get it off my chest and can forget about it. Sometimes, they tell me, I say the most awful things. I don't even remember. It doesn't matter. I don't really mean anything by it. It's a release. And I can make up for it later by being extra nice.

The dissociative reaction is actually a form of temporary amnesia in which one can blot out an embarrassing or humiliating memory. When reminded of a moment of lost self-esteem, the man who responds with, "Did I do that?" is a man who is probably suffering a dissociative reaction. He could well continue: "It's just as well that I don't remember. I don't ever want to think about it again."

Subconsciously, he is remembering. He may protect himself with fantasies or daydreams of glory. In extreme cases, he may enter a *fugue* state in which there is a temporary loss of personal identity. He acts in an outrageous way that he would never do normally, does things that his conscience would ordinarily forbid, and then, coming out of the state, remembers nothing about it.

Some of the worst aspects of people in this state are violent temper tantrums, manipulation of other people, self-dramatization, egocentricity, a preference for fantasy over reality. The afflicted are emotional liars and cheats not only to others but to themselves as well.

Conversely, they can be beguiling, seductive, imaginative, and charming. Some of the most memorable figures in fiction have been classic examples of people suffering from dissociative reactions. Their names have passed into the language as archetypes: Don Quixote, Walter Mitty, Don Juan.

My marriage was on the rocks. I was driving my wife right up the wall. I knew what I was doing. But I couldn't help myself. She's a very relaxed woman. If a book's out of place on a shelf, I just have to set it right. The same thing with an object on a table. Finally, she blew. I couldn't blame her, and I couldn't stop by myself. But we're getting it all together now. We're into meditation. And it's really working.

An *obsessive-compulsive* reaction is a response to anxiety over the possibility of acting upon conscious and repugnant thoughts, generally of an aggressive or sexually perverse nature. The nervous energy that might go into action is displaced to meaningless and often trivial ceremonies.

Handwashing, touching, rearranging objects in a room, repetition of clichés, acquisitiveness, preoccupation with meaningless details: These are some of the traits to be found in the obsessive-compulsive personality. They are the collectors, the pillow-fluffers, the string savers, the ashtray emptiers. There is a concentration on trivia that is counterproductive, wasteful of both time and energy.

The obsessive-compulsive man is often aware of his shortcomings but unable to control them. He looks to things outside himself to order his existence, to motivate his actions. As a result, he is likely to believe in the power of prayer, astrology, the occult, EST (Erhard seminar training), TM (transcendental meditation), or any other faddist cult that might help him "to get his head together" without analyzing himself, probing his own depths to find out why he is falling apart. There is an adherence to excessive morality that does not alleviate persistent doubt about his own worth. His life is a pendulum swinging between the extremes of vacillation and inflexibility.

> Life just ain't worth living since my wife passed on. I'm a religious man. I know she's with God. But somehow it doesn't help. Nothing does. All I can do is pray that I'll be permitted to join her soon. It's so empty without her. Nothing matters any more. Not even my kids.

A *depressive reaction* is triggered by the loss of a beloved person or object or ideal or valued abstract concept. A critical self-depreciation leads to despair and feelings of helplessness. A neurotic depression displaces any normal show of grief, as the sense of loss turns in upon the mourner and becomes self-loathing.

The depressive personality is incapable of normal activity or even the ability to concentrate on anything beyond his own despair. Initiative is stillborn; past failures are exaggerated beyond any semblance of reality. Guilt stifles a healthy expression of anger. An unbearable sense of worthlessness sometimes evokes dangerous thoughts of self-destruction.

The differences between "normal" and "neurotic" reactions are not very great. Given certain stresses, most of us will (or already have) react neurotically: this will occur in any so-called normal person when tension is applied to his specific area of vulnerability. The difference is in depth, duration, and the degree of incapacitation. In most instances, neurotic reactions are socially acceptable or dismissed as idiosyncrasies that are occasionally deemed "interesting" or even "fascinating." They are often channeled into creative activity.

We say of the neurotic:

"He's so sensitive."

"He's different because he's artistic."

"You must treat him with kid gloves."

"When he acts up, you've got to forgive him. He's not like the rest of us. He's a creative guy."

So special is the treatment that some people simulate neuroses as attention-getting devices. But the act is self-defeating, for it ultimately leads to genuine neurotic behavior.

The neurotic is able to make an adequate social adaptation and continues to function in the "real" world. Indeed, the uninvolved onlooker is often unaware of the extent of his distress. In the final analysis, the difference between normal and neurotic behavior can only be assessed subjectively, in terms of the depth of despair, pain, and incapacitation suffered by the individual.

Help is possible only when the neurotic is ready for it and feels that he needs it, that he cannot go on without some relief. There are times when trying to cure a neurosis will so disorient a man who has come to terms with his behavior patterns that it is wiser not to tamper with his delicate equilibrium.

There was a famous playwright who was severely depressed by his homosexuality. He entered analysis and began to function successfully as a heterosexual. His depressions were gone. He married happily and had children. But though he could interpret other people's plays as a competent director, he never wrote another play to equal his work before analysis. Friends claim that he became depressed again shortly before his death and began to wonder if his happy heterosexuality was worth the price he had paid for it in creativity.

Nobody could satisfy that final doubt for the writer. When it comes to our own neurotic reactions, we must be the arbiters of their depth and our needs for help.

DRUGS AND ADDICTIONS

Without two or three cups of coffee, I can't get started in the morning.

I need a cigarette to steady my nerves.

I still like to start the day with a Coke. It's a habit left over from when I was a kid down home.

The drink in the club car makes life possible.

Jesus, I couldn't get through those business lunches without a martini or two.

We've given up drinking. All we have is white wine.

A Valium a day keeps the shrink away.

I'm not hooked on sleeping pills. Most weeks I don't take 'em more than once or twice.

I only use dexies to keep my weight down.

In 1964 the World Health Organization defined "drug dependence" as "a state arising from the repeated administration of a drug on a periodic or continuous basis. Its characteristics vary with the agent involved, and this must be made clear by designating the particular type of drug dependence in each specific case—for example, drug dependence of morphine type, of cocaine type, of cannabis type, of barbiturate type, of amphetamine type, etc."

Most of us are addicts (have a dependency or habit). With almost no alteration of meaning, caffeine, nicotine, and alcohol can be included among the drugs. To a lesser or greater degree, they all work upon the sensory perceptions of our nervous systems in the same way as any of the opiates, and we repeatedly administer them on a periodic or continuous basis.

The limited, spasmodic, rare use of all but the hardest drugs will not harm the healthy body or mind. It is the effect on them of habitual use that one must question. Even the mildest drug is evil at the point when we stop taking it, and it starts taking us. The more dangerous ones have the hook built in, and most of us are taken from our first experiments with them. These must be avoided, no matter what social pressures are brought upon us by others to try them or what state of inner stress makes them suddenly viable.

Opium

Crude opium is the juice of the poppy seed. It has been used medicinally for thousands of years. In *The Iliad,* Homer described it as "inducing forgetfulness of pain and the sense of evil." Thus, it is clear that even the ancient Greeks were aware of opium's dual powers: the relief from (1) pain *and* (2) the sense of evil, our personal devils, those mental or spiritual problems that are robbing us of tranquillity.

In 1806, morphine was first extracted from opium. It was ten times more powerful than its source both as a medicine and in the depth of false euphoria that it produced. Extremely habit-forming, it had a built-in law of diminishing return. Pleasure could not be sustained at a prescribed dosage. The more that was taken, the more that was needed to keep the high.

Still, morphine did not begin to be a problem until 1843, when the hypodermic needle was invented. During the American Civil War, physicians took aim with needles filled with morphine, and used the wounded as a shooting gallery. Pleasure replaced pain, and the doctors were extolled as saviors.

When the veterans came marching home, they brought their habits with them, and the miserable addiction was called the "soldiers' disease." Unemployment, devastated cities, a nation torn apart: like soldiers after every war, they felt cheated by a system that had promised much more than it could deliver. They were heroes no more, and frustration approached psychological impotence. For those who had learned of the marvelous escape in a morphine-laden needle, there was an easily available solution. Like all addicts, they were eager to turn on their buddies who had not experienced the escape of drugs. And this country experienced for the first time what it was to experience after each of its subsequent wars—a vast number of young addicts eager to get stoned on anything from alcohol to the opiates.

Heroin

In 1898 America went to war with Spain, and in that same year medical science made another of its significant breakthroughs in the world of opiates. The returning veterans from that war were greeted with the news that heroin had been isolated from morphine. It would soon be the source of greater misery than any other drug in history.

Known in street language as "smack," "horse," "shit," or simply "h," heroin's euphoria doesn't last as long as that of the parent drug, but it comes on much more quickly and is three times as strong, with a high of such intensity that it has almost completely replaced morphine among the addicted.

Heroin can be sniffed, but the most common way of taking it is by injection. Injecting it into the muscle may serve for beginners, but "mainlining" is the name of the game for the seasoned user. A tourniquet is usually tied around the upper arm, causing the veins beneath it to swell, and the drug is injected directly into one of them. We've all seen pictures of the equipment necessary for mainlining: the silk tie, the teaspoon, the eye-dropper, the paper of white powder, the needle. There's something akin to ritual here, a form of ritualistic self-mutilation.

Ritual seems to play a part in all forms of drug dependence. There are exotic "head shops" for buying a whole range of equipment. One can find a variety of papers, pipes, holders, and rollers for the potheads as well as specially crafted implements for sniffing cocaine. Lights, decor, music, incense: they all play a part in the drug culture, lending an abstract sexuality to an abuse that so often ends perversely for the male in sexual abstinence or, worse still, temporary impotence. Metaphorically speaking, the high substitutes for the ejaculation. In the case of heroin, the metaphor can be extended to the phallic nature of the needle and the orgasm of heroin it shoots.

There is no doubt that heroin provides a fantastically euphoric escape for those overwhelmed by emotional or environmental problems. But there's a terrible retribution. In common with morphine, there is an acceleration factor in the drug. The addict needs an ever-increasing amount of heroin to sustain the same high. Each descent is accompanied by a more crushing depression than the one before. The times between fixes become unbearable. The dependence outstrips all moral considerations. To support his habit, the addict will bankrupt himself, ruin his family, lie, cheat, steal, and even kill.

At the same time that his morality is atrophying, his health is degenerating. He loses all interest in food, and malnutrition sets in. If he has been "shooting up" the same vein, it collapses. His sense of personal hygiene diminishes, and there is a good chance that he will use a germ-infested needle that will cause infections, abscesses, possibly jaundice or hepatitis. He will certainly become sexually impotent. His life expectancy will be terribly foreshortened, and he may achieve the ultimate high—death by O.D. (overdose).

These facts are readily available to the potential user. No matter how young he is, he's aware of the dangers. Why does he take the first trip? Some might say that it's a macho thing. He thinks he can lick it, that he'll have the joy without getting hooked. Others might point out that death is a fantasy to the young, something that can never touch them. There's some truth in this. But there's something more. It's the same reason why older addicts return even after going through the pain of withdrawal and rehabilitation. A former addict who currently works in a rehabilitation center commented:

We have to concentrate on breaking the dependence on the drug. Most centers don't have the loot or the facilities to dig into the sociological, environmental, and psychological factors that are the roots of most addiction. Withdrawing a man from drugs, giving him some cursory therapy, maybe getting him into a methadone program, and then releasing him back into the world is often a bust. Man, it's the world and not the drug that's the disease.

Tobacco

Despite the significant hazards of heroin, it is not the most dangerous addiction. Tobacco claims first place among the deadly habits of men. Next to war, it has probably contributed to, if not been responsible for, more male deaths than any other cause. We all have been exposed to the statistics on lung cancer, emphysema, and heart disease, to say nothing of the lesser perils of fire and accident. In the latter category, it is interesting to note that smokers have four times more accidents than nonsmokers. And yet, we persist. Almost half the male population consumes a dangerous amount of tobacco each year in spite of the warnings clearly printed on the package. A majority of these men would be quick to denounce drug dependence as a major problem of our times. The denunciations obviously do not extend to their own addictions.

Alcohol

When we talk of drug problems, we generally mean heroin, marijuana, cocaine, etc. We have laws regulating them and penalties for abuse. Actually, the most serious drug problem in the Western world involves a substance that is readily available from any number of sources and perfectly legal in every part of the world except a few countries in the Mideast. It is alcohol. At the beginning of this decade, there were 5,500,000 known alcoholics in the United States, and an additional 4,000,000 who showed a distinct alcoholic pattern. Compared to that, there were less than 150,000 active narcotic addicts.

Our literature, films, stage, newspapers, and periodicals are rife with graphic and harrowing stories about the tragedy of alcoholism. Unfortunately, a few pages after a documentary story on the horrors of delirium tremens or cirrhosis of the liver, there will often be a smashing advertisement for some whiskey that implies elegant sexual conquest via spirits (a rather dubious claim, as a degree of intemperance can usually be spelled *impotence*).

The purveyors of the legal lethal drugs, alcohol and tobacco, spend millions in advertising that is aimed largely at playing upon the sensibilities and insecurities of the male. Smoke this, and you'll be just like that brawny cowboy. Serve her a glass of that, and the gorgeous lady will fall into your bed. It's all aimed at the male market. The majority of those killed or ruined by abuse of these drugs are also male. One might even make a case for a link between these two facts. The death merchants of the tobacco and alcohol industries have been socking it to us men for years.

It makes no sense! My uncle's a real alkie. He can't hold a job. His wife walked out on him. But he can't give up the booze. And nobody can make him. He has the right to drink as much as he wants. The guy down the street —a two-packs-of-cigarettes-a-day man, everybody was warning him for years. Didn't do any good. He could buy his poison anywhere. Cheap, too. Now he's in the hospital. Lung cancer. He ain't never comin' home. Yet, if I light up a joint—which doesn't harm anyone, including myself—I'm breaking some fuckin' law.

Marijuana

Now let us look at the inconsistencies of our attitude toward cannabis, the extremely pleasurable derivative of the hemp plant. It goes by different names in different parts of the world: marijuana, hashish, kef, dagga, charas, ganja, bhang. In American slang, it's pot, tea, grass, weed, Mary Jane. The World Health Organization reported, in 1969, that the derivatives of cannabis were not physically habit-forming, but that they were drugs of dependence. It recommended that they be kept under legal control. The same organization has said much worse about both tobacco and alcohol. Two wrongs may not make a right, but it does seem logical that so long as the latter are readily available and legal, there is no justification for the same not being true of marijuana.

Keeping marijuana illegal has not significantly decreased the number of those already on the drug, nor discouraged those who want to try it. The illegality might even be part of the attraction to rebellious youth, just as Prohibition significantly increased alcoholism among their counterparts in the nineteen-twenties.

One might ask if there are any real reasons for keeping the drug proscribed, aside from pandering to that potent mixture of private interests made up of equal parts of the underworld and the puritans. Extreme abuse can bring about exactly the same results as alcoholic abuse: extreme swings in mood, depression, anxiety, bouts of paranoia and other psychotic reactions lasting for several hours. This loss of control can obviously be physically and emotionally dangerous, leading, in some cases, to suicide and acts of extreme violence. Less physically extreme is the loss of social, emotional, and professional motivation and the restriction of one's relationships only to those also on the drug.

The foregoing are extreme reactions to cannabis. They happen far less frequently than the same results among the imbibers of alcoholic beverages. Depending upon the individual and the amount consumed, the worst that usually happens are an eye irritation, palpitations, a constriction in the chest, thirst, extreme hunger, and a lessening of co-ordination and perceptions similar to that experienced in any form of intoxication.

The psychological effects very much depend upon one's mood at the time one takes the drug. Often this takes place in a sympathetic group in which the joint or pipe is passed around and smoked communally. As the high comes on, the group atmosphere prevails. Inhibitions are lowered. Talkativeness increases. Abstruse thoughts come easily, and one can follow them out to their often inane conclusions. Fits of giggling are frequent, and the most childish things become the height of wit. For some, there may be some pleasant hallucinating. For others, the drug acts as an aphrodisiac, although that is probably only an extension of the lowering of inhibitions.

The ambience is extremely important to the pothead. Whether it's Beethoven or Beatles, many profess to a heightened pleasure in listening to music while smoking. Others experience a harmless turn-on from watching fantastic Technicolor epics while high. Among the special favorites are space films like *2001: A Space Odyssey* and *Star Wars* and Walt Disney's *Fantasia* and *Alice in Wonderland*.

If not abused, marijuana does not seem like a terribly dangerous indulgence. Keeping it illegal contributes to its one disastrous side effect. Marijuana users are usually susceptible to the suggestion that they try something a little harder, a little kickier. As they have frequent recourse to criminal suppliers who want to hook them into the harder and more expensive habits, they are constantly being tempted to give heroin or cocaine a try.

It is in susceptibility that the dangers of cannabis become more acute than those of alcohol and tobacco. Drinkers need not be smokers, may never have smoked, nor are they tempted into smoking by the man at the corner cigar stand or another smoker. Conversely, a man can smoke three packages of cigarettes and never touch a drop of alcohol. The overwhelming majority of those into the heavier drugs (e.g. heroin, cocaine, LSD) first entered the scene via pot.

I was feeling no pain that night. I'd had two or three joints and a couple of drinks. All those famous names. It was a wild scene. A gossip columnist's idea of heaven. And they were all tripping on coke. When this model comes up with her little spoon and suggests I take a sniff, I figure—sure. Like, why not? Look at all these celebrities sniffing away. Man, it blew my mind. I've been high before. But this was sky time.

Cocaine

Cocaine ("snow" or "coke") is the "in" drug among the celebrated and affluent heads. As early as 1934, Cole Porter was writing in one of his most urbane lyrics: "Some get a kick from cocaine."

"Kick" is the operative word, for it acts as a great stimulant, a high in the truest sense of the word. Exhilaration might be a better description of its primary effect than the euphoria experienced with other drugs.

Cocaine is obtained from the leaves of a coca bush that grows wild in Peru and Bolivia. Indians of the region have been chewing the leaves for centuries, not simply for pleasure but for the ability imparted to withstand pain, hard work, hunger, and thirst. When taken orally, it produces an anesthesia in the mouth that retards sensations of hunger and thirst.

Coke makes a direct attack on the central nervous system, stimulating the cortex of the brain to produce deceptive sensations of increased mental power and energy. Fatigue seems to melt away. It makes discothèquing all night long very possible. A sense of extreme well-being mingles with delightful hallucinations. Because hunger disappears, diets become a painless exercise for the thin-is-in crowd.

The results are feelings of inordinate pleasure. The trouble is that paradise is too rapidly lost and displaced by depression and unutterable enervation. The impulse is to increase the dosage to sustain or recapture the mood, and therein lies the danger. In addition to the brain, the spinal column is attacked. Ultimately, there is the possibility of depression of the entire nervous system, convulsions, and death from respiratory failure.

In 1977 the National Institute of Drug Abuse labeled cocaine a "serious drug of abuse" and "significantly more dangerous" than marijuana. Fortunately, the Institute continued, the cost keeps it a relatively modest health hazard (cocaine was selling about $2,000 an ounce, or $10 for a single dose, with effects lasting about thirty minutes).

The Institute was "concerned about cocaine in the potential." In 1977 eight million Americans had tried the drug at least once, and about one million had used it within the last month. Dr. Robert L. DuPont, of the Institute, says that their findings run "contrary to street mythology" and hoped that the study would "deglamorize cocaine." He adds that there is "a kind of casualness about drug use now that worries me, and in a sense cocaine is riding on the coattails of marijuana." Dr. DuPont has supported the decriminalization of marijuana and stresses: "Cocaine is not like marijuana. . . . The closest analogy is the amphetamines."

The NIDA report underscored the rare but real possibility of death and the greater dangers, to the heavy users, of anxiety, sleeplessness, depression, sometimes paranoid feelings and hallucinations or "a cocaine psychosis with associated violence." The report gave no absolute figures for the amount of cocaine that can safely be used, and it did note that "occasional single-dose snorting rarely produces complications sufficiently severe to require medical intervention."

Although cocaine is not a physically addicting drug, it is capable of causing psychological dependence. "Realistically," the report concluded, "most individuals are unable to afford the quantity of cocaine necessary to produce such adverse reactions. . . . After a few days, the pleasurable effects give way to an intense anxiety state with gross paranoid features, including auditory and visual hallucinations."

As can be seen, the risk is not great to most of us who might be tempted into an occasional snort, because we cannot afford to make it a habit, and it is not addictive in the way that heroin is. But it does not bode a very glamorous end for those famous and beautiful people with their gorgeous hand-crafted silver snorting spoons hanging like flashing pendants from chains around their necks.

Sniffing poppers can make the most ordinary sex fantastic. You're stretched out, floating. It's like it's never going to end. And you never want it to. Sex is the greatest high. And when you come, it's like a million shooting stars. There's no big letdown later. You're just sort of pleasantly flaked out.

Amyl Nitrite

For those who are into marijuana for its libidinous properties, a new underground partner has become popular in the last few years. Amyl nitrite ("poppers") is a volatile, rapid-action blood-vessel dilator. It gives quick relief from attacks of angina pectoris (a severe but temporary cardiac pain). Amyl nitrite is sold commercially packaged in ampules which are snapped open and held under the noses of those who've had an angina attack. The snapping sound gives rise to its slang name of poppers.

Each ampule contains a single dose of the medicine, but that amount would constitute an overdose in its sexual role. For use during sex, the ampule is snapped open and quickly thrust into an empty inhalator which is kept capped, except when in use, to seal in the rapidly evaporating vapors. These inhalators are usually the emptied commercial packages for those vaporous medicines, like Vicks, sold without prescription for the temporary relief of stuffed-up noses.

For the fetishists, special inhalators are available in sex shops specializing in kinky sexual devices, such as leather straps, wrist bands, underwear, masks, cock rings (metal rings slipped over the penis and testicles during the flaccid period that add a painful charge to erection), and enormous dildos (plastic or rubber penises). These shops usually cater to homosexuals, who are probably the largest consumers of amyl nitrite for sexual purposes, although it has recently had an enormous upsurgence of use among heterosexuals. These special inhalators are made of metal and suspended from a leather thong which is tied around the neck.

A whiff of amyl nitrite sends a sudden rush of blood to the head due to its vasodilating action. When this occurs during the sex act, it gives the illusion of slowing things down, of a floating languorous headiness. It usually has no ill effects on a healthy male body, but this does not mean that it is not a potentially dangerous drug. It should not be used by anybody with a tendency to glaucoma, heart disease, or migraines. All the nitrites cause falling blood pressure, flushing of the skin, headaches, and occasional nausea.

Those addicted to them sniff poppers frequently during each sex act. There needn't be a cannabis prelude, but there often is. Pot and poppers have become necessities to many men who are jaded, inhibited, or unfeeling to be fulfilled by ordinary sex, to experience the pleasures of a simple ejaculation, in some cases to sustain an erection under ordinary conditions. The pot gets them psychologically aroused during foreplay, and the popper keeps them aroused during coitus. For these men, sexual partners are often incidental, and masturbation, in company with the drugs, gives them an equal amount of pleasure.

Because of the widespread abuse, the Food and Drug Administration has required prescriptions for its sale since 1969. In 1975, only 5,000 prescriptions were written, but approximately 330,000 boxes (each containing 12 ampules) were sold, worth profits of one million dollars to the amyl nitrite manufacturers, Eli Lilly and Burroughs Wellcome. They're worth considerably more on the black market, where they sell for ten dollars a box.

The FDA control of amyl nitrite has simply sent users off to buy butyl nitrite, which has the same effects and can be bought without prescription.

It is listed, by the United States Pharmacopoeia, as a "chemical reagent" and is thus outside the jurisdiction of the FDA. It is openly sold as incense and deodorizers in bookshops, boutiques, and the sort of sex shops we've already described. Some of the brand names are: Rush, Locker Room, Bullet, and Jac Aroma. It is often sold in liquid form, which makes it much more dangerous than amyl nitrite. Although it is supposed to be sniffed, it could be fatal if accidentally swallowed. The victim would go into shock and die of vascular collapse if treatment were not immediately administered. Butyl nitrite is so hazardous that it even prompted the pro-drug magazine *High Times* to issue a health warning about it.

> Believe it or not, it was the good old U. S. Army Air Corps that first hooked me on speed. When I was a fighter pilot, they gave it to me to keep my weight down and my energy high. And that's how ye Pentagon doth make junkies of us all.

Amphetamines and Barbiturates

Amphetamines are a group of synthetic drugs that work as stimulants of the central nervous system. Known as "uppers," "speed," or "pep pills," benzedrine was the first one introduced into the market, and it was quickly followed by dexedrine, methadrine, biphetamine, desoxyn, dexamyl, and edrial. The simple nicknames of bennies, meth, and dexies gave way to a rainbow assortment of names, deriving from the colors of the pills: purple hearts, French blues, black bombers, whites, and Christmas trees.

They have valid pharmaceutical purposes in helping to control diet, treating chronic depression, relieving muscular rigidity in some forms of Parkinson's disease, and making alcoholics susceptible to the psychological suggestion of abstinence.

During World War II they were prescribed for combatants engaged in operations requiring lengthy periods of alertness. The returning veterans had a lot of postwar catching up to do at school and in their occupations. They found the necessary extra spurts of energy in the pills to which the armed forces had introduced them. When reed-thin fashion models became the vogue, both they and their imitators found the solution to weight problems in the same pills. Hollywood stars were fed amphetamines to give them the enormous energy that characterized their performances and to keep them slenderly photogenic.

So amphetamines entered three spheres containing great numbers of immature, rebellious, and unstable characters who would prove very sympathetic to drug experimentation: schools, high fashion, and show business. These remain the areas in which enormous drug subcultures exist.

Although there is no physical dependence formed, there can be an enormous psychic dependence on the false sense of energy and alertness given by the amphetamines, and, for those hooked, the side effects become part of life. These include at various times: sleeplessness, anxiety, jumpiness, as well as occasional nausea, vomiting, cramps, and diarrhea. In cases of extreme abuse, paranoia or schizophrenia may result. A prolonged depression has been known to lead to suicide. In most cases, however, the chain reaction of drugs sets in, and amphetamines lead directly to barbiturates.

Barbiturates are depressants that reduce the number of messages sent to the brain by the nervous system. The relaxation of impulses relieves anxieties and makes sleep possible. They have been widely prescribed for a range of problems, includings tension, epilepsy, and insomnia; they are also effective in hypnosis and as an anesthetic. They come in many forms characterized by the length of their effectiveness: long-acting (six hours or more), e.g. phenobarbital; intermediate (three to six hours), e.g. tuinal and amobarbital; short (up to three hours), e.g. secobarbital or seconal and pentobarbital or nembutal. There are also ultra-shorts, but they're only used as intravenous anesthetics.

As a group, the barbiturates are called: barbs, goofballs, candy, or downers. They are individually named by colors—blues or blue devils (amobarbital), yellows (nembutal), red birds (seconal), and rainbows (tuinal).

There's not much I can say about drugs. It's not my thing. I look at my children and their friends and think something should be done to regulate them for their own good. The kids, I mean. Me? What I take is for medicinal purposes only. I have a weight problem, and the doctor prescribed some dexadrine to help control it. In my business I don't get enough exercise. The big lunch is always a temptation. A chocolate bar just for energy. I have trouble winding down. At night, my mind's still going a mile a minute. I have the phenos just to help me sleep. But, as you can see, it's all medicinal. Doctor's orders.

The strains of the modern world make men particularly susceptible to the upper-downer elevator of amphetamines and barbiturates. The former counterfeits energy so that they may face the fiercely competitive, stress-filled world of business, and the latter extinguishes the tensions in sleep. The result is a psychic seesaw, with such conflicting messages being sent through the nervous system that breakdown is a real danger.

Sustained use of barbiturates leads to tolerance, a condition in which increasingly large doses are necessary for them to work. The ready availability of the drug, combined with the depression it produces, has greatly increased the number of suicides by overdose. The mixture of alcohol and barbiturates can be fatal. An evening of drinking capped by a large dose of barbs has been responsible for many accidental deaths. When the user decides to break his habit because of the many negative aspects of barbiturates, the withdrawal can be as painful as it is with opiates. It should be done gradually and under medical supervision.

Tranquilizers

Tranquilizers are rapidly replacing barbiturates as the most commonly prescribed relief from tension and anxiety. Although they have no anesthetic factor, they do retard the stresses that so often cause insomnia and thus permit a natural state of sleep. They are also taken to relieve the anxieties of the day. Without promoting either the drowsiness that accompanies barbiturates or the nervous energy that comes from amphetamines, they do seem to make problems more manageable and solutions easier to find. Tranquilizers are available only on prescription, and the most widely used are: meprobamate (Milltown or Equanil), Librium, Atarex, Valium, and Oblivon.

The drawbacks of tranquilizers are dependence and tolerance. Overindulgence has been known to lead to impairment of consciousness, muscular weakness, lack of co-ordination, respiratory depression, low blood pressure, and a subnormal body temperature. There can also be painful withdrawal problems.

By this point, it must be clear that even the mildest form of pill-popping can have very serious consequences. Drugs are necessary for the treatment of our physical ailments. Something more is probably required for those illnesses of the psyche that make a problem of coping with day-to-day life.

My daughter was the sweetest kid you ever saw. Perfectly normal in every way. She got in with the wrong crowd. This punk gave her some LSD. It was the worst kind of trip. Schizophrenia. Three suicide attempts. For the last five years she's been in and out of institutions. I tell you—there was nothing wrong with that girl until that little bastard gave her that stuff. If I ever get my hands on him, I'll kill him.

Hallucinogens

Except for those introduced to the hallucinogens under scientific supervision for research, the majority of those who have experimented with them have had previous experience with milder drugs such as cannabis.

LSD (lysergic acid diethylamide) is the best known of the hallucinogens or psychedelic drugs. Frequently called "acid," it is also known as "sugar" (a drop on a sugar cube is one way of taking it) and "zen" because of the alleged mystical experience.

Mescaline, an active ingredient of the peyote cactus, and psilocybin, derived from a Mexican mushroom, are often used for their hallucinogenic properties. Psychedelic experiences have also been reported after sniffing a variety of substances from ether through nitrous oxide to model airplane glue, and from chewing the seeds of a number of garden plants.

The noted English novelist and essayist Aldous Huxley lectured and wrote about his experiences with mescaline. He said:

> For years, my failing eyesight had forced me to dwell in a gray world. The full experience of color was a dimly recollected memory. From the very first experience of mescaline, it returned more vivid, more dazzling, more vibrant than ever.*

The psychedelic trip is regarded as unique by those who have experienced it. Good or bad, it seems to have been so different from anything they'd known before that it has remained with them long after, sometimes altering their view of the world. At its best, it can induce a peerless serenity far beyond the euphoria of other drugs. At its worst, the "bad" trip terminates in violence, suicide, or a psychiatric institution. The extreme variations depend upon psychological expectations (what the tripper brings with him), personality quirks, mood, locale, trust in the person administering the drug.

The initial physiological changes are similar to those experienced from any stimulant to the central nervous system: tingling in the extremities, high blood pressure, dilated pupils, palpitations, loss of muscular control, a rise in the threshold of pain, increased body temperature, excited mental responses.

There seem to be certain psychic reactions that are experienced by all trippers: a sensation of floating and being suffused in light even when the eyes are closed, colors glowing radiantly beneath the lids; an alteration in perceptions of time, space, and shape. Reality gives way to illusion which, in turn, may become hallucination. Music often becomes a visual experience, and light a musical experience. There is an attempt to simulate the latter in the light shows that are so often a part of hard or "acid" rock concerts. On a less ostentatious level, the effect is used in most discothèques.

* An interview with the author of this book that took place in New York City, in October 1950, at the Warwick Hotel.

The users have trouble articulating the more intensely personal responses.

It liberated me. I saw where I fit in. I am one with the universe. And I must be true to myself. Do my thing.

There is a change in one's view of oneself. A feeling of oneness with the universe. At the same time, one is outside of it. Floating in infinite space. A place where time is meaningless. And so beautiful. A part of the stars and planets. I felt I could never again feel ugly, unwanted, insecure. I am one with a world beyond time.

•

I was pissing, and shitting, and puking. I had to kill all the devils who were tormenting me, or they'd kill me. It was a nightmare. And I was in it and out of it all at one time. And it would never end unless I broke out, mutilated my guards. It was awful, the worst experience of my life. Later, they told me they had to pin me down. Me, who has always been on top of things. In control. Never again.

The stripping away of defenses, on a bad trip, leads to a private hell, a nightmare, in which neuroses tumble over into psychotic behavior. Madness, self-mutilation, even murder have been not infrequent results.

Unfortunately, there has been so much negative publicity generated by the abuse of LSD that the public tends to look askance at some of the notable scientific achievements of its use in psychotherapy. Administered by professionals, in controlled situations, there have been encouraging results from experimenting with it in the treatment of alcoholism, narcotic addiction, autistic children. It has also given a new sense of inner peace, and an ability to cope with the inevitable, to terminally ill cancer patients.

In fighting man's addictions, we tend to concentrate on the drug involved and the crimes against himself and society that come from his pursuit of it. We are incensed by the violence perpetrated to support habits, by the pointless suicides and madness brought about by drug abuse. We worry about the lack of motivation and the loss of a sense of reality that go along with a dependence on cannabis, alcohol, or cocaine. We are disturbed by the cyclical nature of drugs as evidenced by the way experimenting with a relatively harmless one so often leads to playing with the more dangerous varieties.

We are so much more involved with effect than with cause that the solutions we come up with generally are based on legal action. We make the drugs illegal. We treat addicts and pushers alike as criminals. We submit the addicted to forcible withdrawal, which inflicts great psychic pain without genuine hope of lasting cure. All it really does is remove the drug for a period and then return the supposedly rehabilitated junkie to the psychological and sociological environment that made it a viable alternative to his surroundings. Sometimes we place them in programs such as the methadone program, which only substitutes one addiction for another without supplying a motivation for change.

Obviously, the best way to treat the drug problem is to find out what there is in a man's life that turns him on to such self-destructive escapes. Many people believe that it's the pain of poverty or racial oppression that attracts people to drugs. But cocaine and the barbiturate-amphetamine cycle are generally upper-class addictions. Cannabis and alcohol know no class or racial barriers. It would seem that both rich and poor, oppressed and oppressor, are caught up in the drug world.

There will be no real solutions until man begins to look in as well as out. It's too easy to say it's entirely a social problem. Cure the ills of our world, and you will cure addiction. Not quite. Equally at fault is man's ignorance of his body and its capacities. There is just so much stress that it can take. When the nervous system starts sending out signals of growing neuroses, the drugs that bring temporary relief are no more a real solution than blinding himself would be considered a cure for partial loss of vision.

6

THE RESPIRATORY SYSTEM

I'm going to introduce this section by telling you about an extraordinary (at least, *I* think extraordinary) thing that has happened in the course of writing, doing the interviews, and researching the sections on drugs, the respiratory and the cardiovascular systems. I've given up smoking. Until now, I was not living in a vacuum. I'd heard statistics, read articles, seen commercials *ad nauseam*. I'd tried to give up smoking before. It never worked. I'd hear that sinister voice telling me that it was a matter of life or breath and reach for another cigarette. I'd be lighting the second of the day as I read the latest finding of the ghoulish Surgeon General in the morning paper.

But this time the evidence was overwhelming. There isn't a thing that can go wrong with the respiratory tract that isn't made worse by smoking. The same is true of much that can go wrong with the cardiovascular system. And to top it off, I really resented being in the same addictive category as a junkie.

I'm not going to be a psalm-singing reformed whore about it. I don't feel particularly healthier or more virtuous now and I went through quite a period of feeling distinctly less healthy for want of a cigarette. Rare is the day when I don't miss or long for one. But it just doesn't make any sense to have one any more.

You may wonder about the pleasure factor for somebody who enjoys smoking. Well, I really enjoyed it, but I realized that I'd actually begun enjoying it less and less for a long time before I stopped. It was because I'd been trying to have it both ways: health *and* cigarettes. When I first started to smoke, there were a few cork-tipped brands, but there were no filtered cigarettes in the popular market. Manufacturers were concentrating on strength and taste and aroma: they weren't in a race to see who could make a cigarette least like a cigarette by removing tar and nicotine, the basic qualities of tobacco, and cutting its length down by a third with some dreadful "cotton-wool" filter.

In the old days, a good cigarette was like good wine. You lit up and inhaled that marvelous aroma. The tart acid-velvet taste filled your mouth. You could feel the warmth going down inside you. As you exhaled, you got that wonderful aftertaste, that memory of a good experience. That was a Lucky, or a Camel, or a Chesterfield in the old days. And that was smoking!

With the health scare, I followed the advertisements to cigarettes with less tar and nicotine drawing the line at about 1 mg. of nicotine and 15 mg. of tar. Anything below that was just a bad habit. Because they had no taste, the aroma seemed more stink than scent. I may have had more breath, but I needed it to drag on the weed in order to get so much as a hint of the old zing.

Kicking the habit is never fun. The first thing a smoker has to bear in mind is that he's an addict, and he's going to have some painful withdrawal symptoms. If the tobacco junkie needs help, there is hypnosis, as well as all manner of clinics, devices, classes. None are guaranteed in every case, but all have had a fair degree of success. It depends on motivation. If a smoker really wants to stop, he will. If his need for tobacco outweighs all other considerations, then he won't and probably shouldn't. He knows the consequences.

Cold Turkey was the route for the majority of ex-smokers. They just stopped. Some went on diets at the same time, fearing the gain of weight that comes of satisfying a frustrated oral craving, figuring that they're going to be in hell anyway and a little more irritation won't make that much difference. Others took to chewing furiously on sugarless gums which acted as their support drug, their methadone. Others walked around muttering: "I want to live. If I take just one cigarette, I'm going to die."

All went through periods of disorientation. Their minds would wander at parties, business meetings, during telephone conversations, during all of those times when they were accustomed to reach for a cigarette as a prop. But after a few days, that passed and they found, to their surprise and relief, that they were capable of having a conversation and following a thought through to its logical conclusion without the prop of tobacco.

For former tobacco addicts, in common with ex-alcoholics or heroin addicts, there is usually no such thing as a "moderate" habit. One may delude oneself into believing that one is sufficiently cured to have one cigarette occasionally. It *is* delusion. One cigarette inevitably leads to another, and another, and another, and soon the addict is back at his old habit.

In conclusion, I only want to add that I am opposed to legislating against cigarette smokers (especially in long-distance transportation) until we have legislated against all of the pollutants that now befoul our air. We all breathe the harmful equivalents of several packages of cigarettes a day simply by living in the vicinity of a major highway, population center, or industrial park. Cleaning up that mess will only take money and effort. The tobacco addict has a much more difficult emotional problem to cope with before he can stop. Most of us do very little about the greater foulness we breathe every day. Surely, we can indulge the addict for a few hours of flight during which his nerves may underscore his needs, and he will do far less to pollute our air than the automobiles that we drive.

The purpose of the respiratory system is to take in the life and energy-supplying substance oxygen, and to excrete carbon dioxide. This act links all of nature in what is known as the "carbon cycle."

Our chief energy and heat-producing nutrient is carbohydrates, and our major source of it is plant life (fruits and vegetables). The oxygen that we breathe is used to ignite the carbohydrates that we eat, thereby releasing the life-sustaining elements in them. In the process, the residue is carbon dioxide, which we return to the atmosphere when we exhale. This is true of all animals. The carbon dioxide is used by plants to produce carbohydrate, and so we see that nature has forged a chain that links all life on this planet.

The respiratory system consists of the folowing parts:
the nasal cavity
pharynx (throat)
larynx (containing the voice box)
trachea (windpipe)
bronchi
lungs

Breathing is a reflex action controlled by the nervous system, specifically a small section of the *medulla oblongata* (basal part of the brain).

It is healthier to breathe through one's nose than through one's mouth, because the hair follicles in the nose filter out larger particles of dust, and a warming, moisturizing process starts in the nasal cavities. This continues as the oxygen passes down through the pharynx, and by the time it reaches the trachea it is saturated with a vapor that equalizes both temperature and

The Respiratory System

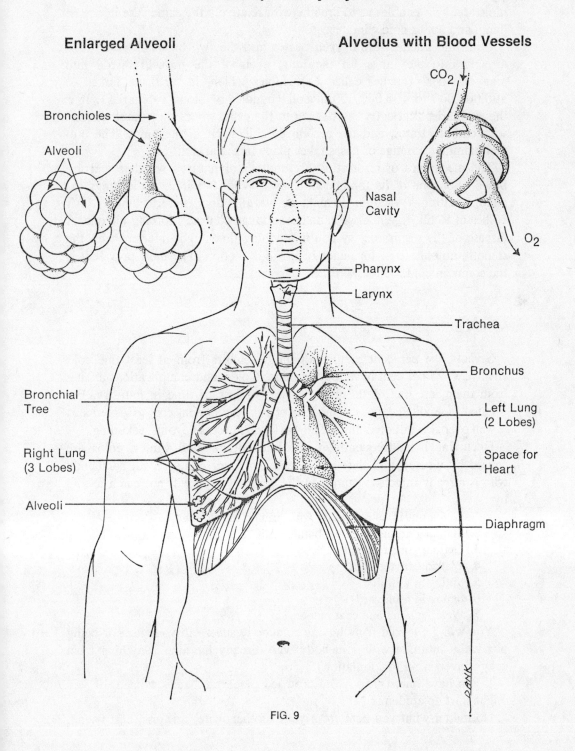

Enlarged Alveoli

Bronchioles

Alveoli

Alveolus with Blood Vessels

CO_2

O_2

Nasal Cavity

Pharynx

Larynx

Trachea

Bronchus

Bronchial Tree

Left Lung (2 Lobes)

Right Lung (3 Lobes)

Space for Heart

Alveoli

Diaphragm

FIG. 9

moisture. This enables us to breathe with relatively the same ease in dry or damp and hot or cold climates.

From the trachea, the oxygen passes into the two bronchi, which lead directly into the lungs. In the lung, each of the bronchi divide into many smaller branches called bronchioles which, in turn, are linked to 300,000,000 to 400,000,000 alveoli (bundles of blood capillaries). It is the capillaries that carry the oxygen to the cells, where they make contact with carbohydrates, and the carbon dioxide back to the lungs. The life-maintaining exchange of gases takes place in the alveoli.

The mechanics of respiration are another of nature's wonders and are based upon one of its fundamental laws. When we inhale, the lungs expand, creating a vacuum (which, as we all know, nature abhors). Air rushes in to fill it. When we exhale, the lungs contract, forcing air out. A disease of the respiratory system is anything that might interfere with the smooth, automatic performance of this dual action. The most prevalent is the common cold.

COLDS

Seventy-five per cent of the population suffers from at least one cold each year; 25 per cent have four or more. Colds, and complications arising from them, are one of the major causes of loss of time in industry. Estimated in medical expenses and loss of pay, the annual cost to Americans is well over two billion dollars. The worldwide cost is beyond reckoning.

Occurring most frequently in the late autumn and winter, colds are caused by viruses, and they are spread by direct contact with somebody who is already infected. Rumor to the contrary, you will not catch a cold by:

1. Going out in cold weather with insufficient clothing
2. Standing around in a wet bathing suit
3. Getting your feet wet
4. Walking in the rain
5. Sitting in a draft
6. Skiing in a blizzard
7. Wearing a hat and coat indoors

You will get a cold from having somebody sneeze in your face or being physically intimate with somebody who already has one (anything from cozy conversation to copulation).

If you have one, try to avoid crowded places and sexy women, or you might start an epidemic.

No matter what you hear from your mother, wife, mistress, best friend,

TV commercials, or local vitamin addict, there is no sure cure for a cold—neither aspirin nor chicken soup nor vitamin C.

At most, these remedies relieve symptoms. Aspirin will *temporarily* relieve achiness and reduce fever, if there is any. The same is true of antihistamines. The use of antibiotics can actually have bad side effects. Some people have allergenic reactions, and others build up resistance, rendering the drugs worthless for fighting more severe infections. Nose sprays and drops give temporary help by shrinking the nasal membranes, but the aftermath is generally still greater swelling. This may impede or destroy the valuable germ filters in the nose and pharynx. Vitamins and large doses of liquids have no proven worth. Special diets do nothing except, in special cases, facilitate the passage of food through sore throats.

A cold usually runs its course in three to ten days. In the early or severe stages, bed rest and warmth are advisable; above all, avoid coming in contact with other people, for you're in an extremely contagious state. Hot baths temporarily reduce nasal congestion and stuffiness by dilating the blood vessels in the skin and increasing the flow of blood through them. Mild analgesics (aspirin, Anacin, Bufferin, etc.) will reduce achiness. But that's about all you can do.

Get a lot of rest. Keep away from others. Pamper yourself. Let your natural recuperative powers do their work. Don't be a hero and ignore it. There's nothing manly or attractive about a cold. A sneeze is not a citation for heroism, and the complications can be serious.

ALLERGIES

Because they have the same symptoms, many people mistake their first attacks of allergies for spring or summer colds. However, allergies are not communicable and are relieved when the sufferer is separated from the thing to which he is sensitive. There are those who hold that allergies are hereditary, and others who claim that they are psychosomatic in origin. Neither view has been completely substantiated. Many sufferers outgrow childhood allergies, while others only develop them in adolescence and adulthood. They respond well to treatment by oral antihistamines or injections.

INFLUENZA

Influenza, a severe and highly infectious viral respiratory disease, usually occurs as an epidemic that rapidly spreads to large segments of the population, sometimes, on a global level. Most cases are communicated by direct contact, although indirect contamination is possible via linen, the preparation and serving of food, hand-to-hand contact, etc.

Influenza is caused by a number of different viral strains of varying severity. Most cases follow a similar course, coming on suddenly with chills, general achiness, and extreme fatigue. Within twenty-four hours the temperature rises between three and six degrees above normal and remains constant for about a day.

There is little or no congestion or runny nose, as in the common cold, and sore throats are rare. The chief complaints are headaches and muscular pains. There may also be a dry, hacking cough and some mild laryngitis. If you are a self-diagnostician, bear these symptoms in mind and call a doctor at the first sign of them. Complications can set in that might lead to pneumonia or bronchitis.

There is no specific treatment for influenza. Drugs do relieve symptoms, control fever, and may inhibit the pneumonia bacteria, which is the major cause of death. But the disease must run its course.

Every man should have an annual flu shot. It may not control the virulent strains that cause specific epidemics, but it is effective protection against the nonspecific type that recurs every winter. The serum only offers protection for up to twelve months; a new inoculation is necessary every year. Influenza is hideously debilitating, causing loss of income, faculties, and intimacy. Most important, it also causes loss of life.

PNEUMONIA

It is criminal to disregard respiratory infections, from the common cold on up, for they can lead to the most fatal one of all, pneumonia. Added to symptoms similar to those of flu, there are, in various combinations, a severe cough, heavy brown sputum, rapid pulse, breathing difficulties, cold sores, severe chest pains, a bluish tinge to skin, nails, and lips. There are both bacteriological and viral pneumonias. There are no preventives. Vaccines are only effective on limited types and among small groups of those exposed to them.

It is essential that treatment begin at the first symptoms. The mortality rate in untreated cases is 30 per cent, but medication reduces that figure to 5 per cent.

During the severe stages of all the infections we've been discussing, there is a period when even the most avid smoker loses his taste for tobacco. It's a good time to start breaking the habit, but, unfortunately, most smokers measure the date of their recovery from the first day that tobacco again tastes good to them.

BRONCHITIS

Bronchitis is an inflammation involving a dysfunction of the bronchial filters, called cilia. These hairlike structures sweep micro-organisms and foreign bodies out of the tubes. The inflammation, which can be viral, causes the glands to secrete mucus and other serous fluid that clog the cilia, making us cough so that we may expectorate the foreign material. It usually occurs in the aftermath of a cold, influenza, or strep throat. It can be precipitated by dust and a host of pollutants in the air, cigarette smoke being a prime offender. It is related to a condition commonly known as "smoker's cough."

Bronchitis should not be ignored. If untreated, it could become chronic or lead to pneumonia and, if there's any predisposition, to cardiac and pulmonary failures. The first symptoms are a dry cough and chest pains. These are followed by the bringing up of viscous material. If some traces of blood appear in it, a severe spasm of coughing has probably ruptured a small blood vessel. It's not serious and will heal by itself.

The first treatment for bronchitis is to get plenty of rest and keep away from places that have dusty or foul air. Tobacco is anathema, even the inhalation of other people's smoke. Depending on the severity of the condition, some antibiotics may be necessary. Usually steam inhalation, bronchodilators, and cough medicine are sufficient to bring relief and a cure within a few days.

The condition becomes chronic when a persistent irritation causes permanent damage to the bronchial tubes and destruction of many of the cilia. Again, cigarette smoke is a major offender, especially among men. The adult male is more susceptible to respiratory ailments than women. The common cold may seem like an insignificant irritation, but we men must never ignore it. We must avoid any possibility of the chain reaction of cold to bronchitis to pneumonia or emphysema.

EMPHYSEMA

I was a very active man. Healthy as a horse. Listen, I did everything in a big way. Drinking, screwing, smoking. When I look back, my downfall started with a little bronchitis. I didn't feel much like smoking. I should've quit then and there. Not me. The minute I started to feel a little better, I was back on the weed. Up and doing my thing again. Well, you know, things started to slide for me. I got this kind of smoker's cough. It wouldn't go away. But what the fuck, it wasn't killing me to bring up a little phlegm in the morning. Then they told me that it was chronic bronchitis, and it wasn't going to go away. And I had to give up smoking. Je-sus! That was killing me. I couldn't do it. I was always sneaking a drag when nobody was looking. So next came emphysema. And I'm not living so hard any more. I gave up smoking, because I don't have enough strength to inhale. And that goes for drinking and screwing, too. Shit, it's a major safari to make it to the mailbox.

Emphysema could almost be categorized as a male specialty disease. The overwhelming majority of victims are men between the ages of forty-five and sixty-five. It is usually preceded by chronic bronchitis and begins with a wheezing that accelerates until the slightest physical exertion results in gasping for breath. The descent continues until the sufferer is totally incapacitated.

There is no cure. A dry, warm climate may help. But it won't cause any miracles. Antibiotics aid in fighting off the recurrent bouts of pneumonia to which emphysema victims are prey, and drugs will relieve the bronchospasms. Nothing can prevent the inevitable death from heart failure or from an acute aggravation of the infection.*

Men must realize that they have a fatal weakness in the chest. Whether cardiac or respiratory, it's our major killer. We must stop doing things that endanger this most delicate of all parts of our bodies.

LUNG CANCER

The most fatal of all respiratory diseases is lung cancer. Of all forms of cancer, it is the most common in men. The only cure is surgical removal. Success of this operation is so remote statistically that surgeons report that only less than 10 per cent survive for five years or longer.

Let's not delude ourselves by pointing at Winston Churchill and George Bernard Shaw, who smoked their way into ripe old ages. Name five more. To bring this section back to where it began, with cigarettes, smoking is one of the direct causes of most cancers. No matter how clean or filtered it may be, all tobacco smoke contains carcinogens capable of setting off can-

* Asthma is another contributing cause of emphysema. It is essentially an allergic condition but incalculably worse than hay fever. Asthmatics can be helped by adrenaline, but the condition flares up again with sudden changes in temperature and emotional disturbances. An even climate and an even state of mind are essential.

cerous growths in any portion of the body that the smoke reaches. Cigarette smokers are seventy times more likely to have lung cancer than nonsmokers. No matter what kind of gambler you are, those are sucker odds. Smoking cigars rather than cigarettes is different only in that the cancer is more likely to appear in the mouth, larynx, or pharynx.

As urban dwellers are more likely to get lung cancer than those residing away from the cities, there is ample evidence that air pollution also contributes to the fatal disease. Yet, we continue to pollute the air and seduce each other with alluring tobacco advertising. Programs to rid us of these evils don't get through Congress. They offend big business and would cost the money that must be used to develop neutron bombs that preserve property while destroying people. We men are still running most of this country, and this is how we're doing it. One wonders—is insanity another male specialty disease?

7

THE CARDIOVASCULAR SYSTEM

The heart is a fantastic machine. It has been called the greatest pump
ever devised. As long as life persists, it is a study in perpetual motion. It
begins beating before birth and does not stop until the moment of death.
Together with the blood vessels, it composes the cardiovascular system.

The heart is divided into four chambers: the left and right auricles (or
atria) and the left and right ventricles. The pumping operation is actually
two simultaneous actions. In the first, oxygen-laden blood is pumped from
the lungs through the heart and into the rest of the body. The pulmonary
veins bring it from the lungs into the left atrium. It passes through a valve
into the left ventricle. From there, the aorta, the major artery of the body,*
carries it into the bloodstream and disperses it to all of the cells of the body
by way of a network of smaller arteries and capillaries.

In the second action, blood containing waste products is pumped from
the body through the heart and into the lungs, where the waste is replaced
by oxygen for the cycle to begin anew. Waste-laden blood enters the right
atrium by way of two major veins. It passes through a valve to the right
ventricle, from which it is pumped through the pulmonary artery into the
lungs.

The pumping motion is measured in heartbeats. It normally beats from
sixty to eighty times a minute. The smaller the heart, the more frequently it

* Arteries carry blood from the heart to the rest of the body, and veins carry it back to the
heart.

Cardiovascular System

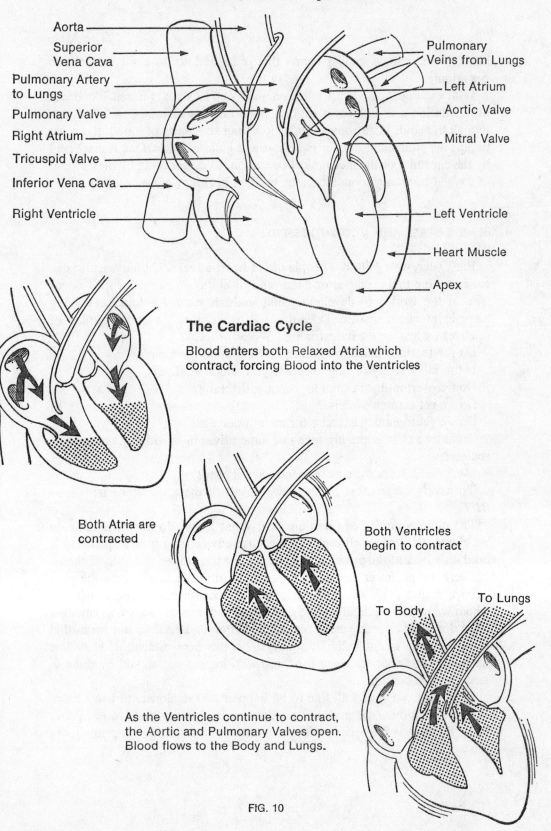

Aorta

Superior
Vena Cava

Pulmonary Artery
to Lungs

Pulmonary Valve

Right Atrium

Tricuspid Valve

Inferior Vena Cava

Right Ventricle

Pulmonary
Veins from Lungs

Left Atrium

Aortic Valve

Mitral Valve

Left Ventricle

Heart Muscle

Apex

The Cardiac Cycle

Blood enters both Relaxed Atria which
contract, forcing Blood into the Ventricles

Both Atria are
contracted

Both Ventricles
begin to contract

To Body

To Lungs

As the Ventricles continue to contract,
the Aortic and Pulmonary Valves open.
Blood flows to the Body and Lungs.

FIG. 10

beats. Women have smaller hearts than men and six to eight more beats per minute.

With each beat, the heart takes one-half cup of deoxygenized blood out of circulation and replaces it with an equal amount of refreshed blood. Although the adult male body contains less than six quarts of blood, the heart pumps the equivalent of over two thousand gallons a day. One is staggered by the enormity of the mechanical operation, to say nothing of the amount of oxygen necessary to maintain the body in healthy working condition.

HEART DISEASE AND MODERN LIFESTYLE

Each year, over 650,000 people die of heart attacks. Cardiovascular diseases are the major causes of death and disability in the developed countries of the world. In developing and underdeveloped countries, the big killer is infectious disease. Does that tell us anything about the quality of the lives we lead in the industrialized Western world?

Do the tensions place too great a burden upon the heart?

Is the killer really the age of anxiety in which we live?

Do we overindulge in smoking, eating, drinking?

Do we get enough exercise?

Do we get too much exercise for men of our age?

Should we change the hierarchy of imperatives in our highly competitive society?

Must we all learn to relax, unbend, take it easy?

To a very large extent, the answer to all of these questions is: *Yes—BUT.*

The more complicated questions are: What do we do about it? How do we change? It's so much easier to dispense advice than to act upon it. We need only look at the principal advisers of our time to see the truth of that.

There are no fewer instances of cardiovascular diseases among the physicians, analysts, philosophers, mystics and soothsayers of every stripe to whom we turn for guidance. The doctor who advises us to give up smoking often drops his cigarette ashes on the prescription. This does not mean that what they say is not valid; it simply indicates how difficult it is to live healthily in our society, even for those who know what should be done to keep in good condition.

Obviously, we would all like to be happier and healthier, to live longer. We would enjoy small personal revolutions in the way that we order our lives. But this is impossible without a larger revolution in the priorities of the world.

Speaking in a different context, a friend of mine once said: "If you can't have what you want, want what you can have." Let us apply that to longevity. Are we really in such a dreadful way as the articles that we read would seem to indicate? The answer is *no*. We are retaining our vigor and health longer and experiencing greater longevity than ever before. Do we need more? The answer is *perhaps*. But first we must learn how to handle our longer lives. Old age is already assuming such proportional significance and creating so many problems that geriatrics and gerontology are becoming major fields of research. The world is already terribly overcrowded. Shouldn't we be contented with what we have, leave well enough alone? By living still longer, mightn't we run the risk of having some madman drop bombs to solve the overpopulation problem?

Most men are not too concerned with any of the aforementioned questions. They want to live even longer. If it comes to choices due to overcrowding, they would rather put a curb on birth than age, especially as they are the ones who are aging.

What does all of this have to do with cardiovascular diseases? The longer we live, the more likely it is that we will die of them. More of us are already dying of cardiovascular diseases, which is largely due to the fact that more of us are living to the ages when we are susceptible to these diseases.

Until the age of thirty-five, accidental deaths outnumber those attributable to heart by six to one. By fifty-five, heart has overtaken accidents by three to one.

By sixty-five, cardiovascular is fifteen to one over accidents. Other significant alterations have cancer at five to one over accidents, and respiratory diseases (comparatively low until this age) at three to one over them.

It is in the ten-year span after sixty-five that cancer and respiratory diseases kill more men than they do at any other period. Nevertheless, their combined toll is less than half that of cardiovascular disease in the same period.

After seventy-five, cancer is responsible for 10 per cent fewer deaths than it was at its peak, and respiratory diseases are reduced by about 30 per cent. Accidents have stabilized at the same figure they were ten years earlier. Cardiovascular deaths have increased by approximately 50 per cent.

Many conclusions can be drawn from these figures, but most of them are hypothetical. Nobody positively knows the secrets of a man's life cycle. We are told positively that smoking, cholesterol, anxiety, and lack of exercise are major contributors to cardiovascular accidents. When a man is in his early thirties, he is likely to be suffering from the severest kind of anxiety, as he tries to make his way in the world and starts to raise a family with attendant worries about mortgages and the education of his children. If he smokes, he's probably at the peak of that habit during these years. He's likely to be lunching and snacking on junk food high in cholesterol, and just as likely to be getting less than half the amount of exercise his body was accustomed to a decade earlier when he was finishing college.

Let's turn the clock ahead two decades to the man's early fifties. Twenty per cent of the former smokers in this age group have quit; another 10 per cent have cut back notably. Our man is likely to be among them. He is much more aware of his diet and has eliminated much cholesterol, because he's eliminating foods containing them in an attempt to save the remnants of his waistline. Very likely he's finished paying for the mortgage and for the children's education, and his career is more a holding pattern until retirement than a battle to get ahead, so his anxieties are considerably lessened. If he ever was athletically inclined, his increased leisure time is apt to be used in a revival of participation in light sports such as jogging, golf, or tennis.

The younger man is living much more dangerously, from a cardiovascular point of view. According to the experts, he's doing all the wrong things. Of the deaths that occur in his age group, only one in nine is from heart.

The older man is making a sincere attempt to do all of the right things. In his age group, a little less than one out of every two deaths is from heart.

It would seem, then, that age is an important factor. This does not deny the extreme importance of the other things we've mentioned. The tense smoker with high cholesterol is an endangered species. We can take some chances while we're young, but we've got to reduce risk as we age.

There is some indication of a hereditary tendency to heart disease, but for the vast majority of us, those born without congenital conditions, the cardiovascular system will continue to perform very competently until late in life—if we'll only give ourselves a little tender loving care.

THE "HEART ATTACK"

The worst thing about it was the name. I remember when I was a kid, a guy had a heart attack. And he was out of it for good. And there I was in my thirties, and I had one. But I recovered. Good as new, the doctor says. But the name lingers on. And I hate it. "He's doing fine," they say, "for a guy with a heart condition." "I hope he isn't doing too much," they say. "He had a heart attack." I cringe. I can't stand it. I want to scream. I'm fine. In the pink.

The nomenclature is often more frightening than the cardiovascular episode it describes. People use the term "heart attack" with an abandon that is often inaccurate and always terrifying to the victim and his family. Clinically, it is a coronary disease: specifically, a hardening of those arteries, branching off the aorta, that supply blood to the heart muscle.

One of the symptoms of coronary disease is angina pectoris: a severe but temporary attack of cardiac pain that may radiate to the arms with constrictions around the chest. The significant point is that the pains are *temporary* and may not signal coronary defects. They may come from some form of strain like exercising too strenuously. No matter what the origin of the angina, people often carelessly say of the victim: "He had a heart attack."

Any cardiac pain is too often described by the all-encompassing term "heart attack." The same is true of disturbances in rhythm and occasionally even spasms of shortness of breath. Let somebody once have suffered any kind of heart incident, no matter how small, and chances are that anything that befalls him that's even remotely related will be described as a warning or attack. This sort of amateur diagnosis is dangerous. The psychological effects can be much more harmful than the physical episode.

I can go for a long time without thinking about it, and then something happens, and it's back on my mind. The worst thing about the recuperative period was that, no matter how reassuring the doctor was, there was something emasculating about having had a heart attack. A suspicion that, from then on, I'd somehow be less than a whole man. I began to wonder if I would ever be able to do the same day's work I was used to doing. I worried about sex. Would it ever be like it was? Would it ever be as good again? Psychologically, I had aged a hundred years.

The heart attack victim has many fears to overcome during his period of recovery. The psychological pressures are often worse than the illness. They often prove totally groundless. There is every reason to expect a return to normal and fulfilling and active lives. Treatment for all types of heart disease has improved radically over the last few years. There are many instances of patients who once surely would have died who are now back at work with every reason to expect a healthy and happy old age.

We ought to make an effort to remove the expression "heart attack" from our vocabularies. It's tired and overused and has come into disrepute. If we have any of the symptoms, we should lose no time in finding out exactly what's wrong, and then we should call it by its rightful name. The real thing doesn't sound as bad when it's called a coronary disease. As for temporary pains in the area of the heart which are of no specific origin, let's not dignify them more than we would a nonspecific temporary pain in any other part of our anatomy.

HEART FAILURE

Heart failure is another of those frightening and misleading terms. It sounds so absolute and fatal: the heart fails, and that's it, the end. We started calling it that when it really was as awful as it sounded. That is no longer true. This is not to imply that heart failure is not a very serious disease. It is. But each day there are more and more cases of recovery and return to normal and rewarding lives.

I have an enlarged heart. Some doctors say it's congenital, others that it's hereditary, still others that it's the result of rheumatic fever when I was a kid. The truth is: nobody knows for sure. One day it just failed. My lungs filled with fluid. I was choking, couldn't breathe. They rushed me into intensive care, a cardiac unit. The big thing was to get the fluid out and make certain pneumonia didn't set in. For me, cold weather's the bad time. A bad cold, flu, bronchitis—any of that can set it off again.

Heart failure is actually a dysfunction in the pumping mechanism of the heart which prevents it from delivering sufficient quantities of oxygen to the various parts of the body. This causes an accumulation of fluid, usually in the lungs and/or legs. There are many precipitating factors. It can be induced by faulty heart valves, illnesses with high fevers, the strain of overeating, severe dieting, too much exercise, coronary diseases.

High blood pressure can bring on any of the cardiovascular illnesses. High blood pressure (hypertension) most often starts in the early thirties, but no age is exempt from it. It may be hereditary or it may arise from unknown causes. Temporary bouts of it can be brought about by tension, danger, overexcitement, too much exercise, overeating. Whether or not this is dangerous depends upon the condition of the heart, how often it happens, how long each attack endures, and how high the pressure goes.

Because it has been established that high blood pressure endangers the heart, brain, kidneys, and glands, it is absolutely essential for every adult to have his pressure checked periodically. If there is any tendency to or history of hypertension, one must try to hold it in check by keeping slim, exercising moderately, and limiting one's intake of salt. When the pressure is chronic, certain drugs will help to control it.

CORONARY DISEASES

Coronary diseases may not always lead to heart failure, but they result in a certain amount of sclerosis (hardening) of the arteries. There may also be a myocardial infarction, which is death of tissue in the heart muscle. The dead tissue is replaced by rigid scar tissue that permanently weakens the heart. It is not as dire as it sounds. Actually, most men have or will have suffered minor coronary infarction by the age of forty without having noticed it. With the passage of years, the incidents become more serious.

Arteriosclerosis is a sclerotic condition usually associated with hypertension. A hardening of the arterial walls causes an inadequate blood supply to reach the brain. The memory fails; there is great anxiety; strong personality traits become distorted and exaggerated; there is giddiness and headaches and possible incontinence. The ailment generally, but not necessarily, occurs in old age.

THE STROKE

Since the stroke, my father's been a vegetable. There's no hope for him. He'll never move or speak again. It's tearing the family apart emotionally, to say nothing of the financial drain. Medicare doesn't begin to cover what we consider proper attention for our father. And there's no end in sight. His heart is very strong. You begin to wonder—where's the morality in keeping him alive? He doesn't know he's living. Then you hate yourself for thinking it. He's my father. Everything I am, I owe to him. But like this—that's not my father any more. That's just a blob. There is a case to be made for euthanasia. But how would you live with yourself after? How are you living with yourself with things the way they are? You can't bear to see him. And you can't walk away from him.

A cardiovascular accident, or stroke, is a failure of the blood supply to reach a portion of the brain. They are much more common in men than in women. The section of the brain affected goes out of operation. At worst, there is less of faculties, speech, and total paralysis.

Recovery from a stroke depends on age, vigor, and the size and location of the damage. It may take years and leave partial paralysis and impaired mental and vocal powers. Rarely does one regain complete control. The victim is usually left with a limp, a partial loss of use of a hand, a slur in speech, or a distorted facial expression.

PREVENTION

Every day new research and breakthroughs are bringing hopes of recovery to victims of heart (and related) diseases. From the heart transplants pioneered by Dr. Christiaan Barnard in South Africa, to the work of the American Heart Association, an enormous amount of creative medical research is being focused on this area. The government is contributing to the effort through the United States Public Health Service and the federally funded National Heart Institute. But first and foremost, it is up to us. We must learn to help ourselves, to take care of our hearts. There are certain rules:

1. Regular checkups on blood pressure and electrocardiograms.

2. If you can't stop smoking, switch to low-tar cigarettes. The chance of heart disease among heavy smokers (two or more packages a day) is more than five to one over nonsmokers in the 40–50 age bracket.

3. Try to maintain the right weight for your age. In every group, there is 30 per cent greater chance of heart attack among men who weigh twenty pounds more than they should.

4. Cut down on weight by cutting down on foods with high cholesterol, which are generally very fattening, too. Although nothing has been proved conclusively, there is ample evidence that they lead to sclerotic conditions and hypertension.

5. Try to exercise on a regular basis, giving proper attention to your age and medical history. (See the chart on page 30.) If there's been previous heart disease, consult a doctor before embarking on any regime.

6. It is an illusion that we need less sleep as we age. For the sake of your heart, you need more rest with every passing year.

7. Tension and stress contribute to a susceptibility to heart disease. Try to learn to relax, to walk away from anxiety-provoking situations. Know your own weaknesses in this area. That's the beginning of strength.

We are all responsible for our own health and well-being. Our bodies are in our safekeeping. If we don't want to lose them, then we must love them.

8

THE GASTROINTESTINAL SYSTEM

The gastrointestinal system is the elaborate mechanism that ingests food, processes it for use by the body, and eliminates its waste matter. Along the way, there are probably as many hazards to a man's well-being as there are mines around an enemy encampment in wartime. Before discussing how the parts of the system work, and the traps contained in them, let's discuss the subject with which it is most concerned: food.

One of the greatest works ever written on the pleasures of food was Anthelme Brillat-Savarin's *The Physiology of Taste*. In the eighteenth century the great French gourmet proclaimed a philosophy of eating that still holds true today. He maintained that the two elements most essential to eating well are time and thought. He might have added that this also holds true for healthy eating. Unfortunately, time and thought are two of the things that we seldom apply to our choices of foods.

THE AMERICAN DIET

I don't have the time to waste sitting around fancy restaurants. A pizza or a hot dog on the run—maybe a sandwich at my desk. That's about it.

•

Coffee and juice, maybe a slice of toast—that's breakfast on the days I have expense-account lunches. I know it's supposed to be bad for me. But I also know I've got to pack the drinks and meal away in the middle of the day. I can't stint, or the guy I'm lunching with gets suspicious, thinks I'm going to pull the lean-and-hungry look on him. I drink a little too much. That's okay. I figure he's drinking a little too much too, so we're quits. The food is the *spécialités de la maison.* I don't pay much attention to that. It's only to get a quick fix on sobriety. The only important thing is matching the restaurant to the client, so he'll be suitably impressed.

It has often been said that some people live to eat and others eat to live. There's a third category to which men seldom belong; these are the people who eat *properly* and generally live longer.

Like the fellows we've just quoted, most of us are midday gastronomical victims of our livelihoods. There might be some relief if the evenings brought a healthy change. They almost never do, for at night we're at the mercy of our lifestyles.

As concerned as she may be about us, the busy mother or working wife seldom has time to worry about balancing our diets.

I once told her that her spaghetti was the greatest this side of Napoli. So I get it about once a week, even if I had linguini for lunch.

It's no easier on the "swinging single." If he hasn't got a date, it's a frozen-food special or hamburger before doing the bars, or going to a film, or staying home with television or a book. If he does have a date, what he eats usually depends upon one or a combination of four things:

A. His finances
B. How much he wants to impress her
C. Her experiments with *haute cuisine*
D. His experiments with *haute cuisine*

Unless he is a health food faddist, neither the married nor the single man gives much thought to the nutritional value of what he eats unless he is ill. We seem much more concerned with getting better than staying well.

The women with whom we are involved are not much wiser than we are in this respect. The solution to eating badly for both sexes is usually the crash diet. This can sometimes be as good for our emotional lives as it is for our waistlines. The couple who diets together generally stays together, at least for the period of austerity. The problem is that, together or apart, the diet is no proper solution. We have to change our eating habits or the weight will return, and the diet cycle will begin all over again. This bouncing up and down is emotionally frustrating and bad for our hearts. We've got to remember that no system of the body exists as a totality. How and what we eat are affected by and affect every part of us.

Like Brillat-Savarin, we must develop a philosophy of eating. Let's return to basic types of eaters. Although some American women, trying to emulate a fashion-model slimness, may eat to live, the American male seldom does. We are surrounded by too much abundance. Restaurant and food advertising appeals directly to us by boasting of "man-sized portions." Has anybody ever seen an ad for "woman-sized portions"? It becomes almost a matter of masculine pride to be like the distressed male in the old Alka-Seltzer commercial and moan: "I ate the whole thing."

Food can be delicious, decorative, dietary, deleterious, or a combination of any of these four. We've all had memorable meals made up of foods that looked beautiful, had provocative aromas and tantalizing tastes. The thick soups, the rich sauces, the pastries and desserts that were works of art, the wines and liqueurs: they were feasts recollected with pleasure. Aside from the memory, the only thing gained was weight. With few exceptions, every time a chef is called a genius, a nutritionist shudders.

For those of us who live to eat, these great meals are generally not the rule but the exception. Most of the men in this category are gourmands rather than gourmets. They eat out of compulsion, tension, frustration. Food is a displacement for sexual energy or professional inadequacy. They eat anything at hand, and what's most readily at hand might be called *nutritional pollution:* the proliferating junk foods, the cheap candies and cakes, the packaged snacks, the pizzas, hot dogs, and chain-store hamburgers.

Everything in our national heritage conspires to make us eat. Even our most cherished national holidays are reduced to excuses for gorging. The deep significance of the day runs a poor second to the ritual of eating at Easter brunches, Thanksgiving Day feasts, Christmas dinners, New Year's parties, and Fourth of July picnics.

Food is ubiquitous. We never even take a drink without hors d'oeuvres, potato chips, popcorn, dips, pretzels, peanuts, crackers, cheese. We go on health food kicks and then allow the manufacturers to ruin them by catering to our weakness for rich garnishes. Cottage cheese gets creamed, yogurt has sugar-laden fruit preserves added, whole grain becomes carbohydrate-laced Granola. In living to eat we're becoming a nation eating to die.

American men are naturally energetic. We run, jog, walk, play tennis, football, baseball, do calisthenics, and swim. Many of us do it as part of a regular regime; yet there is a higher percentage of overweight men in this country than in any other country in the world. We have to start applying as much time, thought, and energy to healthy eating as we do to healthy exercise.

Eating to live used to be an exercise in boredom. This is no longer the case. Browse through a health food store, and you'll find all kinds of delicacies that are both delicious and nutritious. The great French chef Michel Guérard has devised what he calls *cuisine minceur*. It's a revolutionary approach to the great foods of France that doubles the value to us by halving the calories without sacrificing the flavors. If you cook for yourself or even as a hobby, buy one of the books based on his discovery. If you don't go near a stove, get one for whoever does prepare your meals.

The most important advice to anybody who wants to look good, feel well, and keep healthy is to watch the portions. Enormous quantities of even the most nutritious food does not do any good for any of us. In eating, less is more. Bulk does not equate with benefit. When we are really in need of food, the body gives us the signal through hunger pangs and cravings. Our bodies are not warehouses.

Food should satisfy three basic requirements:
1. Be a source of energy
2. Be a source of strength
3. Take care of structural and functional needs

To do the job well, we must make certain that we take in a sufficient amount of the nutritional substances found in food, which are: carbohydrates, fats, and proteins, with lesser amounts of minerals and vitamins. In order that we may do this, we must know where to find these things and how to balance our diets so that we have sufficient quantities of all and excesses of none. Proportion is as important to diet as it is to architecture. A philosophy of food starts with a knowledge of what we eat and how we eat. Fulfillment of self, even in the area of nutrition, is not satiation; it is enlightenment. We are, indeed, what we eat, both in external appearance and internal well-being.

The search for a perfect diet is futile. Foods are too complex. They contain a bewildering array of nutrients, some acting at cross-purposes with others. To help us to live healthy and possibly longer lives, the things that we need to know are the values of the individual nutrients, the good and bad sources, the dangers of excess if any, the surprisingly small amount we need. We can then find our way to a sensible diet and dispel some of the myths. We'll learn that, rumor and speculation to the contrary, there are *no* vitamins that will make us more potent and sexier; steak is not the best source of protein but is a possibly dangerous source of the wrong kind of fats; an excess of vitamin supplements can be lethal; a baked potato with the inevitable dollop of butter is not diet food; no nutrient in the world will cure baldness; vegetarianism is not healthy unless one really knows the full nutritional content of each vegetable and fruit and balances them as carefully as one should balance the more traditional "meat and potatoes" diet.

THE NUTRIENTS

Proteins

Function: The basic chemical unit of the living cell. The only source of nitrogen essential to the growth and repair of the body. Responsible for 80 per cent of the dry weight of our muscles, 70 per cent of skin, and 90 per cent of blood. Aid in the distribution of food and drugs. Essential to the maintenance of the correct balance of vital fluids in the brain, spine, and intestines.

Good sources: Protein comes in the form of over twenty chemicals that are essential to the body; these are called amino acids. The best sources are those foods containing *complete proteins*—that is, all of the essential amino acids. These are found in all animal products and by-products. Within this category there is a subdivision—those complete protein foods, also containing a high degree of fats, which are not as good for us as those with low fat content. Vegetables contain *incomplete proteins* and seldom supply all amino acids. It is also good to shop among the complete proteins for those containing good supplies of essential minerals and vitamins. The best sources are poultry, fish, lean meats, milk (fortified skimmed or partially fat-free), cheese (low-fat or skimmed-milk varieties), and low-fat natural yogurt. Other good sources are whole grains, dry nuts, bean sprouts, soybeans, wheat germ, and brewer's yeast.

Bad sources: Beef, pork products, creamy cheeses, heavy cream, meals made up only of vegetables (unless one has learned which to combine so that the result equals a complete protein), pastries, all baked goods made from bleached or polished grains, peanut butter, the oilier nuts such as cashews, walnuts, etc.

Requirements: About 65 grams, or 2½ ounces, a day. Excess amounts of it are of no value, because the body does not store it for future use.

Carbohydrates

Function: The body's chief source of energy. Used even while we sleep to fuel the functioning of all the automatic activities of the other systems of the body. Particularly important to the respiratory, nervous, and cardiovascular systems. Important for the digestion of proteins and carbohydrates themselves.

Good sources: Carbohydrates are composed of sugars and starches which the body converts to sugar. To some degree, they are found in almost every food. Valuable sources of concentrated carbohydrate are starches, because these foods also contain large amounts of other nutrients. Although raw fruits and vegetables contain substantial quantities of sugar rather than starch, they are also good sources, because they have so many other values. The best sources, then, are cereals, bread (particularly whole grain), potatoes (cooked in their jackets), fruits, rice, and grains (raw grains are good sources, but cooked grains are better, because the protein in them only metabolizes when cooked).

Bad sources: Candy, desserts, cakes, ice cream, and sugar. No matter what the health food people say, honey, molasses, and sugars (natural, raw, and brown) are equally bad.

Ill effects: Too much sugar causes tooth decay, withdrawal of necessary sugar from the blood, obesity, probably diabetes, heart disease, irritability, and fatigue. (Although there is an initial spurt of energy, the overstimulation brings on ill effects.) Too little carbohydrates causes us to use protein, vital for other functions, as a source of energy. Although the evidence is inconclusive, there are indications that an overabundance of carbohydrate may also play a part in causing high blood pressure, liver and kidney diseases, circulatory problems, and inflammation of the gall bladder.

As American men consume more sugar than any other nutrient, we have to be particularly careful. If we can't curb those sweet teeth, we must try to eat a little protein with our sugar stuffs: milk with desserts, cheese and biscuits with alcoholic beverages. Because we digest protein more slowly, this will slow down the rate of absorption of sugar into the bloodstream.

Requirements: Carbohydrate and fat are our sources of energy. The amount we need is measured in calories. The average man uses 1,600 calories a day just to perform his normal bodily functions. How much more he needs depends upon his size, age, the type of work he does, and to a lesser degree, the amount of physical exercise he gets. A good average for most men is 3,000 calories a day. For those who do sedentary work and get little or no exercise, about 2,300 is sufficient. For those in heavy labor occupations, it can range up to almost 5,000 a day. Bear in mind that these figures include *both* fats and carbohydrates as well as the traces of these in other foods. Little calorie counters are available in most bookstores. It's a good idea to get one not only for losing weight (reducing calories so that we burn up the energy stored as fat in our body) but also to maintain weight so that we are certain to have enough to get through our tasks without invading our supplies of protein.

Fats

Function: An important source of energy. Insulation for the body. Protection of the vital organs. Carrying the fat-soluble vitamins (A, D, E, and K) as well as essential fatty acids.

Good sources: All fats can be made liquid by heating. Saturated fats are those that harden at room temperature. The best sources are the highly unsaturated or polyunsaturated fats, and these include all vegetable oils except olive oil. This means that the relatively inexpensive corn, soybean, and safflower oils are every bit as good as the very expensive oils, such as sunflower, found in specialty and health food stores. There are many excellent and healthful products in these stores, but there are an equal number of fraudulent items. Make it a practice to read all labels and know exactly what you're getting for the often exorbitant prices you're paying. Margarine is another excellent source of fat. Again, read the label to make certain it is unsaturated; otherwise, you might just as well use butter.

One can't be expected to give up all saturated fats, so we include cheese, eggs, whole milk, and butter in our good list. Lean meats, poultry, and fish all have quantities of fat and are better than the fattier varieties of beef, pork, and lamb.

Bad sources: Cream, solid shortenings, cocoa butter, coconut oil, and palm oil—all of which are used in many cookies and cakes of the store-bought variety, as well as in nondairy milk and cream substitutes (be sure always to ask for real milk when you order coffee or tea in restaurants). All fatty meat products, especially chain-store hamburgers and hot dogs. The saturated fats are bad for us because they contain a high degree of cholesterol, which is linked to heart and sclerotic diseases. Cholesterol is not all bad. It performs many important body functions, including the repair of ruptured membranes and the production of sex hormones. Perhaps there is something to the myth of the stereotyped rugged, sexy male and his preference for steak, fried potatoes, whiskey, and apple pie à la mode.

At any rate, our body manufactures cholesterol, as well as getting it from food sources, and generally makes enough to satisfy most of our needs for it. Don't make its healthy qualities an excuse for ignoring its harmful effects.

Requirements: See the requirements for carbohydrates on page 90.

Vitamins

General information: Vitamins are specific organic compounds found in foods. They were first isolated at the beginning of the twentieth century. A lack of them can lead to insufficient growth in the young. There are also specific diseases traceable to this, called "vitamin-deficiency diseases." Among them are scurvy, beriberi, rickets, night blindness, and pernicious anemia. For purposes of classification, they are divided into two groups: fat-soluble and water-soluble. The former include vitamins A, D, E, and K. The latter include vitamin C and the diverse group known collectively as B complex. *Only very small quantities of vitamins are necessary in the diet,* and usually a well-balanced diet will satisfy all of our requirements. Except for certain illnesses and special diets to lose weight, additional dosages of vitamins in pill form are about as beneficial as any other placebo.

Vitamin A. A deficiency can cause night blindness and subsequent atrophy of the conjectiva, alteration in the growth of bones and teeth, and general susceptibility to disease due to changes in the skin and mucous membranes. There is also some likelihood of an interference with the reproductive process, which is as close as it comes to being a "sex" vitamin.

A very small amount is necessary to well-being, and we generally are provided with all we need from a diet that includes liver (or cod liver oil), whole milk, fortified margarine or butter, fortified skimmed milk, hard cheeses such as Swiss, Jarlsburg, or Cheddar, eggs, apricots, carrots, parsley, squash, kale, and other dark-green and yellow vegetables.

Vitamin D. It plays a large part in strengthening teeth and bones and is necessary for the absorption of calcium. A deficiency leads to rickets, a disease in which calcification is retarded.

Large amounts are necessary but, fortunately, it is synthesized in the skin by direct exposure to sunlight. When the sun is filtered by weather as in winter, pollution, clouds, or by windowpanes, other sources may be necessary. Most of the foods mentioned as containing vitamin A also contain D. Oil-packed fish, such as sardines and tuna, are also well supplied with it. In the absence of these in the diet, supplemental doses may be necessary.

Vitamin E. Although there is no evidence that we need this vitamin, it does help stabilize membranes and, thus, aid in the healing of skin wounds. It has been called a "sex vitamin" by those who take as conclusive evidence of human frailty the findings of experiments on rodents. The lack of it has induced sterility in some species of rats. *There is no evidence that this is also true in men.*

It is found in wheat germ oil, green leafy vegetables, eggs, and brown rice. Specific dosage has yet to be determined. Despite the lack of any proof of their beneficial qualities to men, the sale of vitamin E capsules has developed into quite a profitable business for the pharmaceutical companies.

Vitamin K. It is essential in the production of prothrombin, a substance manufactured in the liver and necessary to the proper clotting of blood. Lack of it has been known to lead to hemorrhages.

The necessary daily quantity has yet to be determined. It is found in green leafy vegetables such as spinach and lettuce.

Vitamin C. This vitamin is necessary in large quantities. Also known as ascorbic acid, it has proven effective against the disease of scurvy, an ailment of the blood that has the clinical features of hemorrhaging, oozing of the gums, bleeding spots under the skin and around the hair follicles on the skin. It also aids in the formation of red corpuscles and helps the healing process of wounds and broken bones. It is needed for strong teeth and bones. *There is no evidence that it will help to cure colds.*

The best source of vitamin C is citrus fruit. It can also be found in strawberries, leafy vegetables, and tomatoes. Because so much is necessary, supplements should be taken by those on diets deficient in these foods.

Vitamin B Complex.

Vitamin B_1 (thiamine) is necessary to prevent beriberi. As it is part of the enzymes that break down carbohydrates, small deficiencies lead to a loss of appetite.

Vitamin B_2 (riboflavin) is sometimes called vitamin G. It is important to the oxidization of carbohydrates. A deficiency can lead to lesions on the skin and tongue. It is also believed to play a part in the proper functioning of the eyes.

Vitamin B_6 (pyridoxol, pyridoxamine, pyridoxine) is necessary to the formation of red blood cells. It also helps to metabolize amino acids.

Vitamin B_{12} (cyanocobalamin) is the most complex of all vitamins. It is necessary for the manufacture of red blood cells, and injections of it are a known cure for pernicious anemia.

Niacin (nicotinic acid) is one of the B vitamins, complex although it is not numbered. It is an effective antidote to chilblains and migraines, and serves as a preventive of pellagra, a deficiency disease symptomized by inflammation of the tongue, skin eruptions, neuritis, a species of anemia, and changes in the spinal cord.

Folacin (folic acid). A deficiency of this vitamin can cause a reduction of white blood cells and a species of anemia. The disease associated with it is sprue, which is characterized by indigestion, inflammation of the tongue, and difficulty in absorbing nutrients.

There are other B complex vitamins, such as biotin and pantothenic acid, about which so little is known that we need not trouble ourselves with them here.

The B complex vitamins are found in most foods, particularly in proteins, whole-grain breads, liver, wheat germ, brewer's yeast, milk, and lean meat. Some are manufactured in our own systems. A well-balanced diet should supply all of these vitamins that we require.

Minerals

The body needs a constant replenishing of minerals because they are excreted daily in significant quantities. Bones are the great storehouse of minerals. When we draw on this source without replenishing it, there is danger of softening the skeletal structure. Calcium, chlorine, iodine, iron, magnesium, phosphorus, potassium, sodium, and sulfur are the minerals most essential to the human body. To a much lesser degree, we need flouride to help prevent tooth decay. This is most true for children and, for their sake, it is often added to drinking water. The infinitesimal quantities of other necessary minerals, including zinc, copper, chromium, manganese, and cobalt, find their way into our systems in a variety of foods that are parts of our normal diets.

Calcium is necessary for strong bones and teeth, blood clotting, nerve and muscle tone. Milk and milk products are the greatest sources of it. It is also found in eggs, green vegetables, and blackstrap molasses.

Iodine is an essential regulator of the thyroid gland.

Sodium and chlorine. Both are regulators of the water balance in the body.

Iodine, sodium, and chlorine are all found in iodized table salt. Most of us consume much more than we need. Unless you are on a salt-free diet, you need not worry about alternative sources. By the way, cutting down on salt will not cause weight reduction except for the most fleeting period.

Iron is an essential ingredient of hemoglobin, the substance in the blood that transports oxygen from the lungs to all the other parts of the body. Iron is found in lean meats, egg yolks, green vegetables, liver, and grain products which have been fortified with it after its removal in the milling.

Magnesium helps in the formation of bones and teeth and is required for the functioning of certain enzymes. Magnesium is supplied in grain and vegetable-rich diets. It is also found in seafood and chocolate.

Phosphorus plays an important part in metabolism. It is supplied by dairy products, lean meats, and animal organs such as kidneys, liver, and brains.

Potassium is related in function to sodium and chlorine. It also plays a part in nerve and muscle tone. Seafood, meat, and vegetables are important sources.

Vitamins and minerals in pill form will never substitute for a balanced diet. Without the basic foodstuffs, we do not get bulk, fiber, and roughage, which are important for the regulation of the digestive organs, particularly the intestines.

Liquids are necessary for keeping the water balance in the body. They are also required for flushing the system clean of harmful waste products. We should all drink at least eight glasses of fluids a day. One of the best is plain water, because it not only contains no additives but is also a repository for certain necessary minerals.

WEIGHT CONTROL

When I was a kid I was real wiry. I ate like a horse and never put on a pound. Now look at this pot. I've joined a gym. You name the diet, I've tried it. Nothing helps. It takes a year and a day to take a couple of pounds off, and they're back on in no time.

Spare tire, middle-age spread, beer belly: there are many descriptives for what happens to most men once they pass their mid-thirties. Weight becomes a problem. Part of it is due to chemical changes in the body. We metabolize food at a different rate and have to eat more to produce the same amount of heat and energy.

Young boys eat more junk food, loaded with carbohydrates and fat, than most adults, but they burn up the calories in the act of growing, in the physical activity and exuberance that are a part of that time of life.

In our twenties, the metabolic rate is slowing down. We're not as wildly active, but a compensating awareness of our physical appearance has begun in late adolescence. Sexual pursuit has become part of our lives and, with it, the desire to be physically more attractive. At the same time, we're embarking on careers, and appearance is an important factor in the job market. We try to keep up a routine of exercise at the same time that we watch our diets.

The mid-thirties finds us in another life condition. Most of us have found our mates and our professional niches. We've started to become a little negligent about how we look. Firm muscles are not as important as firm financing on the mortgage. A flat stomach is not as important as an inflated income.

We don't seem to have the time for exercise. We work out when we think about it, which is not as often as it used to be. In the warmer months we may play some tennis or golf or swim once a week. Perhaps we go bowling on Wednesday or Thursday night, but the beers usually undo the benefits.

Our eating habits have changed. We're back on the junk foods and candy of our childhood—this time in an effort to get spurts of energy or relieve our nervousness and tension. We drink more, and alcohol is pure carbohydrate. A half bottle of wine or a few healthy drinks have as many calories as we should be having in a complete meal.

Chemical changes in our bodies, a laxity about our appearance, less exercise, bad eating habits: they add up to a weight problem. It's a good idea to watch one's diet at any age. After thirty, it's crucial and becomes more important with each passing year.

Dieting must become a way of life for the middle-aged man, not simply a crash program when we've passed the point of no return on our belts. Information is readily available about what we should weigh for our height, and the amount we should eat to maintain that weight within our given modes of life. Whether one counts calories or carbohydrates, diets come down to limiting what we eat. The crash diets that fill the magazines should be avoided, because they are often unbalanced and may eliminate essential nutrients along with extra pounds. Most of them are designed to fatten the reputations and pockets of dubious nutritionists rather than slim your body. Whether putting on weight, losing it, or maintaining it, a diet must be a proper balance of those elements necessary to sustain life and health.

Overeating leads to obesity, a condition in which we take in far more food than the body needs for growth, repair, and energy. This decreases our performance at work, because the body's bulk interferes with the coordinated use of our muscles. It places an enormous burden on both the circulatory and cardiovascular systems—another example of how the systems interrelate. The fat acts as insulation, interfering with the release of body heat. For many reasons, fat people are susceptible to infectious diseases, as well as to such degenerative diseases as hypertension and atherosclerosis. It interferes with a good sex life not merely because "nobody loves a fat man," but because the bulk limits the sexual positions and is too enervating to permit any athletic enthusiasm.

We think of malnutrition as a disease of the poor. Actually, many wealthy people suffer from it, because of an excessive zeal in maintaining that "lean and hungry look" that Julius Caesar so mistrusted. It is caused by a deficiency in one of the essential nutrients. When carbohydrates and fats are eliminated from the diet, the body begins to use proteins for energy, causing a breakdown of essential tissues and emaciation. The body temperature and blood pressure may be reduced to a dangerous extent. The reduction in blood proteins may result in edema (swelling from accumulation of fluids). There is an increased susceptibility to infectious diseases, especially tuberculosis.

We like to think of thin men as wiry, energetic types. The energy is of an unhealthy, nervous type. It is soon exhausted, leaving in its wake fatigue, mental apathy, and a disinclination for physical exertion. Thus, we see that, though the emaciated man may look better in stylish clothes, he is no more sexually adept out of them than his obese brother. He is often too tired and too apathetic to be a good lover and, more frequently than other men, has to resort to artificial stimulants to make the sexual scene.

THE DIGESTIVE SYSTEM

More than thirty feet of tubing links the oral opening with the anal opening. From the mouth, food passes swiftly through the pharynx into the esophagus, which passes through the chest and ends in the stomach. Food generally remains in the stomach from three to five hours. During that time, peristaltic movement pulverizes larger tough particles and glandular secretions begin to prepare it for absorption.

From the stomach, nutrients are moved into the small intestine, a coiled tube from twenty-two to twenty-five feet long. It is there that the process of digestion is completed and most of the absorption takes place.

The first nine to twelve inches of the small intestine is called the duodenum; it contains the pancreatic and bile ducts, which bring vital secretions from the pancreas and gall bladder, respectively. The gall bladder is the storehouse for the digestive agents manufactured in the liver. These include body-manufactured cholesterol, which occasionally solidifies, causing the painful condition called gall stones, and bile, which is most important in its effect on fats.

The pancreatic juices are essential to the digestion of all three major food categories. Insulin is one of the pancreatic hormones. It has a specific function in the metabolism of sugar. A malfunction results in *diabetes* (actually, *diabetes mellitus*), an excess of sugar in the bloodstream, or *hypoglycemia,* too little sugar in the blood.

The appendix is located near the entrance to the large intestine. It's a wormlike sac that may be a vestige of man in a less developed stage, for it serves no function in our bodies as they are now constituted. When it becomes infected, the dangers are in the side effects such as peritonitis, gangrene, and rupture of the appendix wall. If surgery should prove necessary, one should have no hesitation. It's a simple operation that removes nothing that is useful.

The large intestine is a tube of much wider diameter than the small but of considerably shorter length, only four to six feet. It is divided into the cecum, colon, and rectum, which terminates in the anal passage.

By the time food reaches the large intestine, all of the vital properties have been absorbed into the body except water. The water is removed in this tube, and the remaining waste matter (feces) is propelled toward the

The Digestive System

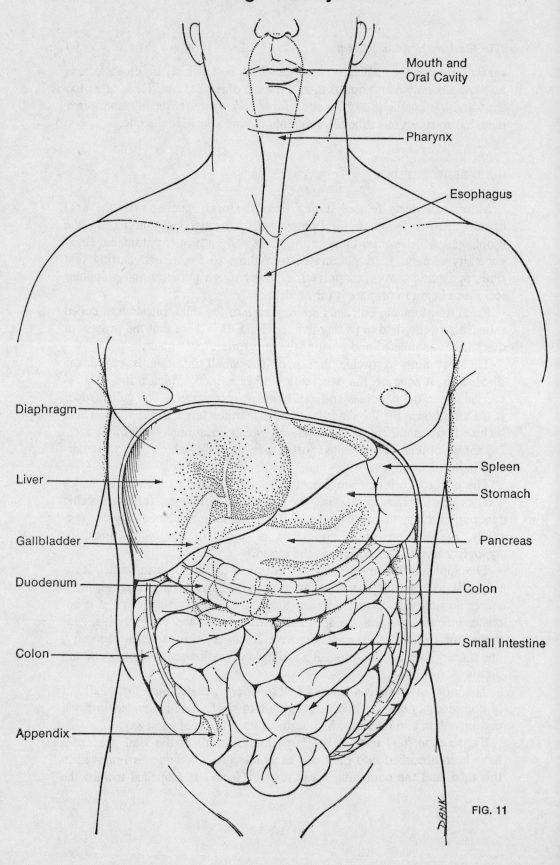

Mouth and Oral Cavity

Pharynx

Esophagus

Diaphragm

Liver

Gallbladder

Duodenum

Colon

Appendix

Spleen

Stomach

Pancreas

Colon

Small Intestine

FIG. 11

anus for excretion. It has taken food fifteen hours to make its journey through the body.

ULCERS

Medical science has yet to isolate the cause of many of the diseases of the gastrointestinal system. In some, there seems to be an allergic reaction. In others, there are dysfunctions in vital organs. Still others manifest themselves in benign or malignant growths. In diabetes, there seems to be a definite hereditary link, since 25 per cent of patients have a history of it in their families. However, this link can be no more than a tendency. There are cases of two diabetics having children who never develop the disease.

There is one constant through most of these ailments. Tension either aggravates the condition or is suspected of being a precipitating cause. There is a link between the nervous system and the gastrointestinal system that is even deeper than those automatic digestive responses that work on signals from the brain. Our state of well-being, how tense or relaxed we are, often dictates what and how much we eat. It also has a definite effect on how our bodies handle that food.

The ulcer is one of the most common gastrointestinal disorders among people who are in situations of stress or tension. Ninety per cent of the sufferers are male. In our fantasies of power, we like to comfort ourselves with the cliché that there are men who *give* ulcers and men who *get* them, and that we are in the former category. Any man uptight enough to give his underlings ulcers is uptight enough to get one himself.

How do you tell a man to relax, when he doesn't seem to know the meaning of the word? How do you tell a man to get out of an ulcer-making situation, when contemplation of getting out is likely to cause as much tension as the situation? How do you tell a man that he's on a collision course, when he's either chosen to be on it or is forced to be on it for what seems like a lack of other options?

"You're giving me an ulcer!" Men groan it with a mixture of torment and pride that's almost exclusively a masculine trait. Although there is some degree of fear, an element of whistling in the dark, they don't really believe they're going to get one, for that only happens to other men. And there is also that element of pride that they're coping with a situation that might in lesser men provoke an ulcer. Perhaps that element of false pride would disappear if men truly knew the dangers inherent in an ulcer, the nature of one.

Most of us have heard of cases of perforation, of serious operations, even of death. But we like to push all of that to the back of our minds. We think of ulcers in terms of bland diets, relaxation, and tranquilizers. Even many who have mild cases tend to say "I've got an ulcer" in a way that they'd never say they had those other male specialties, cancer of the lungs or a heart condition. They wear their ulcers like purple hearts, as proof that they've fought courageously in the front line, been wounded but live to fight on. Yet, ulcers can maim, kill, ruin lives. Before priding ourselves on the decoration, let's examine the wound.

An ulcer is simply a breach in the surface of the skin or of the membranes inside the body. Rather than heal through our natural recuperative powers, it spreads through the tissue. The ulcers with which we are concerned are the peptic ulcers: the *gastric* (in the stomach) and *duodenal* (in the duodenum).

The duodenal ulcer can occur anytime after twenty; the gastric usually does not make its appearance until after forty. The former make up 80 to 90 per cent of all cases of peptic ulcers, but females are slightly more likely to get gastric ulcers. The fact that women usually do not develop ulcers until after the menopause suggests to some researchers that the female hormone, estrogen, may have some immunizational powers.

Although tension and stress are major contributors to the development of these ulcers, other factors may also help to induce them. The only one of these that bears no relationship to anxiety is membership in the blood group "O." A family history of ulcers might also seem unrelated, but an examination of the nature of that family usually finds that its members are volatile and tense people. Excessive drinking and consumption of rich foods, a tendency to stomach acidity, a personality of the same type that is likely to develop heart attacks (highly competitive, intensely ambitious, compulsive): these are the other contributors to peptic ulcers, and they all relate in greater or lesser degree to anxiety.

An ulcer is diagnosed by x-ray. The symptoms are pain when the stomach is empty that abates after eating, nausea, indigestion, and vomiting.

The general treatment is a controlled diet, eliminating alcohol, caffeine (tea, coffee, colas), and spicy or rich food. Every two hours there are snacks of soft, bland foods. At the onset, the patient should be confined to bed and, at all times, he should take antacids to neutralize the stomach juices.

If the condition does not improve, surgery may be necessary. This might entail cutting away the part of the stomach in which the ulcer is lodged or diverting the flow of aggravating gastric juices past the ulcer.

When the ulcers block the passage of food, the patient has to be fed intravenously until the swelling subsides. If it does not subside, surgery must be performed.

Sometimes the ulcer may rupture a blood vessel. Blood is passed through the feces or vomited. If the bleeding cannot be controlled within a day, surgery has to be performed.

Perforations are much more likely with duodenal than gastric ulcers. The ulcer has eaten right through the wall of the stomach or duodenum, releasing gastric juices into the abdominal cavity and possibly precipitating fatal peritonitis. The patient's situation is very serious, and surgery must be performed within eight to ten hours after the perforation. The prognosis is often not good.

These are the risks we run with ulcers, but what is the alternative? The only one that comes to mind is a re-examination of our priorities as males. It seems to me that we must start with a reassessment of our masculine priorities. Women are redefining their roles in society in a revolutionary way. Many of us see the justice of their cause and are helping them. Part of that help should be directed toward ourselves, for their sake as well as our own. Our longevity and health are part of their fulfillment. When those of us with a propensity to afflictions of the ulcer type say that we are staying in situations that propel us toward them because we have a responsibility to those we love, we are obviating our major responsibility—which is good health, moving away from those entanglements that endanger it, as we would move away from a plague-ridden area. If being male means anything, it has to mean some sort of control over our lives and well-being.

COLITIS

A disease that often goes along with ulcers is colitis, an inflammation of the colon. The type to which men under stress are most susceptible is called psychogenic colitis. The regular variety can be linked to infections, protein and vitamin D deficiencies, and/or allergy. The precise causes are unknown. In both types the symptoms include fever, blood or mucus in the feces, diarrhea, and abdominal pain. If untreated, anemia and malnutrition can result. It generally develops into a chronic condition with frequent relapses. Occasionally surgery is necessary.

Everything we've already said about ulcers in relation to man's condition can also be said about colitis. The pain of the ailment can be much more extreme than the pain of separating ourselves from those situations which give rise to it. We've got to learn that there is sometimes greater strength in severance than in perseverance.

After the colostomy, my first thought was that I was glad to be alive. My second was, what kind of life is it going to be without sex? How could I ever show myself naked to a woman with that damned thing attached to me?

Of all the forms of corrective surgery, contemplation of a colostomy gives rise to the greatest amount of fear and fantasy in most men. We will discuss the anxiety connected with a prostate operation in the next section. Many men do not find that as awesome, because they will not be living with visible evidence twenty-four hours a day.

Treatment of growth, obstruction and adhesions low in the rectum sometimes makes restoration of bowel continuity impossible. Sometimes this is a temporary condition, but often it is permanent. A colostomy becomes necessary. A tube is inserted into the colon through an opening of the abdominal wall. A plastic or rubber bag is attached to the end of the tube in which the feces is collected, and the patient has to remove and cleanse it after defecation.

There are some minor adjustments that have to be made concerning the sort of trousers and underwear that he can wear. There are two major adjustments that sometimes call for psychotherapeutic help.

The man will be much more involved with his own excrement than he ever has been before. Everything in our cultural heritage makes this repugnant. We've been brought up to think of this human function as "dirty." As a result, the colostomy bag makes many men feel vile and somewhat less manly.

The second adjustment is to his own appearance. He finds his own image in a mirror rather bizarre and wonders how any woman, even his own wife, will ever be attracted to him. He worries about the bag possibly coming loose in the middle of intercourse. He has lost control to a large extent. What happens if he defecates as he reaches orgasm. The excitement does not make the possibility seem too remote.

People have been telling him for years that presidents and celebrities in every field have had colostomies with no waning in admiration and love for them. They're as attractive after as they were before. It may sound like cold comfort, but it is very real comfort. He is no less a human being than they, and those who loved and admired him before will go on loving and admiring him. Bluntly, he is still capable of all the things of which he was capable before his operation, except moving his bowels in the normal way. He must learn to accept this as a part of his life. His virility is intact, his mental capacities are as great as ever. His potential is the same as it ever was. After all, nobody ever counted the way he relieved himself among his virtues.

DIARRHEA AND CONSTIPATION

Diarrhea and constipation are symptoms rather than diseases. If they are chronic, they are usually symptomatic of other ailments of the gastrointestinal tract. Tension and emotional problems often bring on attacks. We've all heard of soldiers getting diarrhea on the eve of battle. "Uptight" can mean just that in relation to constipation. When one is very tense, the muscles contract, making bowel movements very difficult. We'll close the subject with one observation. "Regularity" is often a question of habit. One man's diarrhea may be another's constipation. For some, it's normal to relieve themselves three times a day; for others, once in three days. When changes in habit occur, see a doctor if they become chronic. If not, you can take any of the medicines recommended by a pharmacist and try to relax, to anticipate the situation that might bring it on, and avoid or learn to cope with it.

HEMORRHOIDS (PILES)

Hemorrhoids, or piles, are among the most common disorders of the gastrointestinal tract. They are enlargements of the veins in the walls of the rectum (internal hemorrhoids) or under the skin just outside the anal opening (external hemorrhoids).

Although a hemorrhoid may develop singly, they usually come in clusters. They are generally the result of straining during defecation, and constipation is often a precipitating cause. Because extremely tense and uptight people often have constipation and squeeze or strain during bowel movements, this type is particularly prone to hemorrhoids.

At first, the internal variety drops down through the anal opening only during or just after a difficult elimination. If they are ignored, they often enlarge and emerge while standing or walking. They protrude permanently in extreme cases.

Hemorrhoids often ulcerate, causing blood and mucus to appear in the stool, but the bleeding stops almost immediately. Itching and burning in the anal and rectal areas are common complaints. At worst, there can be almost unrelenting pain. Because the symptomology is often that of more serious ailments, they should never be ignored.

In the majority of cases, hemorrhoids can be successfully treated by regulating bowel movements in conjunction with rest, release from tensions, the application of lotions or ointments, frequent sitz baths, and sometimes the injection of an astringent. Only the most dire cases require surgery.

As we've seen, a healthy gastrointestinal system is dependent upon what we eat and our states of mind more than anything else. Change is always possible. Sometimes it's necessary. A man's first responsibility is to himself. Only when he assumes that responsibility can he take on responsibility for others.

At first, eating properly takes time and thought. Soon after, it becomes a habit, a way of life. At first, refusing to remain in a situation that causes tension and stress may seem selfish, or cowardly, or irresponsible. A little deeper thought reveals that staying healthy, free of the anxiety-provoking ailments such as ulcers and colitis, can be the most generous, courageous, and responsible thing we can do for ourselves and those we love.

9

THE URINARY AND REPRODUCTIVE SYSTEMS

There is a very old, slightly off-color story that, in my adolescence, seemed an example of devastating wit. In a way, it illustrates why we are discussing the urinary and reproductive systems as a single unit.

A man is beating his penis against a fence, shouting angrily: "I'll show you who's boss! I'll show you!"

A friend passes by and sees him performing this strange act. He asks: "Are you crazy? Why are you doing that?"

"I was just in bed with a beautiful blonde. Everything was going great. When it came time to fuck, my cock wouldn't get a hard on. But I'm getting even. Now it wants to pee, and I won't let it!"

One of the ways men and women differ anatomically is that, in the male, the reproductive and urinary systems share a common channel. In the female, urine is eliminated through the vaginal orifice that a man enters for reproductive purposes, but that is the only thing shared by the two systems.

In the male, the urethra is the joint reproductive and urinary duct. It carries urine from the bladder, through the prostate, along the penis for elimination through the opening at the tip of the penis (the *meatus*). Sperm enters the prostate from the testes, where it is mixed with prostatic fluids to become semen. In orgasm, the semen also travels along the urethra for ejaculation through the meatus. The male urethra is 8 inches long; the female, only 1½ inches and functions solely as a urinary duct.

The penis, then, is the dual-purpose, uniquely male outer organ of the body. It has been the source of envy, myth, trauma, pleasure, and pain. It is the only organ (of either sex) that, in certain religions, has been made a god and in others worshiped as a religious artifact. Indeed, it has occasionally been referred to as "the godhead."

CIRCUMCISION

In some cultures circumcision is a religious rite analogous to the Christian sacraments. Like baptism, it takes place shortly after birth (e.g. the Hebraic *birth*) or, like confirmation, around the time of puberty (e.g. many African tribal rituals). This may be the reason for the sometime confusion of the sexual, hygienic, and cultural significance of circumcision.

A man is born with the head of his penis (the *glans*) covered by a sheath of flesh called the foreskin (or *prepuce*). Circumcision is the surgical removal of this covering. Its mystical significance has played a part in various cultures that have flourished in every part of the world except Europe.

The foreskin has no sexual significance for the healthily formed male. It neither impedes nor increases his coital pleasure. With erection, the foreskin naturally rolls back to uncover the head of the penis and, from then on, plays absolutely no part in any sexual activity. The head usually has extreme erogenous sensitivity, but the foreskin has none. It is as useful as one's appendix and, like the appendix, can sometimes be troublesome enough to need surgery.

The condition is clinically known as *phimosis*. It is the inability of the prepuce to retract over the glans either in erection or by being rolled back manually. It is usually caused by adhesions of the foreskin to the head or by an abnormal narrowing of the preputial orifice (the opening at the top of the foreskin), and it can easily be corrected by circumcision.

If one is not circumcised, it is necessary to roll back the foreskin manually in order to clean the area under it. A white sebaceous secretion gathers there, known medically as *smegna,* and in street language as "cheese." When it is not washed away, the foreskin takes on a most offensive odor and can even become inflamed. There is also a possible link between smegna and cancer, although that has not yet been fully substantiated.

THE PENIS

The Empire State building was the great phallus of New York City. As long as it was the tallest building in the world, the city was the greatest in the world and prospered. The minute they put up the World Trade Center, the gods got angry and the city began to decay.

Half whimsically and half in earnest, the above observation was made by a young man at a literary cocktail party. The cultural and artistic pursuit of phallic symbols has become a popular intellectual pastime. We often find esthetes and critics shouting "phallic symbol" with the same urgency that a golfer reserves for crying "fore."

With all of the values, in excess of function, that have been assigned to the penis down through the ages, it's little wonder that some of us have been accused of being obsessed with it, and some women of suffering from penis envy. Yet, when it is anatomically separated from the mystique, the penis is not a very formidable organ. It is composed of three layers of erectile material that is activated by signals from the nervous system and sometimes, superficially, seems to have a life of its own, refusing to become erect on command in one situation and losing erection in another.

The layers are encased in skin and subcutaneous tissue devoid of fat. Alas, it is one of the few parts of the body that will not gain weight no matter how much we eat. Actually, the fatter one gets, the less impressive the penis looks proportionately, to say nothing of the mechanical difficulties that corpulence might present in intercourse positions.

PENIS SIZE

Did you get a look at the new kid in the locker room? He's hung like a horse.

•

When I was a child, I remember standing next to my father at a urinal. His prick looked enormous. I thought, no matter how much I grow, I'll never have a thing that big. I was in awe of him for years. Even after puberty, I felt inadequate.

During adolescence, and among those who remain sexually arrested in that stage, there tends to be a preoccupation with size. We think in terms of myths and stereotypes, equating size with power, of building muscles and growing taller, of large men with large penises that women will find irresistible.

The adolescent locker-room talk is in terms of inches, and we secretly (sometimes openly) compare sizes. The judgments are usually made on a view of the penis in its flaccid state, which is deceiving, for it bears no relationship to the erect organ. One that measures a little over three inches at rest can easily swell to seven inches in erection, and one that measures over four inches may only expand to less than six inches.

No matter what the height and breadth of a man, the average size of an erect penis is between five and seven inches, and a man who is over six feet tall can measure the smaller size, while one well under average height can have the more impressive dimension.

There are abnormalities. The largest recorded erection is twelve inches, while the smallest biologically functioning penis is less than one inch. Despite the myths that all blacks, or Jews, or Latins are well endowed, and all Orientals or Anglo-Saxons are not, there is no evidence of racial variations. The same averages and statistics are universally applicable.

As for giving a woman pleasure, the proof is in the doing and not the dimension. The female vagina will accommodate itself to any but the most abnormally large or small penises.

THE TESTES AND PROSTATE GLAND

When we think of sexual intercourse and reproduction, we usually think in terms of the functioning of the outer genitalia: the penis and the scrotum which carries the testicles. In a sense, the penis has the fun, and the testes do the work.

The testes perform two functions: they manufacture sperm and the male hormone, testosterone. Testosterone controls the secondary sexual characteristics such as growth of body hair, muscular frame, depth of voice.

When we are sexually aroused, the sperm travels through ducts to the prostate gland, where it is metabolized by the seminal fluids. Without this action, the sperm would be sterile. Other prostatic fluids are added to manufacture the viscous, milky liquid, *semen*, which is ejaculated through the urethra.

Prostatitis is an inflammation of the extremely important prostate gland. The condition can be either temporary or chronic. An enlargement of the prostate is possible at any age, but the likelihood increases after middle age.

The symptoms are the same for both conditions. There is usually retention of urine, while the desire to urinate increases. When one does urinate, the elimination is slow, spasmodic, lacking in force, and often followed by dribbling. If the condition is severe, there will be considerable pain. Prostatitis can often be treated by prostatic massage and chemotherapy. An enlarged prostate (*prostatitis hypertrophy*) is a far more serious ailment.

The conditions causing surgical removal of the prostate are:

1. A severe enlargement of any origin

The Urinary System

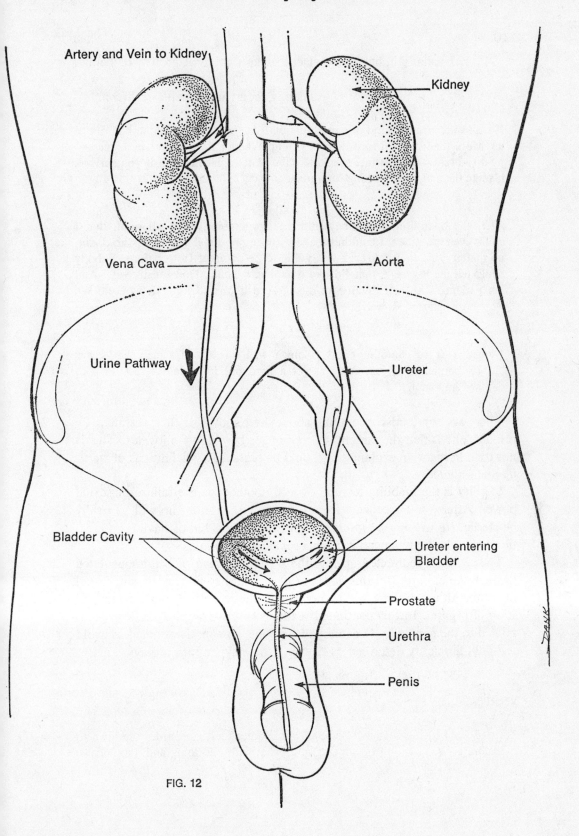

Artery and Vein to Kidney

Kidney

Vena Cava

Aorta

Urine Pathway

Ureter

Bladder Cavity

Ureter entering Bladder

Prostate

Urethra

Penis

FIG. 12

2. A hormone imbalance that causes an unnatural growth of benign cells

3. Cancer of the prostate (frequently occurring in men over fifty)

We all suffer from a kind of cancer-phobia. The big "C" scares the hell out of us. More than heart. More than anything. When I think about it, I guess— next to brain—the prostate seems like the worst. I mean, even if you survive, it's like the end of everything for a man.

•

After the operation, when they told me I was going to be all right, that I could even enjoy sex, I couldn't make it for a long time. There was no doubt, no matter what they said, sex was going to be different from before. Nobody could tell me it wasn't, that I'd like it as much. Thank God for my wife. And her patience with me. Finally we did it. And it was all right. It worked. We were both satisfied. It was fine.

•

I hated it. It was shooting blanks. Somehow, I was less of a man than I was before. Sometimes I just couldn't get a hard on. It made me feel so goddamned impotent.

There are some misconceptions about the removal of the prostate. The primary one is that the patient will no longer be able to enjoy sex. This is not true. Perhaps an explanation should be prefaced by definitions of *sterility* and *impotence*.

Sterility is the inability to reproduce. Impotence is the failure of sexual power. After a man recovers from a prostate operation, he will generally be sterile. *He will not be impotent*. He will be capable of having an erection and of both giving and receiving sexual satisfaction.

The semen is redirected up into the bladder instead of being ejaculated through the urethra. But this does not mean that he will stop having sexual pleasure. Although there will be no "come," he will still experience the ecstasy of orgasm. In this continued sexual pleasure (despite sterility), it is related to the female hysterectomy, which one woman, determined to avoid self-pity, flippantly described as "turning the playpen into a playground."

VENEREAL DISEASE

I had just become engaged. Some of my buddies took me out on the town to celebrate. We did a lot of boozing and, what with one thing and another, we decided to pick up a couple of hookers and party. About two weeks later, I noticed this little sore on my cock. I panicked. I knew what it could mean. I went to a doctor and he confirmed my suspicions. It was syph. That damned bitch of a whore! Thank God, my fiancée had the curse, and I hadn't touched her for over a week. Anyway, they shot me up with penicillin, and I was cured. I thought—now I don't have to say a word to my girl. No such luck. The stuff stays in your bloodstream for a long time. And when we went for the blood tests to get the license, there it was. What a scene! It almost broke up my marriage before it started. For over a year, you never saw a more faithful husband. I wouldn't even look at a copy of *Playboy*.

There are ways of preventing the contraction of venereal diseases. Simple treatments and quick cures are readily obtainable. Despite this, they remain a major health hazard in the United States, often reaching epidemic proportions, especially gonorrhea. It is estimated that there are over 1,750,000 men (but only 650,000 women) in the United States who have the disease. The estimate for the number of victims of syphilis, the other major form of venereal disease, is much lower. Instances of both syphilis and gonorrhea may be much higher, because actual figures are not available. Many people have the diseases and do not know it, because they either cannot recognize the symptoms or they do not appear in an identifiable way. In the case of women and gonorrhea, there are no symptoms at all.

After I was treated and no longer communicable, I got a call from this guy from the Public Health Service. He wanted to see me and talk to me about it. I put him off. I had nothing to say, especially to somebody I didn't even know. He kept calling. At home. At the office. Finally he wore me down, and I agreed to talk to him. He was a real hellfire-and-damnation type. Very unnerving. And then he wanted a list of all the people I'd been intimate with during the contagious period. He wanted to make sure they knew. He'd be very discreet, wouldn't even bring me into it if I didn't want it. I told him to go screw himself. What kind of a bastard did he think I was? I'd already told them myself. It was terrible, but I did it. All and all, it was quite a session. And it wouldn't have happened if it weren't for my goddam doctor. He reported my case. Somebody I knew also had it. His doctor gave him penicillin and let it go at that. That's the way it should be. Do they really think a man's going to keep quiet? That's stupid. If you're infected and don't tell a girl, you can keep passing it back and forth like ping-pong. It's not like the measles. You're not immune after one dose. Hell, nobody wants to be Syphilis Sam spreading an epidemic. If it's a one-night stand with somebody you just picked up—that's tough for her. But it's part of the bar game. No health service is going to locate a girl you can't locate yourself. Besides, it could as easily have been her who gave it to you as the other way around.

Although doctors are required to report cases of venereal disease to the Public Health Service, fewer than 20 per cent do. They take their chances on the fundamental decency of their patients and do not want to embarrass them by submitting them to investigation. With married people, they can be fairly certain that notification of mates will take place, but it can be a risky business with the unmarried, especially the more promiscuous singles.

I was seventeen when I first got the clap. I refused to believe it, although I really recognized the symptoms from a sex hygiene course at school. Still, I ignored them. I guess I was scared of what my family would think. My mother and father. I tried to tell myself it was something else. The burning sensation when I urinated wasn't unendurable. The discharge—well, I was a horny kid —I thought—it's only that I can't stop coming. But there came a time when I couldn't hide it any more. The stains were all over my sheets. My parents must have discussed it, because the first thing I knew, my old man takes me aside to give me a lecture on masturbating in bed. If I have to jerk off, why don't I go to the bathroom? It's not nice for my mother to have to handle the messy sheets when she changes the linen. Jesus, I thought, my mother! What if she touches the stuff, and I give it to her? It knocked me out. I had to confess. And the roof fell in! You know, a funny thing happened after that. I began to boast about it to my friends. It made me a big man in their eyes. You know, I also have the sneaky suspicion that my father was boasting about it to his friends. My son, the macho whoremaster.

There are many cases of venereal disease that are not reported because of religious guilt or familial shame. Both syphilis and gonorrhea are degenerative diseases, and to ignore or hide them is to lay oneself open to dreadful physical disabilities and possible death.

When I was a kid my mother used to tell me not to sit on toilet seats unless I covered them with paper first—and to be careful about the glasses I drank from and the silverware I used. If I didn't listen to her about these things, something terrible would happen to me. She was obviously thinking about VD, but she never said it—which only made it worse. I don't think I ever sat full on a strange can until I was eighteen.

The old myths about toilet seats, dirty silverware, dishes, drinking glasses, etc., are all untrue. Venereal diseases are generally spread through sexual contact, although there are some extremely rare instances of infection from dirty underwear or sheets or towels. It is because of the almost exclusively sexual means of transmission that this group of very different infections is classified in the same category.

I was leaking like a faucet. I went to the doctor, and he confirmed it. I had the clap. I guess he thought he was being comforting when he told me: "Listen, better a dozen doses of gonorrhea than one of syphilis.

Syphilis is the most potentially dangerous of all venereal diseases. It is caused by a bacteria that requires warmth and moisture to live and thrives in the linings of the genitalia, rectum, and mouth. The disease has three stages, with a latent period between the second and third. The corkscrew-shaped microbe (*spirochete*) enters the body usually through sexual intercourse (vaginal or anal), mutual masturbation, fellatio, or cunnilingus. As this microbe dies the moment it leaves the body, it can only be spread via direct contact.

In primary syphilis, the spirochete enters the body at the point of contact and reproduces at an astonishing rate. Within a matter of hours, it is already in the bloodstream and journeying through the body. The length of incubation can last from less than ten days to ten weeks.

Symptoms generally do not begin to appear until the third week. A primary sore develops at the point of entry. It is a painless little sore which oozes a highly infectious but colorless liquid containing the contaminating microbes. If one is fortunate, the sore is immediately apparent, but often it is no larger than a pinhead or internal and goes unnoticed. Later, the glands in the groin *may* swell, but as no pain is involved, this second symptom may also go undetected. Even without treatment, the symptoms disappear leaving no scars. But the disease is still in the body and growing daily more virulent.

Secondary syphilis may follow directly or after a hiatus of several weeks. At this point, the spirochete is lodged in the skin, mucous membranes, eyes, and nervous system. In 51 per cent of secondary syphilitics, the first symptoms are a general feeling of being physically run-down manifested by headaches, queasiness, loss of appetite, a certain edginess, unspecified pains in bones and joints, a sore throat, and occasionally a low-grade fever. There can be swollen nodes in the groin and around the breasts. A rash may appear on the arms, legs, palms, and/or the soles of the feet. This rash neither itches nor contains boils or blisters, and may go unnoticed or dismissed as any of a number of common skin disorders. But it is constantly emitting the highly infectious colorless liquid. Often, the skin shows no signs of infection, and the only lesions appear in the hidden mucous membranes of the mouth and genitalia.

One of the great dangers of syphilis is that, in the primary and secondary stages, it resembles so many other infections that it has been called "the great imitator." The genital sores resemble at least sixteen other diseases;

the mouth sores look like twenty-three other infections; and the skin lesions, any of at least forty. Many are so trifling that, when the symptoms disappear of their own accord, the victim forgets all about them. It is a luxury that those who like to swing, or are in anyway promiscuous, cannot afford.

Any persistent lesion, no matter how slight, on the genitalia, lips, tongue, inner surface of the mouth, or even on the finger, should be regarded as possible syphilis, if you've been at all sexually indiscriminate. Get yourself to a doctor immediately. It's easy to cure and, in the early stages, will leave no damaging aftereffects on the body or in the blood. Blood tests should be continued until you are completely negative. Although caught early and arrested, the tenacious microbes can linger for over a year.

Latent syphilis follows the healing of the sores and disappearance of the other symptoms of secondary syphilis. The condition can last anywhere from several months to a lifetime. There are no outward signs and, with the healing of the sores, a man becomes completely noninfectious, but if the latent syphilitic female becomes pregnant, chances are that she will transmit the disease to the child she is carrying.

It is the quiescence of latent syphilis that makes it so dangerous. It doesn't seem to be doing any damage to either the syphilitic or to those with whom he becomes sexually involved. The only means of detection is blood tests. But it is still there, still capable of attacking vital organs, causing irreparable damage as well as death.

Tertiary syphilis will develop in twenty-eight out of one hundred cases of untreated secondary, or latent, syphilis. Of that number fifteen can expect to be permanently maimed or killed by it, while the disease remains relatively benign in the other thirteen cases.

Almost any part of the body can be attacked. Painful ulcers of the skin and chancres on bones and joints are the least of it. If tertiary syphilis attacks the eyes, portions of the cardiovascular system, or the nervous system, it can cause blindness, paralysis, aneurysm, a crippling loss of control of the limbs, and death.

Penicillin (or another antibiotic for those allergic to it) will cure syphilis in any of its stages. In the early stage the cure will be complete. But it cannot reverse the ravages of tertiary syphilis. Those who are blinded or crippled will no longer be syphilitic or subject to further affliction, but they will remain blind or maimed.

Gonorrhea (or, in the vernacular, "clap" or a "dose") is among the oldest known diseases. It was familiar to the ancient Chinese, Greeks, and

Arabs. The name is based on an ancient belief that the chief symptom of the disease was really no more than an involuntary flow of semen (in ancient Greek, *gonos* means seed and *rhoia,* flow).

Like syphilis, it is caused by a bacteria (*gonococcus*) that thrives in the moist linings of the urethra, vagina, rectum, and deeper recesses of the mouth. Thus, it is practically impossible to contract gonorrhea in any way other than direct sexual contact—specifically, vaginal or anal intercourse. Although a minority cling to the notion that it can be communicated by "soul-kissing," it is more widely held that it is virtually impossible for a man to contract gonorrhea from oral contact (except by performing cunnilingus). The gonococcus lodges near the tonsils. It would indeed take a "deep throat" to give you a dose, and fellatio would seem the safest form of sexual activity with somebody about whom you are dubious.

The incubation period is usually from three to five days after contact. The first symptoms are burning sensations upon urination and a feeling of irritation in that section of the urethra that runs through the penis. This is soon followed by a purulent discharge that is seldom too slight for immediate detection.

If untreated, the disease can spread through the upper reproductive and urinary tracts. Then there is frequent, painful, and uncontrollable urination. Gonorrhea has been known to clear up spontaneously within a year; but, more frequently, untreated cases result in permanent arthritic conditions.

Homosexuals can contract gonorrhea in the rectum, where, like vaginal gonorrhea, it is asymptomatic but still highly contagious during intercourse.

In certain groups, gonorrhea is as common as the cold, with people contracting it as often as two or three times in one year.

The cure is the same as for syphilis. However, there can be complications. Gonorrhea behaves like flu germs in one way. It develops successively stronger strains as forms of treatment come within reach of eliminating it. Veterans returning from Vietnam have brought back a strain that resists normal doses of penicillin. At present, researchers are using gonorrheal discharge in experimental work that may enable them to isolate strains and develop a vaccine.

There are some nonspecific and nongonococcal urethral infections that resemble gonorrhea but are not transmitted by intercourse. They can be treated with antibiotics.

During the period of treatment for both nongonococcal urethritis and gonorrhea, the patient should abstain from both alcohol and sex, as they complicate the condition and inhibit the cure.

The other veneral diseases—such as chancroid, lymphogranuloma venereum, and granuloma inguinale—account for only 1 per cent of the cases of VD. They are transmitted through sexual contact, and all respond to antibiotics in treatment.

In general, one good preventive for venereal diseases is to always wear a condom during intercourse with those whose sexual history is unknown to you and, in these cases, to try to avoid oral or even manual contact.

There is another preventive, but it requires a medical prescription. Take a pill, containing an adequate supply of antibiotic to destroy the microbe, directly after sexual contact with anybody who seems dubious.

VASECTOMY

We cannot finish discussing the reproductive system without mentioning an operation that is becoming increasingly popular among men who have decided that they do not want children. A *vasectomy* is a simple scrotal incision that prevents the passage of spermatozoa. It doesn't inhibit sexual pleasure, nor does it diminish prowess. Its only function is male sterilization.

A great deal of self-examination should precede a vasectomy. Although there have been some cases of reversing its effects by surgery, involving stitching back together the severed sections of the vas deferens (the duct carrying sperm from testes to prostate), it is very delicate work and not always successful. A man must be certain that he never wants to have a child. Once committed to vasectomy, he cannot change his mind with new circumstances that might change his outlook.

THE URINARY SYSTEM

The urinary system is composed of:
  Two kidneys
  Two ureters
  One bladder
  One urethra

The kidneys are the great filtering system of the body and its major channel of excretion. Their importance to our well-being cannot be overestimated. One fifth of the blood pumped out of the heart goes to them. They rid the body of nitrogenous waste and excess water by eliminating a drop

The Reproductive System

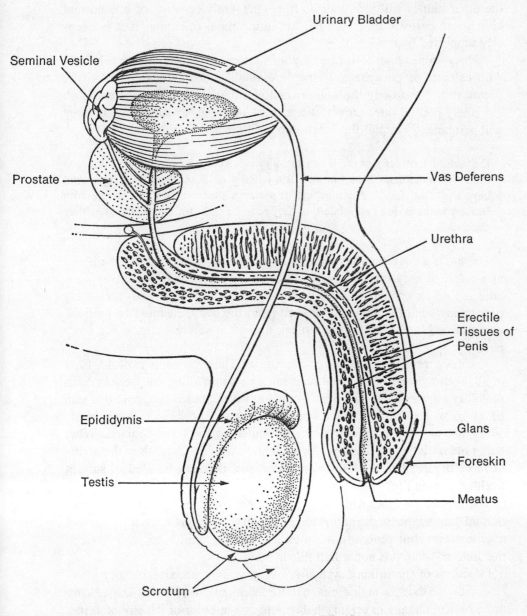

Urinary Bladder

Seminal Vesicle

Prostate

Vas Deferens

Urethra

Erectile Tissues of Penis

Epididymis

Glans

Testis

Foreskin

Meatus

Scrotum

FIG. 13

of urine every half minute. They are vital to the maintenance of both the water balance and acid base of the body.

When one kidney is damaged irreparably, it can be removed by surgery; the other kidney will take over its functions. Only one half of one normal kidney can perform all of the life-sustaining renal functions, if it is properly supported by surgery.

Kidney stones can be formed by an abnormal congealing of uric acid with calcium or phosphate. If they are small enough, they can often be passed out of the body through normal elimination, but the process is an extremely painful one. Larger stones must be removed surgically, or they will permanently impair the functioning of the system.

I'm one of the lucky ones. When my kidneys went, my brother donated one of his for transplant. Now I'm fine. But when you think of all the people who have to be on the dialysis machine, it seems a shame that more people with healthy kidneys don't stipulate that they're to be used for transplant after they die.

Uremia is a condition in which toxic substances accumulate in the blood as a result of a dysfunction of the kidneys. The patient is treated by periodic use of an artificial kidney apparatus. It is a painful and enervating process in which the blood is removed from the body, cleansed by dialysis, and returned to the body. It is a bleak and often severely depressing prospect.

A kidney transplant is a better alternative. The problem is twofold. First of all, both red and white corpuscles must be compatible, and perfect compatibility only exists in identical twins. However, there is support that can be given where this does not exist. The second problem is availability. There are not enough kidneys being donated to meet the demand. What better memorial could there be, for somebody who has died, than the giving of those organs, like the kidneys and corneas, that can be used to sustain health and even life?

The ureters are tubes which carry the urine from the kidneys to the bladder, an expandable organ that acts as a reservoir. It has a capacity of well over one pint, but generally the muscles contract, and it empties through the urethra, when it is about half filled.

Infections of the urinary system are very serious matters, for they interfere with the body's major channel for elimination of toxic waste. Any pain, radical change in urinary habits, change in color or density of urine, must be checked out immediately with a physician. If caught in time, even the most serious conditions need not be disabling or fatal.

Sometimes problems of urinary incontinence or abnormal retention are psychological.

When we went on those raids in Vietnam, we were all so nervous we were peeing in our pants all over the place.

I don't know why, but when I go into a crowded john in a theater or restaurant, and I have to stand at the urinal with all those strangers, I can't go, no matter how badly I have to take a leak.

The more we discover about ourselves, the more we realize that many of our problems are the result of anxiety and stress rather than physical disabilities. We begin to see that the roots of a well-ordered and functioning body are often found in the ability to adjust to our emotional and intellectual reactions. We must learn to live with all of the tensions to which we are daily exposed. If we don't, what start as warnings from our nervous systems can degenerate into crippling disorders.

10

THE ENDOCRINE SYSTEM

The endocrine system is the last system of the body that we will investigate. It differs from the other systems in that its parts are not physically linked to each other (e.g. stomach and intestines, prostate and urethra, etc.) but exist in remote parts of the body connected only by means of the bloodstream. The endocrine system is composed of the endocrine glands, which are:

1. The pituitary (located beneath the central part of the brain)
2. The thyroid (located in the neck on either side of the trachea)
3. The parathyroid (located around the thyroid)
4. The pancreas (located in the abdomen)
5. The adrenal (located just above the kidneys)
6. The testes (in women, the ovaries)

They become a system by virtue of the interrelationship of their functions and controls over each other, and by the similarity of their design.

All of the endocrine glands are ductless and produce substances called hormones which are secreted directly into the bloodstream. These hormones have several vital functions:

1. Maintain the body's stability
2. Control growth
3. Develop secondary sexual characteristics
4. Insure the healthy functioning of each other

Only minute quantities of hormones are ever secreted into the blood-

The Endocrine Glands

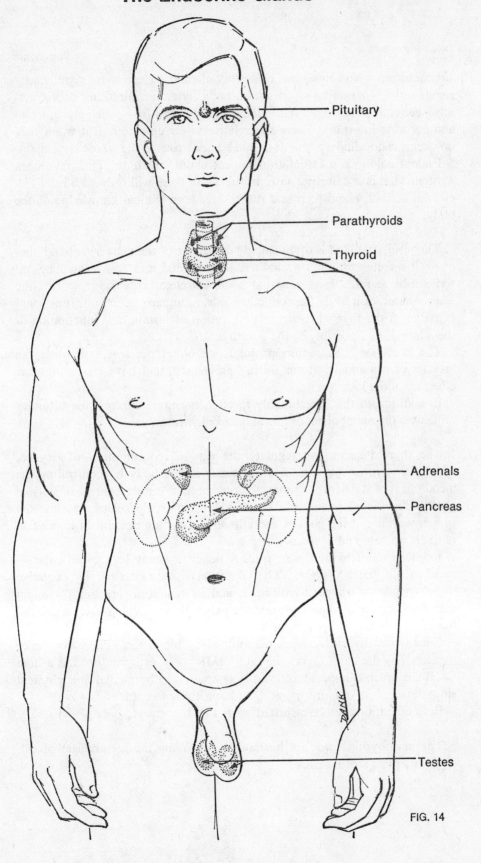

Pituitary

Parathyroids

Thyroid

Adrenals

Pancreas

Testes

FIG. 14

stream at any given time, but these tiny chemical messengers significantly regulate the functioning of the entire body by either inhibiting or accelerating cellular metabolism. The glands operate with an amazingly graceful and accurate interplay. There are relatively few disorders. But when they do occur, endocrinal dysfunctions can be disastrous to the whole system.

Endocrinology is a fascinating subject about which volumes have been written. That is not our purpose. In this book there will only be a brief discussion of each gland to round out the reader's clinical knowledge of the body.

The pituitary gland is often called "the leader of the endocrine band" because it secretes so many hormones. It is divided into two parts. The anterior lobe secretes hormones that control skeletal growth, growth of the testes, maturation of the reproductive cells, mammary secretion, functional activities of the thyroid, pancreatic secretion of insulin, the functioning of the adrenals and possibly of the parathyroids.

The posterior lobe secretions influence blood pressure, stimulate the muscles of a woman's uterus during pregnancy, and have an antidiuretic effect upon the kidneys.

In addition to this, presumably through hormone control, the pituitary influences the metabolism of fats and carbohydrates.

The thyroid secretions regulate the rate of consumption of oxygen, which, in turn, affects almost every tissue in the body by controlling the metabolism of nutrients. Among the other functions are control of normal growth and development of the brain and musculoskeletal system; the proper working of the gonads and adrenals; a certain amount of regulation of the heart rate and nervous system.

Iodine is required by the thyroid. A deficiency may lead to an enlargement of the gland (*goiter*). The condition is characterized by excessive thyroid secretion (hyperthyroidism), and its symptoms are loss of weight despite an extremely healthy appetite, palpitations, bulging eyes, a lack of tolerance to heat, and nervousness.

Changes in thyroid rate are determined by blood test. They were once measured by the basal metabolic rate (BMR). Hyperthyroidism has a high BMR. Its reverse, hypothyroidism, is symptomized by mental and physical sluggishness, loss of hair, dry skin, and sensitivity to cold.

Both conditions can be adjusted by diet and/or drugs.

The parathyroids produce hormones controlling the metabolism of calcium and phosphorus.

Insulin is the chief hormone of the pancreas. It controls the metabolism of carbohydrates. A lack of it causes diabetes. It can be controlled by injections and stabilization of diet.

The adrenal is actually two glands in one. The *medulla* (inner portion) receives impulses from the nervous system and, in times of mental stress or physical shock, secretes hormones that constrict the blood vessels, increase the heart rate, and raise the concentration of blood glucose, thus playing an important part in helping the body to sustain assault.

The *adrenal cortex* (outer portion) secretions regulate the metabolism of nutrients, control the level of sodium and potassium, and have an effect on secondary sexual characteristics.

The testes (male gonads) produce two hormones: testosterone and androgen. In addition to supporting the manufacture of sperm, testosterone controls the growth and development of secondary male characteristics: penis, prostate gland, seminal vesicles, beard, body hair, and the potential for baldness.

Androgen stimulates the development of muscle, skeleton, and viscera and accounts for the superior musculature and stature of males. Secondary sexual characteristics will not develop if there is an androgen deficiency during puberty. If this occurs after maturity, a partial regression is possible. A pituitary defect may be the cause of this lack. Externally administered, laboratory synthesized testosterone can rectify the situation by substituting for the organically produced androgen.

HIS SEX

11

SEXUAL ATTITUDES

What turns you on. That's all that counts.

·

I look at my son and wonder. When I was his age, I was a husband. I'd never slept with my wife before our wedding. And I'd only known two girls sexually before. Since then I've had one experience, and I was too drunk to really enjoy that. Now, don't get me wrong. I love my wife. But I'd like a crack at being young again today. Man, I'd fuck, fuck, fuck!

·

If there was an Olympics for making out, I bet I'd be up for a gold medal. I'm the high-score man on my team. But you know, sometimes I get a funny feeling that I'm so busy making time that I've forgotten how to make contact.

·

The trouble with the girls today is they want their liberation, and they want a meaningful relationship at the same time. You just don't know where you stand any more. I'm all for equal rights and the rest of it. But there's still such a thing as traditional roles.

·

When I get married, I want what my parents had. None of this open shit.

•

Sometimes I think I missed a lot by getting married so young. But then, I think I gained a lot. We grew up together. Shared learning things. Now, when the sex isn't the greatest, there's so much more we have together to fall back on.

•

When I meet a girl and like her—sure, I want to go to bed with her. But I want something more to happen between us. Before, after, even during. Otherwise, it's not much. You can always get laid.

•

I don't know where this sexual revolution is. And it's not because I haven't been looking. I don't lose much sleep in other people's beds. With most girls, it's still the same old courting drag. And most of the time I don't make out.

•

I'm not all that interested. When I get married, I want to have had some degree of experience. But I don't want to be jaded. And the woman I love, I don't want to be frightened that every time I walk into a room I'll come face to face with somebody with whom she's had intercourse. I want cleanliness and decency in my relationships. These are the things I believe in. That's the way I was brought up. And looking around, I'm glad of it.

The majority of men think a great deal about the sex act, about what turns them on, but they don't think very deeply about its essence: *Sexuality*. What is sexuality?

Is it a sin or a blessing?

Is it a duty or a pleasure?

Is it dirty or divine?

The answer to all of these questions is: *yes*. Depending upon the time, the culture, the individual, the situation, sex can be any of these things—and often, kaleidoscopically, many all at once.

Ultimately, we may be recalled as the age of sexual enlightenment as much as the atomic age. Some have called what has happened a revolution; others have been more conservative and termed it liberation. The description doesn't matter. What we have actually achieved is a sexual recognition. Instead of ignoring or hiding from it, we discuss it. Sometimes it may seem that we discuss it too much. Happily, for most of us, it is one area in which it is not all talk and no action.

Sigmund Freud could be called the father of modern sexual recognition.

Dr. Kinsey is certainly the author of its emancipation proclamation. People like Masters and Johnson could be thought of as the sexual chiefs of state.

Superficially it seems as if a sexual Valhalla has been created, but, unfortunately, it's not true. Ignorance persists. Old ways of thinking still color our actions. Even the intellectually enlightened, those who've read all the books and make all the cocktail party chatter about it, even they have the same emotional and sexual hang-ups that plagued their fathers.

One does not change the patterns of centuries by simple referendum. Sex continues to be governed by laws of state and church rather than by those of human nature and needs. Just or unjust, we continue to humble ourselves before these laws despite our inclinations, thereby setting ourselves up for sexual guilts and even failures.

The guilts and fears of past generations remain with us. We worry about the effects of sex education in the schools and often remain either inchoate or coy when the subject is introduced in the home. We tell obscene stories in the presence of the children on some occasions, and on others we tell them that it's dirty, or sinful, or wrong (choose your favorite guilt-producing word) for them to have natural inclinations and sexual curiosity.

We worry about pornography instead of analyzing what in our society and our natures produces the need for it. We legislate against prostitution instead of dealing with the real problem, which is what makes a man seek out a prostitute. In most cases it is far more complicated than simple sexual release.

There are legislative acts against every form of sex except the most basic missionary-position heterosexual intercourse, and there are religious interdictions against that except when practiced by man and wife for the purposes of procreation. We have banned pleasure and, in the process, have denied one of man's greatest needs: the need for sex.

For centuries we lived in the darkness of sexual ignorance. Now light is as easily procured as electricity. Nevertheless, many of us have yet to learn to reach for the switch. It is darkness and ignorance that is dirty, not sex. All nature is clean, and sex is as much a part of nature as our genitalia are part of our bodies. Life begins with sex, and sex begins with life. We are sexual beings from the moment we emerge from our mother's womb.

In this century we have discovered that the act of maturing, growing up, progresses in a series of well-defined sexual stages. To understand our bodies and the lives in them, we must recognize and understand our sexuality.

12

PREADOLESCENT SEXUALITY

We are born sexual beings, but our infant sexuality is different from that which most of us experience as adult men. A baby does not isolate sex from his other needs. He finds expression of it in all the things that give him pleasure: food, warmth, being touched, held, cuddled. His sexual feelings do not reside only in his genitalia but are manifested in all of his organs and senses. One could say that, as infants, we are total sexual beings.

My pal Charlie has a great way with the women. When he goes after one, he almost always gets her. I can see why, too. It's what the French call *joie de vivre*. He's got it. That guy enjoys everything to the hilt. A meal, a trip, a book, a play. And no doubt about it, a woman. The most recent is always the greatest he's ever known. Nothing is ever so-so, or not as good as the time before. Now is the best. I really envy him.

To their great joy, some men retain remnants of this original sexuality throughout their lives. They find gratification in everything they do, in everything that touches them. In the presence of these men, the observer often feels a palpable sensuality. We can discern this quality in the way they handle objects, enjoy their food and surroundings, look at and stroke the people to whom they are attracted. While their manner draws some people to them, it makes others hostile. We should never react as the latter do. It's much better to try to emulate these men, to reach back into ourselves and attempt to rediscover those wonderful traits that were once a part of all of us. Far from being born in sin, we were all born in innocent sexuality.

As the infant gets older, certain organs take on a special sexual significance. They retain this erogenous sensitivity, to a greater or lesser extent, for the rest of his life. The pleasure he derives from a specific organ may be so strong that a man becomes fixated on it to the exclusion of the others.

THE ORAL STAGE

You see before you the total oral man. I happily admit it. I love to eat, talk, smoke, even chew on the ends of eyeglasses and pencils. And the lady who likes a little head can be the love of my life.

The mouth is the first erogenous zone of which the infant becomes aware. This leads to the first stage of sexual development, *the oral stage.*

At the very beginning of his life, the baby becomes aware of the pleasurable sensation of sucking at his mother's breast or from the nipple of a bottle. The feeling is almost orgiastic. It continues to play an important part in his postpuberty sex life, from the sensually arousing kiss in foreplay to acts of fellatio and cunnilingus that, in some cases, become so exciting that they completely replace conventional intercourse.

Oral erogenicity is often sublimated into compulsive talking, eating, thumb-sucking, nail-biting, chewing on the ends of pencils.

In the film version of *Tom Jones,* one of the most memorable and funny scenes involved the hero and his mistress eating themselves into a state of sexual satiation. Audiences all over the world identified with the implication.

THE ANAL STAGE

Sometimes I love to have a woman shove her finger up my ass and, maybe, massage the old prostate. It drives me wild.

The second stage begins at approximately the time the child starts his toilet training and is appropriately called *the anal stage.* At this point, the child becomes fascinated with his excretory functions and the pleasurable sensations associated with defecation. For a good bowel movement he is rewarded with ego strokes. Thus, approval as well as a stimulating physical sensation become associated with the anal area.

The homosexual pleasure in anal intercourse is often related to this stage of development. Later, we'll discuss the statistics on the number of heterosexual men who have experienced and enjoyed the act of anal sex with a woman. It may come as a bit of a surprise.

> If there was any one reason for my divorce, it was that my wife was a slob. The few times she did bother to dust, she could never put an object back where it belonged. When my things came back from the laundry, and she had to put them away, the drawers looked like a hurricane had swept through them. I know I get uptight about it. But I can't stand things out of place. I can't function that way.

Sublimation of the anal instinct almost literally takes the form of being "uptight." The man is extremely fastidious in the care of himself and his possessions. There is great orderliness and a tendency to acquisitiveness. Unsurprisingly, many authoritarians in the military and government are anal types.

Rebels are often the inversion of anal. They express their disdain for authority figures in the form of slovenliness and a loose lifestyle.

THE GENITAL STAGE

> I really dig a woman who's loose enough to touch me, run her fingers all over my body, caress me with her hands. And I really go ape if she's good to touch too.

There is a prelude to the third or *genital stage* of development. It could be classified as the touch or tactile stage. From birth, the baby enjoys having his mother and others touch and caress his skin. He smiles and responds. His overt pleasure gives ample evidence that the skin is an erogenous zone.

By the time he is one year old, he develops sufficient co-ordination to touch the various parts of his own body and independently administer the sensual stimulation. One of the organs he touches is his penis. This feels especially good, and he begins to touch himself there more and more often.

> My kid had his first erection when he was about a year old. My wife went crazy. She thought she'd given birth to some kind of sexual maniac. She kept

saying, What are we going to do? I told her, Give the kid a gold star and let him enjoy himself.

Not only does the infant have spontaneous erections, but he quickly learns how to bring them on by manipulation of his genitalia. It is a phenomenal experience. It is also a perfectly normal, healthy activity. Sharp parental disapproval can cause a trauma that will have deleterious effects for the rest of his life.

By the time a boy reaches the age of five, he has usually passed into the true genital stage. The penis and scrotum have become the center of his most profound sexual feelings and will remain so from then on. He has probably learned to masturbate without true understanding of the significance of what he is doing. It is likely that he has experienced an orgasmic feeling without emission or ejaculation (which can only happen after puberty).

I'll show you mine if you show me yours.

•

Let's play house. You be the mama, and I'll be the papa. Now let's take off our clothes and lie down and hug a lot.

•

I'll be the doctor, and you be the patient. And I'll take your temperature with my finger. Okay?

Until he reaches twelve or thirteen, the average boy's sexuality is of low intensity. He is curious about his own genitalia and those of his peers and passes through phases of mutual exhibition and games in which he mimics adults in what seem to be intimate situations.

These are minor activities for most boys. The sexual feelings are there, but the drive is not a strong one. There are exceptions. Some boys have strong sexual desires and act upon them. They go well beyond the games stage and become quite vigorous on a sexual level.

13

ADOLESCENT SEXUALITY

MASTURBATION

I'd had erections before. I'd even manipulated my penis and felt very good about it. But this time—I must've been about thirteen—I somehow knew it was different. I can't recall how much I'd heard about masturbation and orgasm at that point. I guess something. Funny, the things you block. Anyhow, I just kept pumping. Faster and faster. I felt like my head was going to blow off. And then—wow—then! I was king of the hill.

•

The guys I palled around with told me about it. They all claimed they jerked off all the time. And it was great. We were about twelve or thirteen. I don't know. Maybe even younger. If only to conform, I had to have an orgasm. So I went home and I whacked away. I was scared shitless that somebody would catch me at it. It seemed to take forever. When I finally came, it was more relief than pleasure.

•

I was in bed reading this book. There was a scene that I thought was hot stuff, and I began to masturbate. My mother walked in and caught me at it. I thought I was going to die. She didn't say a word. Just turned and left the room. A few minutes later, my father came up. I can't remember all he said. He must've been as embarrassed as hell. In essence, I think it was that it was wrong to masturbate. But if you had to do it, don't do it in bed, where you can get caught or, worse yet, dirty the sheets. Lock yourself in the bathroom, where nobody will see, and there'll be no evidence.

There is a wide range in ages for the beginning of male puberty. Although it generally starts at twelve or thirteen, some can experience it as early as ten, others as late as fifteen. Unless it is handled with tact and enlightenment by their parents, both early and late starters may experience some grave psychological problems.

Adolescence can usually be considered as extending through the teen years, from thirteen to nineteen. For the majority of males, the first sexual experience is masturbation until ejaculation.*

Dr. Kinsey reports:

For boys who have not been too disturbed psychologically, masturbation, however, provides a regular sexual outlet which has alleviated nervous tensions; and the record is clear that these boys have on the whole lived more balanced lives than the boys who have been more restrained in their sexual activities.†

Despite all the proscriptions, myths, and attendant guilts, 58 per cent of all adolescent males have masturbated at least once. Of that figure, 30 per cent began masturbating at the age of thirteen, 45 per cent before thirteen, and 20 per cent at ten or younger.‡

In an average month, 36 per cent of all adolescent males masturbate at least once. Naturally, the percentage is higher among older boys than younger ones.

When I was a kid, I had to jerk off two times a week. It was almost a ritual. Most of the guys did, even those who'd made out. I remember, we once had a group jerk-off. Our version of the fastest gun in the West. It was to see who could come first and shoot farthest.

•

There was one guy on our street who always got very uptight when we talked about sex. We were friendly, so I took him aside and asked him about it. It seems he'd never even masturbated. He'd tried. But nothing happened. I told

---

* We will discuss adult masturbation in Chapter 21.

† Dr. A. C. Kinsey, author of *Sexual Behavior in the Human Male*, quoted in *Sexual Self-Stimulation* by R. E. L. Masters (Los Angeles: Sherbourne Press, 1967).

‡ All figures in this book on adolescent sexuality are from *Adolescent Sexuality* by R. Sorenson (New York: World Publishing Co., 1973).

him to fantasize. He asked, "About what?" I got a hold of some pornography and gave it to him. It only made things worse. He was revolted by it. Now, there was nothing organically wrong with the boy. He's married and has kids now. But he came from the most religious, narrow-minded, tight-assed family I ever saw.

•

Even after I had intercourse, I still continued to masturbate. I occasionally still do. It's not that I don't like intercourse better. There's no comparison. It's a whole other thing. A release of all kinds of fantasies.

Although fewer boys masturbate who've been having sexual intercourse than those who've been inactive during a given month, coitus does not preclude masturbation. Thirty-six per cent of boys who have other sexual outlets continue to masturbate.

Very few masturbators are gratified solely by the manipulation of their penises. External or internal stimuli often provide necessary additional pleasures along the way. Fantasy is the most widely used of these aids. It is in fantasy that the wildest sexual urges can be gratified, extending all the way to the libidinous perimeters of the imagination. Fifty-seven per cent of adolescent masturbators fantasize most of the time, 23 per cent some of the time, 9 per cent sporadically; only 11 per cent never fantasize during the act.

Many moralists protest against pornography on the grounds that it corrupts our youth. I suppose one must then define corruption. It is true that many boys do use erotic pictures as a stimulus during masturbation. However, when I was an adolescent, many of us went to the public library and took out Hemingway's *For Whom the Bell Tolls*. The sleeping-bag scene was the spur to hundreds of masturbatory orgasms. A later group used Nabokov's *Lolita*. I know one man from a religious background who tells of successfully masturbating to visions evoked by the *Song of Solomon* from the Bible. Should Nabokov, Hemingway, and Solomon also be considered corrupting pornographers because of the erotic fantasies of adolescents?

The truth is that each generation finds erotic stimulation in the materials that are available. During World War II, there were probably as many young soldiers masturbating while looking at the photographs of movie-star pin-up girls in chaste sweaters and one-piece bathing suits as there are adolescents today who do it while viewing the no-holds-barred material currently available. As long as there is a real need for this sort of stimulation, it will find a way of being satisfied no matter how many bookstores are closed.

Pot's a groove. Sometimes it makes me real horny. Like, joint and joint go together. Did you ever think of that? When I'm alone and high on some good grass, I take it out and whack away. Man, it's a trip. Outta sight.

The majority of adolescent marijuana smokers enjoy masturbation more than the boys who do not smoke. Twenty-seven per cent of the heads get tremendous pleasure out of masturbation, while only 8 per cent of the nonsmokers admit comparable satisfaction. Those who smoke with one hand while jerking off with the other tend to fantasize in substantially greater numbers (98 per cent vs. 68 per cent), and a somewhat greater number also use erotic pictures. One might hypothesize that the use of marijuana makes one more comfortable with autoeroticism because of a release from the taboos of society. Whatever the reason, there is undeniably a link between the drugs and a high degree of pleasure during masturbation.

I used to feel guilty as all get out whenever I masturbated. I was having a man-to-man talk with my son, and I suddenly realized that he was having the same problems I had. And I thought the kids had come a long way from that. I guess not. I told him all of the things I've always wished my father had told me. It's normal. Relax and enjoy it. I don't know if it helped or made things worse. What *do* you say?

All adolescents feel more uneasy about masturbation than about any other sexual activity. Approximately half of the masturbators feel guilt, anxiety, or concern often, or at least some of the time.

For all of the vaunted permissiveness of our society, this still seems to be something that engenders negative feelings in the young.

These feelings may well go back to the biblical injunction: Man shall not spill his seed upon the ground. Consciously or unconsciously, the bad feelings seem to be handed down from father to son through the generations. Perhaps the wisest course would be for the parent to bring all of his own feelings out into the open, to "rap" with the boy. Whether masturbation is parentally condoned or condemned, it is too often done from a lofty, godlike position. There should be a free exchange between father and son in which they try to tell each other as honestly as possible everything that they feel, and why they feel that way. It is only through getting close to the subject, on a positive footing in their own relationship, that they may be able to cast off the problem.

SEXUAL INTERCOURSE

Going all the way with a girl was everything I ever thought it would be. I've never been so happy.

In contrast to the guilt so often expressed about masturbation, male teenagers describe their first experiences of sexual intercourse as exciting, satisfying, thrilling, and happy. Adolescent girls have negative feelings about it more often than positive ones, but only a small minority of the boys feel guilty, sorry, afraid, or embarrassed.

The newspaper, television, and magazine stories of teenage promiscuity tend to make our imagination run riot. The fact is that 20 per cent of all American adolescent boys have had no sexual experience beyond a kiss. Naturally, the older he gets, the more likely he is to gain that experience. One third of the boys are without it at fifteen, but only 5 per cent are still inexperienced at nineteen.

I don't want to discuss it. Let's just say I'm not ready for it yet.

•

The truth is, I haven't met a girl that I want to have sex with.

•

I'd love to have sex. But I haven't met anybody who wants to have it with me.

Beginning is the difficult part. Once the boy is over his initial fears of rejection and failure, his experience evolves step-by-step until coitus is achieved. After kissing, the first step for novices is touching above the waist, with 95 per cent of all beginners having felt a girl's breast. The next step is touching below the waist, with 56 per cent having felt a girl's genitalia. (But only 32 per cent have had their penises touched. The double standard is obviously already operative.)

The time to begin sex education is at the very first sign of puberty. Of those adolescent males who have had sexual experiences, a startling 17 per cent had their first intercourse at the age of twelve or under. By the time they reach fifteen, 71 per cent are nonvirgins.

A generation ago, finding a satisfactory place for the act was a major obstacle to first intercourse. Today, it most often happens in the home of the boy or girl. The comparatively few reactions of guilt would lead one to surmise that there was probably some degree of parental sanction, even if it was only implied.

I'm glad I did it with her. I really care for her. And she cares for me. We've done it again. Lots of times. It's very meaningful. She's my girl.

•

The important thing is, we didn't lay a trip on each other. We both felt that we were ready, that it was the time to do it. We were right for each other. Any other time with anybody else, I don't think it would have been as good.

The adolescent male is ready to assume responsibility for his sexual behavior. The primary concern of the parents cannot be that their children are having sex: it must be to prepare their children with all of the information that will make it a safe and happy experience for them. The parents cannot shrug off their children's sexuality. It is their responsibility to give adequate information on birth control, sexual techniques and responses—in short, to share with their offspring all that they have learned about sexuality in their adult lives.

HOMOSEXUALITY

There are some guys we think are fags at school. If they do it with each other, and they both want to, that's okay with me. But I'd really let them have it if they tried any of that stuff on me.

Adolescent attitudes toward homosexuality are ambivalent. They are much more tolerant of the abstract concept than adults are; 41 per cent express a neutral approval of boys having sex together, if there is mutual consent. But the majority remain intolerant of the act itself, with 75 per cent finding it abnormal or unnatural.

The figures tend to mitigate against the hysterical fears of some adults that we are rearing a homosexual or bisexual generation. At a very early point in adolescence, boys understand the derision implicit in the epithets "faggot," "queen," "nance," "gay," "queer"—and they are offended when these words are applied to them even in jest.

I've had sex with some of the boys at school. A lot of the others—the ones that call me faggot—would be surprised which ones. But it's all such a big deal that it's better to go downtown and cruise strangers.

In common with many adult homosexuals, adolescents tend to be secretive about their activities, to remain "in the closet." The inner conflicts may be the reason why the figures on the actual amount of adolescent homosexuality are so unreliable. There may be some tendency to opt for the safety of that closet even with skilled researchers. In his survey of four hundred adolescent males, Sorenson found that only 11 per cent had experienced a homosexual relationship. In his much broader investigation, Dr. Kinsey found that 40 per cent of all of his male respondents had indulged in some homosexual activity by the time they'd reached nineteen. The figure was so unexpectedly high that Kinsey carefully rechecked his findings against different sets of criteria. His somewhat startling reassessment was "that the actual figure may be as much as 5 per cent higher."

> When I was about twelve, my cousin and I played with each other. He was a little older, and all he was really doing was teaching me the right way to jerk off. We're both married now, with kids of our own. We never talk about those days. And I'm not sure how I'd react if I found my son doing the same thing with another boy.

The most common age for a first homosexual experience is eleven or twelve. The age of the partner is evenly spread among boys of the same age and those older and younger. Adult males account for only 10 per cent of the homosexual acts of adolescent males. Heterosexual acts, performed on adolescent girls by adult males, are statistically much more common. This weakens some of Anita Bryant's arguments against placing our children in the care of homosexual school teachers. A case could even be made for the reverse proposition.

Homosexual relations account for only a small part of all adolescent sexual experience. Only 8 to 16 per cent of the orgasms of unmarried males are homosexually induced.* Many of the boys who reported homosexual activity had had only one experience.† In the course of sexual events, homosexuality is like the proverbial flower: one blossom does not a summer make.

The most common form of adolescent homosexual activity is one step up the ladder from our definition of no experience. It is mutual masturbation, which could be considered an extension of "I'll show you mine if you show me yours," or "Let's pee together," or "Let's jerk off together." Oral sex comes next: either fellatio or mutual fellatio (commonly called "69"). Anal intercourse is the least frequently indulged-in form of adolescent homosexual activity.

The figure for single-incident adolescent homosexuality makes it unlikely that it leads to adult homosexuality in a majority of instances. If the

* Kinsey, loc. cit.
† Sorenson, loc. cit.

parents among us discover this about our sons, we must be extremely understanding. We must not instill the guilt and anxiety that so often lead to greater confusion and sexual ambiguity. Above all, there must be no condemnation or derision.

If the homosexual incidents are traumatic, we should seek professional help for the boy. He must not be isolated or left to deal with the situation as best he can. If it is the one-incident variety, it should not be made a *cause célèbre* but should be treated with understanding and love. It may well be a case of any sexual port in a storm, as it so often is among adult prisoners and soldiers.

There is one last suggestion for those fathers who have been through similar experiences in their own adolescence. They might try to summon up the courage to discuss this with their troubled sons. It could be a valid demonstration that it does not impair their capacity for heterosexual love, if that is what the boys really want for themselves.

VENEREAL DISEASE

Venereal disease is a real problem for adolescents and one they have not been properly equipped to handle. In the state of California alone, adolescents account for 20 per cent of the reported cases of venereal disease. Yet, of the boys he interviewed, Sorenson found that only 20 per cent had been told anything about VD by their parents.

Parents tend to leave this to sex education classes. As a result, 80 per cent of all teenagers feel that, though venereal disease is a serious problem, it can easily be cured by a doctor. It is in the home, with parental force, that what is taught in the school must be underscored. These diseases have serious consequences (see pages 110–16). Added to them are the possible psychological problems for a young person. For their own sakes, our children must be taught everything about VD and must be confident that they can turn to us for help should they contract it.

BIRTH CONTROL

My wife became pregnant before we got married. I was eighteen. I'm not saying I wouldn't have married her anyway. But I didn't know anything about birth control. Nobody told me. As for her, her people were very religious and didn't talk about those things. I want to get on in the world. But working all day, being a father, and going to night school, too. It's not easy. I don't know if I can hack it.

•

When I make it with a girl, birth control's her problem. I'm not about to stop and ask if she took the pill or anything.

The California statistics are among the most complete in the nation. In 1973, 44 per cent of all the illegitimate births in that state were to adolescent females. A child was born to almost one third of the teenagers married during the previous year. It is hard to believe that pregnancy did not precede the wedding in a majority of the cases.

When we speak about telling our children about birth control, most of us mean telling our daughters about birth control. Eighty per cent of teenage males claim that their parents never told them anything about it. For all of the publicity, too many young girls are not prepared by their parents with contraceptive devices. When this is equated with the number of boys left in ignorance by their parents, we have a very dangerous situation.

Only one quarter of the boys report that they always use a condom, while over one half claim that the last time they had intercourse neither they nor the girls used any type of contraception. Too many parents simply shrug and refuse to accept any responsibility. Some blame it on the times in which we live. Others are too religious or too embarrassed to discuss the facts of life with youngsters. The majority are resigned to the fact that they cannot stop their children from having sex. That may be true, but with a little instruction to our children, they can be stopped from having unwanted babies.

All boys should be told about condoms (politely called "prophylactics"). Parents should make every effort to see that they are used by those indulging in sexual relations. Parents must try to overcome any religious or moral scruples they may have and face the world in which their children live.

If contraception is truly anathema, the boys must be taught about coitus interruptus (withdrawing from the vagina before orgasm). Both boys and girls must be told the facts about female menstrual cycles, so that they may practice the *rhythm method*. No intercourse can take place during the days when the girl is likely to conceive (the ninth to ninteenth days after the period). Both of these are among the least sexually satisfying and most imperfect methods of birth control, but they are better than no control at all.

A teenager is generally so excited and anxious over the possibility of intercourse, that he seldom thinks of asking about the contraceptive methods his girl might be using. Nevertheless, it is his parents' responsibility to teach him about them.

The widespread publicity about the pill makes it unlikely that any boy is so out of touch that he does not know enough to ask a girl if she is on it. He should also be told about diaphragms and IUDs (intrauterine devices). If the girl is prepared with any form of contraception, her parents have obviously enlightened her about the consequences of lack of birth control. If she is not, it is the boy's responsibility to attend to the situation by using any of the methods that have been discussed.

ABORTIONS

One reason I haven't had sex is that I'm afraid I'll make a girl pregnant. And then she'll have to have an abortion. And it will be my fault. I don't want that rap.

•

If my girl gets pregnant, I'd rather that she had an abortion than a baby. I think she feels the same way.

Over one third of all the California abortions in 1973 were performed on women under twenty. More than one half of the teenagers of both sexes are not opposed to abortion, and almost one third of the nonvirgin boys would prefer any girl they made pregnant to have an abortion no matter what the emotional tie. The statistics indicate that adolescent thinking on the subject parallels adult thought. The difference is that they may be less able to handle the trauma. Proper understanding and education at home can protect and help them.

Certainly, federal funding should be made available to help the young to have abortions, as they are among the least able to afford them on their own. It is shocking that the President of the United States should say, in essence, that the burden of unwanted and fatherless children is one of the prices you must pay for being young and poor.

MARRIAGE AND FAMILY

Sure, I want to get married. But not yet. That doesn't mean I don't want to have sex. No matter what my parents say, there's nothing wrong with two people living together without being married. And there's nothing wrong with sleeping around, if you get the opportunity. Maybe my old man would be less uptight if he had a mistress. And I wouldn't mind if my mother tried a lover. I'll bet she was a virgin when she got married. That's one thing I don't want —to marry a virgin!

The moral thinking of an adolescent is often at odds with the teachings of his parents, who often come off as much too uptight in their attitudes. As a result, the boy's sexual models are generally in the group only a few years older than himself, and their opinions help to form his.

Many teenagers think that their parents are on the opposing side in the sexual revolution. Almost three quarters of them believe that the older generation thinks that sex before marriage is immoral. The parents might be astonished to discover that one third of their adolescent progeny think there is nothing wrong with married people having occasional extra-curricular sexual relations (just for the sake of variety), while two thirds do not see the necessity for marriage if two people love each other and are living together.

Over one half of the boys report that it is abnormal or unnatural for a boy not to have sexual relations until he gets married, and almost as many have come to the same conclusion about girls and premarital sex. As far as 50 per cent of American adolescent males are concerned, the cult of the virgin is finished.

Although many adolescents have become very concerned about the problem of overpopulation, it has not affected the marital plans of a vast majority of them. For all of the agonizing they've done over the sexual beliefs of the young, parents will be pleased to note that they still believe in the family. Eighty-five per cent of adolescent males expect to marry and have children. One can only hope that they will manage as well or better than their parents.

What can the older generation take away from all of this information about young men? There is one overwhelming fact that runs like a threnody through all of the statistics. Our adolescent boys are not in revolt against all of the old standards, but they are insisting upon the right to accept and reject for themselves, and to find their own way to sexual fulfillment. They would do this far less painfully and probably much more successfully with our approval and help than with our rejection. Fathers and sons still have much to learn from each other. They can use our wisdom and experience, but only if we give it without condescension, and we can use their resiliency, freedom, and inventiveness, but only if they give it without belligerence. Old and young alike must bring the love they feel for each other into the way they regard each other. We must lovingly respect our right to differ.

14

ADULT SEXUALITY

If the girl's a dog, nothing's going to happen. For me, ugliness is a turn-off no matter how horny I am.

•

Naturally, physical attractiveness is very important. I'm not about to go to bed with somebody I'm not attracted to. And I'm sure the same is true for women. If it's going to be more than a one-night stand, it depends on how free she is in bed, how open to experimentation.

•

The most important thing is that she's got to like to do the things I like to do in bed.

•

We've got to dig each other physically and groove in bed. But there's something more. She's got to have a sense of humor about it. No heavy drama. Sex is having a good time, lots of laughs. I'm into humor. I think it's sexy.

In the beginning of a relationship, most people are attracted by the physical attributes of their potential sexual partners. Sexual behavior and sexual attitudes become equally important components of sexuality as the relationship deepens. The modern man is free to explore his sexuality, articulate his needs, and act upon them. No matter what social level he comes from, he has the right to find sexual pleasure and fulfillment in any way that gratifies him. It is one of the more positive aspects of being alive in our times, for that right was not always guaranteed to all men of all social and economic classes.

Until the beginning of the twentieth century, enjoying sex was the sport of the privileged classes. The wealthy and powerful mistresses and concubines whose hold on their positions was determined by the amount of pleasure they gave in the beds of their protectors. If an ordinary, or common, man resorted to a prostitute or "bad" woman, it was usually for relief rather than pleasure. The "good" woman had no sexual outlets: instead, she had babies. Although many people from the lower classes had healthy appetites and enjoyed sex, very few would have questioned the statement that the primary function of sex is procreation, and most would have been shocked at the suggestion that there were those who found pleasure as, if not more, important.

CHANGING SEXUAL ATTITUDES

This century brought forth a series of events that helped to change the sexual attitudes of the masses. What is called the sexual revolution has its foundations in several things that happened outside the bedroom.

The emancipation of women is probably the most significant change in male-female attitudes in our time. Starting with suffrage, it led to an investigation of all of women's rights under the law. Legal rights led inevitably to a realization of sexual rights. She was not simply the chattel of her husband obliged to do his sexual bidding, an object to be used for his sexual relief and to bear his children. Suddenly, she could say *no* even to her legal mate. He had to make it something she enjoyed as well as he. The pleasure principle entered marital sex. To the enormous joy of both men and women, it spread from there into all sexual relationships.

The invention of new forms of contraception has helped immeasurably by freeing people from the fear of having unwanted children. They are free to indulge their sexual fancies on the broadest possible scale.

Contemporary skepticism has brought about an investigation of the religious and moral sexual scruples of the past. Most of these tenets are not only being questioned, they are being challenged. Nature has provided a new motivation that underscores this challenge. There is a very real danger of overpopulation on this planet. To save the species, one must, paradoxically, stop heedless reproduction. This would once have militated against sexual intercourse. The awakening to our need for sexual pleasure has made many people defy religious dicta against contraception and indulge in sex free of fear and guilt.

Sigmund Freud pioneered work in the field of psychoanalysis that, in the space of this century, has forever changed man's view of his sexuality. Among other things, he now authoritatively knows that sexual repression can be as dangerous to him as an individual as overpopulation is to the world at large.

Until very recently, our culture equated masculinity with aggressiveness, high levels of desire and active pursuit of sexual gratification, physical strength and stoicism. Femininity meant passiveness, emotionalism, weakness, and a small sexual appetite. A woman had to be a virgin until she married, but it was considered advisable for a man to be experienced. After the wedding, he could have discreet extramarital relationships, while she was supposed to remain forever faithful.

Both sexes gave lip service to the double standard, but it was already beginning to be seriously questioned during the last century. One *Belle Époque* Frenchman sardonically observed: "If every man has a mistress, then it would seem a verity that every woman must have a lover, or there would not be enough to go around."

The old sexual delineations have become so blurred in our time that it would be difficult to describe any behavior as exclusively male or female. The only things that remain permanently unchanging are the genitalia of each sex and their functioning. In other areas, each sex has taken over many (if not all) of the actions and thoughts once ascribed exclusively to the other. It is not uncommon for a contemporary woman to call up a man for a date, or for a man to lie passively on his back while a woman initiates and remains the active partner during coitus.

Our sexual attitudes are influenced by variables that are often beyond our control. Among them are gender, age, religion, economic standing, politics, family background, rural/urban residence, education, and means of livelihood. An interesting statistical example is that married, college-educated men are more likely to engage in oral sex and/or masturbation than married grade-school-level men. More predictably, a religious man is likely to be against abortion and premarital sex.

Our sexual attitudes are not always the same as our sexual behavior. Mores do conspire to make hypocrites of many of us. A man may fundamentally think that fidelity is necessary to a good marriage and still be untrue to his wife throughout his lifetime. A very with-it type may believe that an open marriage is the only civilized type of relationship and become insanely jealous if his wife so much as looks at another man.

The conflict between behavior and attitude is one of the motivations for the displacement of one's sexuality into other actions. When a man cannot cope, he has subconscious access to two defense mechanisms: sublimation and repression. To sublimate is to divert sexual energy into external activities that absorb it. To repress is to bury one's sexual desire deep in the unconscious.

So strong is the power of displacement that it has been noted that civilization can be viewed as having been built with diverted (sublimated) sexual energy. Sexuality is not the only anxiety-producing conflict that man displaces. Sexual activity, itself, can actually be a form of displacement. When a man is insecure in his masculinity or anxious about his inability to handle personal, professional, or environmental problems, he may use indiscriminate sex as a form of displacement. He develops a macho façade and displaces his stresses in seduction.

Repressed sexuality is refracted back into the consciousness in a variety of warped or disguised forms. The most common examples are: eccentricities, rigidity, nervous mannerisms, dreams, fantasies, neuroses.

In what follows, we are going to investigate how men are being freed from the need for displacement by the liberal and permissive attitudes that have developed over the last thirty years.

15

THE SINGLE HETEROSEXUAL MALE

When I got married, we all wanted to marry virgins. My wife was one. But my son doesn't want to marry one. It's just as well, because I doubt if he could find one.

Through the years, many polls have been taken that have attempted to uncover our nation's sexual attitudes. In both 1937 and 1959, Roper polls indicated that 22 per cent felt it was all right for both men and women to have sexual intercourse before marriage; 8 per cent felt that it was all right for men only; 50 per cent did not believe premarital sex was right for either sex. A 1959 Gallup poll showed that 68 per cent of a national sampling was against premarital sex for anybody. In 1969, the poll showed that the figure had dropped to 48 per cent, going from a substantial majority to a substantial minority. A 1972 survey* found that, depending on the degree of emotional involvement, 60 to 84 per cent of males felt that it was all right for men to have premarital relations, and 44 to 81 per cent felt that it was also all right for women.

PETTING AND INTERCOURSE

When I was a teenager, in the fifties, we did a hell of a lot of heavy petting, then the fellows got out of the car and masturbated in the bushes. I often wonder what those girls were thinking.

* M. Hunt, *Sexual Behavior in the 1970s* (New York: Dell Publishing Company, 1974).

•

I may never have gotten beyond high school but I've been doing postgraduate work in sex since I was fifteen.

•

Despite the open dorms and alleged permissiveness, I know a lot of the fellows still get their rocks off by beating their meat.

For the last fifty years, petting has been an excellent compromise for the man who believed that he should only have intercourse with his future wife and still had sexual needs while single. The most recent surveys show that there remains a substantial minority who still believe in the old-fashioned ideal of chastity.

Educational level is a major factor in the intensity and degree of petting. By the time the average high-school-level male has reached sixteen, he has had his first experience of sexual intercourse. He does not consider petting an important part of his sensual life.

The average college student does not experience coitus until he is twenty and is dependent for release upon petting, often to orgasm and masturbation.

By 1973, about two thirds of the females between the ages of eighteen and twenty-four were having premarital intercourse about once a week.† It is becoming more and more universally acceptable to indulge in sex before marriage.

While sexual freedom may be on the march, promiscuity is not keeping step. Certain statistics have remained constant over the last thirty years. Men have an average of only six sexual partners during their bachelor years. Over half of the women who've had premarital intercourse have had it only with one man. The vast majority of both sexes indicate that there must always be some emotional involvement.

My fiancée and I have been going steady since we started high school. It was a parochial school, and we do share a common faith. But it's not just our religion that's kept us from having sexual relations with each other or with anybody else. It's our commitment to each other and to the kind of marriage and home we want.

Despite the increased amount of sexual opportunity, one man in twenty is still a virgin at the time he gets married. These males usually fall into one of the following categories:

† Ibid.

1. Devoutly religious
2. Desirous of sex only after marriage (the influence of sexual liberty is steadily eroding this group)
3. Extreme timidity
4. Emotionally disturbed

PROSTITUTION

When I was a young man, most of my crowd had its first sexual experiences with prostitutes. It was really the only way. There were very few young women, with whom we would naturally come in contact, who would allow us to do anything more than some petting. And in those days, not much of that. I suppose my grandsons would never frequent a prostitute except as a last resort in a strange town or as an amusing thing to do. But in my youth, there weren't the sexual opportunities that they now take for granted.

There has been a great outcry against the appearance on the streets of our cities of large numbers of prostitutes blatantly peddling their wares. Many people are blaming the sexual looseness of the period for this significant and unwanted presence in our downtown areas. Actually, sexual freedom is working against the ladies. They're out hustling so hard because it's more difficult than ever to "turn a trick."

Only 3 per cent of all single white males under twenty-five had been with prostitutes during the year 1973. Twenty-five years earlier, Kinsey found that double that number, in the same category, had used their services.

The use of prostitutes is stronger in some segments of single society than in others. For some reason, 10 per cent more men with high-school-level educations avail themselves of prostitutes than men with college-level educations: the latter are more likely to pet or masturbate. Some men have a neurotic need for a prostitute because they are too guilt-ridden to function with a "good" girl, or need to be debased, or need kinky sex, or any of a number of other motivations stemming from psychological maladjustments. There are those who simply do not know how to "score" with girls with whom there is some need for at least minimal social exchange. Members of this group sometimes behave with the gaucherie of the man who meets a very desirable woman. She says: "How do you do?" He replies: "Skip the small talk. Let's fuck."

For many, recourse to a prostitute is simply a rare sexual adventure that has little to do with deep functional needs. It might be prompted by the loneliness of a strange place or merely the whim of an evening.

The sexual liberation of women has diminished the need for prostitutes in all facets of our society. Something very significant has been impressed upon single men in the last decade or two. The decreasing use of paid-for sex has been in direct proportion to the growth of an awareness of the need for emotional involvement in order to experience deep sexual gratification. With the expansion of availability, with the blurring of the "good girl/bad girl" judgmental delineations, single men are learning that there is much more to sexual satisfaction than an orgasm. Sex is not only a function of the body. At its best and most rewarding, it will embrace both the emotions and the imagination.

CONTRACEPTION

Contraception was once exclusively the responsibility of the male. It was up to him to practice coitus interruptus, the rhythm method, or use a condom. As the female moved away from what was so often a passive sexual role, the responsibility shifted. This was natural. Her pleasure and demands were increasing, and she had to protect herself against the consequences. Contraception is currently much more apt to be practiced by the female via the diaphragm, IUD, or the pill.

There are two surgical methods of contraception: the vasectomy for men and the laparoscopic method (known as "band aid") for women.

The first vasectomy clinic opened in 1969, and between 1970 and 1974, approximately 700,000 men had this operation performed annually. Some of the men undoubtedly did not want to be fathers for a variety of reasons, ranging from simple preference, to thinking themselves too old to start raising new children, to fear that some dire hereditary strain might be passed on to another generation.

In 1970, 80 per cent of all voluntary sterilizations were performed on men. With the perfecting of the laparoscopic method, that figure dropped to 50 per cent within the next five years.

No matter what pressures may seem to be put on them by lifestyles or lovers or anything else, no single person, male or female, should submit to sterilization except for medical reasons or, in the case of the male particularly, for over age. The younger singles are not in a position to foretell what their own feelings will be at the point when they meet somebody they care about deeply enough to want to marry.

VARIATIONS IN SEXUAL TECHNIQUE

I love all kinds of sex. If I'm dating somebody who only digs the conventional sort, that's all right with me. But I enjoy going down on a girl as much. And a girl who knows how to give good head, she's the wildest. I've even done the anal act with a chick who said that was her big scene. But I used a condom. Can you imagine? I almost never use a condom doing it the regular way. But I couldn't go up the ass without one. Now, there's a crazy hang-up for you.

The emancipation of sexual pleasure has taken place in the little over three decades since Kinsey first published his controversial report. The males he interviewed had been brought up in, or lived through, the economic and political displacements of a great depression and world war (possibly two wars). Contemporary males (especially those forty-five or under) were reared in a period of affluence, peace, and indulgence, an age of Spock, a time when a youth culture was eroding generational differences between parent and child, when public morality had been undermined by a series of assassinations, Vietnam, and Watergate. The findings of Dr. Kinsey also played a part in creating a changed sexual climate from the one that he measured, although it is amazing how much remains statistically the same as his findings showed. Whether any or all of these factors were totally responsible for what has happened would be impossible to determine, but that they have all contributed to it would be impossible to deny.

Let us look at some of the ways in which foreplay is significantly more satisfying than it was thirty years ago. Although there has been no significant change in male handling of the female genitalia—it was high then (91 per cent) and remains high (90 per cent)—female handling of male genitalia has raced forward to draw abreast of it (89 per cent). The real change has been in oral-genital sex. Almost three quarters of today's single men have given "head" or "gone down" on their sexual partners (*cunnilingus*) and have been gone down on by, or had a "blow job" from, them (*fellatio*). The increase in these sexual activities ranges from 40 to 60 per cent.

Many men find fellatio an exciting means of achieving orgasm. There's nothing wrong with it, so long as their partners are also gratified. The only danger is when both participants in a sex act are not equally satisfied. The ensuing frustration can destroy a potentially meaningful relationship

A single man should not use his sexual partner as a "comfort station," a means of relieving himself with no thought given to her needs. When he does this, he is sending out messages that he is not prepared to give of himself. Manhood is truly achieved by fulfilling a woman, by considering her needs as well as his own, by making more of her than she was before. The less we make of our sexual partners, the less we become ourselves. The cult of macho can be the flip side of effeminacy. Modern manliness is measured by giving as well as receiving pleasure.

The new sexual freedom has brought with it an exploration of all of the erogenous zones as possible sources of gratification. In Dr. Kinsey's time, anal intercourse between heterosexual couples was so rare that he published no statistics on it. By 1972, one sixth of the single men and women who had experienced coitus had also tried anal intercourse.‡

It was not long ago that only a homosexual male would admit that his own anus was an erogenous zone. A freer and more honest appraisal has become general enough for male anal erogeneity to be depicted in our popular culture: witness the startling finger episode between Marlon Brando and Maria Schneider in the film *Last Tango in Paris*.

During the early part of the 1970s, there was a great deal of publicity about "swinging." Hardly a week passed without a new story on the phenomenon. However, the statistics on unmarried partner swapping and group sex indicate that a great majority of single males and almost all single females still feel a need to have sexual practice partnered by emotional involvement. This is underscored by the fact that the majority of those who experimented with these activities did it only once or, at most, a few times.

As in almost everything else, sex often follows fashion. What we read about the "in" group doing is what many of us would like to try for ourselves. In the days when chastity was the mode, a great many men managed to retain their virginity until marriage. Now that experimentation is in vogue, there are those who feel a need to seek gratification in it for its own sake rather than for their own inner needs. They boast of their more *outré* exploits. They follow what is in fashion with the same fervor that women do. They seem to be seeking in diversification what eludes them in commitment.

It is not the bulge in tight trousers that proclaims manhood, nor is a mechanical response a measure of sexual prowess. A much greater role is played by the invisible emotions that activate the whole body. For the vast majority of us, truly fulfilling sex comes with relationship, response, and the interaction of many parts of ourselves in addition to the genitals.

DURATION OF INTERCOURSE

I'm a reactionary at the sexual revolution. I don't give head, and I come too quickly.

•

When I get in the saddle, I like to play the easy rider. I have this thing. I can hold off until my girl's ready. I love it when we pass that finish line together.

‡ Ibid.

The last decade has brought about almost complete acceptance of the great changes that have taken place in virtually every aspect of the sex act. We've not only broadened the variety of permissible and/or desirable behavior, but men have actually lengthened the average duration of coitus. Freedom from sexual guilt and a new consideration for the often expressed needs of our sexual partners have conspired to remove most males from the bim-bam-thank-you-ma'am category.

The length of time between penetration of the vagina and orgasm still varies considerably from man to man and situation to situation. There are and always have been sexual athletes who can and do retain an erection in the vagina for over an hour before orgasm.

The late Aly Khan's legendary sexual prowess was reputedly based upon his ability to maintain an erection in the vagina all night with or without multiple orgasms. The amount of pleasure derived from this feat must have depended very much on the needs of the individual women involved. There were some who must have been inordinately flattered by this bizarre compliment.

Some men still ejaculate within seconds of intromission. If this is a chronic condition, a reputable sex clinic or specialist in the field should be consulted for help. It can be a particularly frustrating problem for the contemporary single man seeking an intimate and enduring relationship.

I guess it must be between fifteen and twenty minutes between the time I enter and the time I come. But who looks at a clock at a time like that?

Three decades ago, Kinsey reported that the average married man had orgasm between two and three minutes after intromission, and that the duration was probably even shorter for single men. Nothing points up the difference in sexuality between then and now more strikingly than a comparison with the contemporary time span for single men between penetration and orgasm. It is estimated to be between ten and fifteen minutes.

Aside from sexual freedom, other things that may affect orgasmic time spans include: the degree of excitement due to the partner and/or situation, the amount of anticipation that preceded intercourse, how relaxed the man is, the desire of the woman to achieve orgasm, the length of time between orgasms.

LIVING TOGETHER VS. MARRIAGE

I believe in marriage. But I'm not ready for it yet. Neither is the girl I live with. The big hassle is our parents. When we go to visit either set, they don't let us sleep together, though they know we do at home. And they keep sawing away at getting married, saying we're as good as married. They don't understand. We're not. In some ways we're better than married. In others—it's different, that's all. You can't measure it by the same yardstick.

•

We love each other. And there are other advantages. We share expenses. God knows, it beats having a male roommate. We both expect to get married. But not necessarily to each other. We can't even agree on where and how we'd like to live. We're working on it, but we may not be able to get together on a compromise. Whatever happens, we both feel it's been a good experience, that we're better people for having done it.

•

I wouldn't want to just shack up with a girl. I want the whole thing. Marriage, family, the values I grew up with. I want to stand up in front of the whole world—*my* world—and say, "This is the woman I want to spend my life with." Anything less is a copout, a fear of commitment, of getting hurt, of showing vulnerability. Well, you've got to be ready to give yourself to another person wholly. And that does make you vulnerable.

•

We lived together for about five years before getting married. There were lots of petty fights before, lots of insecurities, lots of secret doubts of love. Suddenly we're part of something that's bigger than our single selves. I'm aware of my mortality. I'm beginning to take my career, my responsibilities, my *self* more seriously.

•

We broke up after a year of living together over some dumb quarrel. If we'd been married, I don't think it would have happened. We'd have handled our hostilities differently. When you're only living together, it's too easy to say, "Fuck you. I don't have to put up with your shit. I'm leaving."

Since 1970, the number of unmarried people of the opposite sex sharing a household had doubled, from 654,000 to 1,300,000, and that is surely an understatement, for many will not report the status of their private involvements to the Census Bureau.

Although the vast majority of males expect to get married at some point, there is a new uneasiness among young single men about making the commitment to it. As sociologist Richard Sennett put it: "The real issue is not cohabitation but the meaning of marriage. Something about making a lifetime commitment of marriage doesn't work any more—that's what cohabiting shows. The idea of a permanent commitment to another human being has lost its meaning."

A vast majority of Americans, young and old, would totally disagree with that statement. Millions, including the President of the United States, still think of it as "living in sin," something that is injurious to the fabric of both church and society.

Some people blame the trend toward cohabitation on the women's movement, others on sexual permissiveness, and still others on youthful rebellion against the standards of the family. How much any or all of these issues affect the trend would be hard to say. One thing is certain. There is an uneasiness about the state of marriage that is based upon the number of times it fails, and the divorce rate was rising awesomely long before women's rights, or sexual permissiveness, or the youth rebellion became a part of our milieu. At present, one out of every three marriages of couples between the ages of twenty-five and thirty will end in divorce. That's a frightening statistic for any single person contemplating matrimony.

Breaking up a living-together relationship brings up the questions of who owns what and whose apartment it is and even whose dog. They're nothing, however, compared to the problems and expense of working out a property settlement in a divorce. Added to that is the continuing payment of alimony. Until recently, a man could walk away from cohabitation scot-free.

A permanent change in the rules of the game may have been initiated in December 1976, when a California Supreme Court ruled that Michelle Triola had the right to pursue her claim for both support payments and community property from actor Lee Marvin, with whom she had lived for seven years. In the absence of a marriage contract or even a verbal agreement, the ruling makes it possible for the court to infer a contract from the behavior of the two parties. Beyond that, it gives the court the right to examine a relationship to see who contributed what. On the basis of it, the court may be asked to determine the value of services and the justice of imposing the economic obligations of lawful mates on people who have rejected matrimony to avoid such obligations.

If the single man is going to be responsible for paying the woman with whom he's lived out of marriage the same benefits that the divorced man is obligated to pay his former wife, the bachelor may have second thoughts about such an alliance. There is already talk of non-nuptial agreements in which both parties to cohabitation spell out the terms of the arrangement and the responsibilities that may or may not be operative at the end of it. It is possible that affairs will be less likely to lead to cohabitation as a result of these new legal entanglements. It is also likely that they may lead to a lessening of the modern male reluctance to getting married.

If cohabitation continues as a viable lifestyle, future couples entering it will discover what many of those living in it now have already learned. It provides no easy solution to the day-to-day problems of two people living in the same space. Adjustments take as much time and patience as they do in a modern marriage.

16

THE MARRIED MAN

We'd slept together before we got married, but it's gotten much better since the wedding. She tells me she never had an orgasm before me. And I believe it. She didn't have one the first few times with me. She was just faking it. I knew it even before she told me. Now it's great. Every time. Just great.

•

I knew my wife had had a couple of affairs before me. When we were going together, it didn't matter. Even after we got serious, it didn't matter. You know when it mattered? On our honeymoon. We'd had a religious ceremony —not that we're religious. For our families. It must've got to me. It was like I was expecting a virgin. Can you dig that scene? But we were able to work it out. Because we're so open with each other. That's the great thing about marital sex. We've got all the fun and games without any of the lying and cheating you have to do when you're single.

•

I sometimes think my wife had more experience than I did. She certainly knows how to pick up sexual cues—and drop them. She's often more aggressive. More inventive. I think she must've had some great lovers. It doesn't threaten me. What we have exists on too many levels. In bed and out. What I give her, none of them ever gave. What we have together, neither of us ever had with anybody else.

This liberation of sexual attitudes and behavior has made a profound change in the lives of newly married couples. The husband today is likely to have had many more premarital sexual involvements than did his counterpart a few years ago. Perhaps even more significantly, the wife has probably had a fair amount of experience, certainly much more than was the case twenty or thirty years ago. Statistical confirmation is found in the fact that many more young women today experience orgasm early in their marriages than was reported by Kinsey.

Men enjoy their marital sex lives much more than they previously did. The frequency of intercourse is higher; foreplay is more important and varied; there is greater experimentation in coital positions; preorgasmic coitus is prolonged and more mutually satisfying.

SEXUALITY AND MARRIAGE

If we'd tried it out before we got married, we'd have saved ourselves a lot of sorrow. From the first night, I knew we weren't going to make it in bed. I tried, but we weren't sexually compatible. You know, I talked it over with my dad. Can you imagine, he told me that what happened in bed wasn't all that important. Marriage was what was left after you outgrew all that stuff. Boy, that was some comment on my mom and him. Anyway, Susie didn't want to stay with it any more than I did, so we broke up.

The higher divorce rates partially confirm the importance of sexuality in a marriage. Expectations are increased from previous experience, the wide dissemination of information, and the candor with which sex is discussed. The married man is no longer satisfied with a wife who passively endures sex rather than freely participates in it. Nor will a wife accept a husband's selfish and egocentric sexual behavior. She refuses to put up with a man who gets his rocks off while she remains unsatisfied. All of their sexual problems can be aired. Therapy and counseling are available for those who need it.

Neither partner to a marriage is willing to endure prolonged frustration. Divorce is much too easy to obtain and too common to be socially unacceptable in any but the most devout environments.

The shift in traditional roles is gradually causing the elimination of the marital double standard. It was once deemed an indisputable fact that a husband is much more interested in the physical side of marriage, while a wife tends to stress the emotional or communicational aspects. This is no longer true. Women freely admit their need for sex, and men fully realize that communication and emotion are as necessary to them as physical fulfillment. This reversal has heightened their mutual awareness, acceptance, and perception into sensual needs.

Many things have combined to bring about this change. We have already mentioned previous experience and the willingness to experiment. Safer contraception has increased relaxation, pleasure, and consequently, frequency. Prolonged and varied foreplay is recognized as a necessary prelude to gratifying intercourse.

In Kinsey's day, sexual liberalization was having an inverse effect upon frequency. Wives had progressed to the point of declining sex on demand, and a husband could no longer have intercourse whenever he felt like it. Although her own needs were gradually coming into focus, her vision of them was not yet strong enough for her to make the first approach. The result was that he was not getting it as often as he wanted it, and she was not getting it as often as she wanted it, and the frequency of marital intercourse declined.

In the last thirty years, wives have become immeasurably freer in bed. They have discovered that they have the right to act upon their desires. Frequency has increased. Sex has become a much more rewarding experience to both partners.

The adolescent boy has the strongest sexual drive, but even in this age of easy accessibility it is the newly married man in his twenties who most frequently and regularly experiences coitus, with an average of more than three times a week for those under twenty-five. Frequency decreases with time, but even in the over-fifty-five group, men still have sex with their wives on the average of one or more times a week.

There has been a marked increase in the amount of marital sex for men of all backgrounds, educational levels, and occupations. There has been a more marked increase of sex for the religious husband than for those of any other group. Religion remains an inhibiting factor, but the pious man and his wife are having from 20 to 30 per cent more intercourse than they did two decades ago.

PORNOGRAPHY

My wife picked up a book in the market and brought it home. It was so raunchy that I'd have sworn you could only buy it in a dirty book store. And there it was in the A&P. No matter what laws they try to pass, you can't avoid that stuff. It's all around you.

A sexual pervasiveness touches all of us. It is almost impossible to avoid contact with material that provides erotic stimulation. It is only the most cloistered person who does not see pictures and hear language that was considered taboo not too long ago. What were once considered "dirty books" are currently sold in open supermarket displays that children can browse through. Cock, cunt, fuck, shit: the entire array of proscribed words and messages have moved from the public lavatory wall to the pages of "important" literature, to say nothing of their regular use in films and plays that we mistakenly label "adult." In almost every American city there are stores, peepshows, and movie theaters specializing in hard-core pornographic material. Topless waitresses and revues featuring simulated sex acts are featured in countless raunchy bars across the country.

We tend to dismiss this pornographic pollution as having appeal only to callow and inexperienced youth, dirty old men, the deeply frustrated, or the perverted. Statistically, four out of ten married men see or hear erotic material anywhere from once a month to several times a week. Twice as many married men and four times as many married women encounter erotic stimuli in the 1970s as did in the 1950s.

A national survey conducted by the Commission on Obscenity and Pornography found that one third of the interviewees felt that all pornography should not be restricted, and that every adult should be allowed to read or view any and all erotic material. Over one half would agree to unlimited access if it was proven that pornography was not harmful. However, the majority still wished to have erotic material restricted in some form.

What does all of this mean in terms of us, especially those of us who are married? Does it mean that most of us feel that pornography is all right for us because we can handle it (i.e. only our curiosities are aroused), but that it ought to be kept out of the hands of the more impressionable, because it might stimulate them to sexual assault? Does it mean that we don't want it outlawed because we're saving it for the horny day when we might need it? Do we have lofty civil rights thoughts about it and believe that making pornography illegal is the first step toward complete censorship of the arts? Do we actually think that restricting the sexual gymnastics of porno film star Harry Reems will lead inevitably to burning the books of James Joyce?

Pornography was part of the art and religion of many great civilizations. There is nothing inherently wrong with it; it can be extremely beautiful. The only things that are questionable are the purposes of those who create it and our own motives for seeking access to it. We can leave the former to the consciences of those engaged in it. Certainly, pandering to the public has been known to lead to art as well as commerce. What was lascivious in one era was esthetic in another.

> Sometimes, I take my wife to pornos. We don't pet in the theater like we used to at regular movies. But we do get steamed and race right home to do it. We feel it helps to freshen up what was getting a little stale.

•

> I look at the dirty pictures and wonder if my wife would go for that stuff.

•

> We've been married for twenty years. Sometimes I feel the need to fantasize while we're having sex. Pornography provides the stuff for those fantasies. It's harmless enough. I don't cheat on my wife.

•

> I admit it. I go to pornos and sometimes jerk off. I never had much sex in my single days. And that stuff's dynamite. It hasn't hurt my relationship with my wife. If it did, I'd stop.

The reasons for resorting to erotic stimuli differ from person to person. For some, it is a release from frustration, a lubricious accompaniment to masturbation. It is often used as a substitute for involvement, a way of getting it off in an exciting way that precludes troublesome and possibly frightening contact with a partner. In another way, it's a great turn-on. Show her a dirty picture and get her hot.

To many, pornography is the substance of fantasy, for there are those who must fantasize during sex even in a relationship as deeply involving as marriage. Pornography is only dangerous when it becomes a necessary concomitant to all of one's sexual experiences, when it substitutes for reality on an intimate level.

CONTEMPORARY SEXUAL ATTITUDES

For most of us, married or single, the best and most meaningful sex is experienced when the participants are completely aware of and attuned to each other without outside stimuli or gimmicks. Today, within the one-to-one framework, there is enormous latitude for experimentation and innovation without either guilt or embarrassment. Respect for and knowledge of our bodies open the way to increased exhilaration. We're free to express ourselves and to act.

> I like what you're doing. I dig it. It really reaches me. What do you like? Do you like what I'm doing?

The freedom to explore and enjoy sex has affected the married man most in the degree and duration of foreplay.

> When we were first married, we'd kiss, sometimes fondle each other or pet, and then have sex. That was it for everybody in those days. The whole thing, foreplay and intercourse, took less than ten minutes. But I've kept up with things, read the books and articles, and tried to teach them to my wife. I remember the first time I went down on her. She was so shocked I thought she was going to have apoplexy. After a while, she not only admitted she liked it but would indicate that she wanted it. And when I got her to go down on me—that was like winning a landmark decision. Now our sex takes a lot longer than it used to. There's so much to do. We can keep at it for upward of a half hour.

At the time of the Kinsey Report, college men practiced foreplay for from five to ten minutes, while men on lower educational levels often did no more than give their wives a perfunctory kiss and begin intercourse immediately. Only half of the noncollege men fondled their wife's breasts with their lips and tongues (80 per cent of the college men did). The figures were very similar for wives who fondled or manipulated their husband's penis (50 per cent for noncollege and 80 per cent for college). Two thirds of all men on all educational levels avoided oral-genital sex. As for anal foreplay, it was almost never practiced.

In the 1940s and 1950s, younger married men indulged in foreplay more than older ones. This might well be explained by the fact that single college men and adolescents of the period found great sexual outlet and pleasure in petting, and foreplay was often an extension of that into marriage.

Youth and education have led the way. The liberal attitudes of the last twenty-five years have bridged the age-education gap. Today, *all* married men indulge in an average of fifteen minutes of foreplay before intercourse. Ninety per cent of them fondle their wife's breasts with their lips and tongues and have their penis manipulated by them.

It was in the instances of oral-genital foreplay that the most striking changes took place in the 1960s and 1970s. Two thirds of all married couples, regardless of background and education, now indulge in fellatio and cunnilingus.

Among young married couples, there is a definite trend toward universal participation in oral-genital sex, with 90 per cent of all married men under twenty-five indulging in it. This group spends 25 to 50 per cent of the foreplay period doing it. There is also a fantastic increase, among the under-thirty-fives, of manual-anal foreplay, with a lesser percentage having at least had one oral-anal experience.

The contemporary man has discovered that his wife enjoys tenderness, caressing, touching, all manner of tactile displays of affection while making love. Along with the new awareness of his wife's tactile needs has come the realization that his pleasure is also heightened by being touched and caressed.

Foreplay, in all of its manifestations, enriches the marital sex experience. The man discovers that coitus with his wife is more than a form of physical release or duty. He has received and given pleasure that seems to draw all of his bodily responses into his genitalia and, as his penis enters her vagina, he yearns for orgasm while simultaneously wanting to prolong the heightened period of passion. The needs of his body and the sensuality suffusing him create a tension that heightens intercourse, building to a breathtaking climax.

When I feel her quivering under me, her muscles tensing—when I hear her begin to moan and I know that she's coming, that I'm bringing her to climax —it's a tremendous feeling. Then I can release my orgasm—let it pour into her. And I feel great. Terrific.

The active participation of the wife has given a much greater eroticism to coitus. It is no longer merely the mechanical means to the sought-after end of orgasm but, in itself, a source of mutual excitement possessed of a tension that makes the orgasm all the more thrilling. When a couple climax together, it is a coming together in every sense, an action charged with a deep emotional meaning.

To the delight of their wives, married men have extended the length of time of coitus just as their single brothers have. That ten-to-twelve-minute differential has enabled today's married woman to achieve orgasm regularly.

The generations reaching puberty in the 1950s and 1960s were the first to perceive the mutual joys and responsibilities of coitus. The pivotal factor was the liberal environment in which a young man came of age and began to have sexual encounters during that period. He was freer to analyze the mechanics of sex without guilt and to condition his body to respond to his needs. He had a great drive and sexual urgency for orgasm, but by the time he married he was able to control himself by a conscious desire to prolong the sex act.

Physiologically, older men require longer periods of stimulation to achieve orgasm, yet young husbands spend an average of three minutes longer between entry and ejaculation. The older man has conditioned his body differently. His generation thought that they owed it to their wives not to prolong the act. As a result, he usually trained his body to be satisfied with entering quickly, ejaculating as soon as possible, then turning over and going to sleep.

What we've just said might imply that the body can be trained to be entirely at our sexual command. This is not entirely true. Most of us cannot always summon up an erection on demand, although sensitive and exciting foreplay can usually stimulate one, if there is nothing physically wrong.

We must not worry about occasional erectile failures. The more distressed we become over them, the more likely it is that the problem will be repeated. (See Impotence, pp. 206–14.) That mass of nerve endings, centered in the genitalia, are sending and receiving all sorts of messages to and from the brain. A distressed mind can be almost as great a sexual inhibitor as a physical defect. The husband should discuss his sexual problems with his wife. Talking generally releases some of the tension. Her support can be extremely valuable to him. Relaxation and openness enhance all of our sensations.

Failure to have an orgasm every single time is something that has troubled men down through the ages. Some have equated it with a lack of manhood. Others have been humiliated by the failure without realizing that most women are far more concerned with their own orgasms than ours, which is as it should be. Ultimately, we are all responsible for our own orgasms. Nobody unfailingly ejaculates with every intercourse, and that includes the most happily married man with the most understanding wife. Not age or background or desire can guarantee potency 100 per cent of the time.

When we first got married, we only had intercourse in the conventional position with me on top. Lately, we've been experimenting with all kinds of different positions. My wife loves to get on top and do the pumping. I think it's a gas, too.

•

Trying new positions is what keeps our sex life fresh. You've got to keep experimenting, or it gets to be a routine, especially after you've been married for a couple of years. We're always discovering something new about personal preferences—like sometimes I like to be passive, other times I want to do it standing up or even dog fashion.

Because men realize that their wives have desires equal to their own for sexual adventure and innovation, they are much more relaxed about experimenting with various coital positions than their fathers were. A man should feel no reluctance about asking his wife to get on top, to try it on the side, or rear vaginal entry ("doggie style"), or sitting, or even standing, so long as he thinks it will increase her enjoyment as well as his own.

Although the male-on-top position remains the one most commonly used, the others have become pleasurable variations, especially for the younger married couples. Negative feelings about them have been eliminated in the sexually enlightened atmosphere of most modern marriages. No longer does the stigma of abnormal submissiveness attach itself to the male who indulges in woman-on-top intercourse. No longer does a woman feel degraded by rear-entry coitus. All of these potentially joyous sexual variations should be a part of a contemporary marriage.

Clinically, anal entry cannot be classified as a form of intercourse, but the anus is an erogenous part of the body and, for some people, an extremely arousing one, even when they are totally heterosexual. Although it remains one of the strong sexual taboos, almost one quarter of married men under thirty-five have indulged in it with varying degrees of frequency from once to often.

THE IMPORTANCE OF COMMUNICATION

Not only am I comfortable having sex with my wife, but I like it. I don't think it could be any better with another woman. As a matter of fact, I bet it would be a lot worse.

•

We've been married for almost twenty-five years. It's amazing how sensitive she remains to my needs. No, I wouldn't want to swap my sex life for that of any of those swinging singles.

•

I don't know what it is, but lately we can't seem to stop fighting. It carries over. You know what I mean? We get into bed, and most of the time she won't let me touch her. Then I get so mad that we have another fight. Sometimes it's the reverse. She wants me and, out of spite, I won't have sex with her.

Most husbands have extremely positive feelings about their sex lives, with over 90 per cent of all husbands finding gratification in intercourse with their wives. Well over half are totally satisfied with their sex lives, with a majority of the rest expressing a desire for more intercourse. The most dissatisfied are those over forty-five who are of a generation that might have been too late to have discovered the fulfilling freedoms of modern marital sex.

Less than 1 per cent of husbands desire less frequent sex with their wives. This minority is probably in marriages that are not working well on any level.

The desire for more intercourse with one's wife may not only reflect a sexual need. It is quite possible that it is also indicative of a marriage that is not as close as the partners might like it to be. This could be the result of the pressures of work, economics, the omnipresence of children, etc. It should not be something that is suffered in silence. During one of their peaceful times, the husband should sit down with his wife and talk about their problems. It should be a conversation with love not recrimination, an effort to improve or save something very meaningful to both of them.

Although some behavioral scientists have questioned the correlation between sexual satisfaction and closeness in marriage, most of us would agree that it exists to a very strong degree. The two interrelate. Intimate physical contact influences or is influenced by understanding companionship. When either member of a marriage is frustrated or habitually seeks extramarital sex, the guilt and strain can cause a rift that is capable of destroying the fabric of the marriage.

17

EXTRAMARITAL SEX

You show me a traveling man, and I'll show you a cheater. It's not that we're unhappy with our wives, it's being alone in a strange town. After putting up with those dumb-ass customers all day, a man needs a little companionship, a little relaxing fun. Let's face it, it's not hard to find these days. The women come on pretty strong. They like their nookie too. Who am I to say no?

.

Sometimes I can't stand myself. I really love my wife. But, Jesus, I'm only thirty, and here I am with a wife, a baby, a mortgage. I look around at my pals, guys my own age, out there having a ball, swinging with these cool, come-on chicks. Sometimes, not often, I just got to go along with them.

.

I figure I'm not taking anything away from my wife that she really wants. I know she doesn't enjoy sex. I do. So who am I hurting if I take a mistress except—heh-heh—the mistress?

If a man is unhappy with his marital sex life, he is likely to look around for an extramarital fling, but it is not the most significant reason for infidelity. More relevant are such things as: absence from home, abstinence because of pregnancy or illness, a desire for adventure, frustration in one's professional life, fear of loss of manhood, dissatisfaction with a humdrum or routine pattern of existence, emasculating guilt over being a poor provider, fear of getting older, and simple availability.

The contemporary woman is not reticent about making her desires known, and it is most difficult to resist an attractive woman who seems to be making a play for you. There are also many career women who are not interested in marriage, nor are they particularly interested in a long-term relationship with a married man, so it is relatively safe to have sex with them. There is a vast difference in emotional input between an occasional one- or two-night stand and an affair.

The instances of extramarital experiences seem to be among the few things in male-female relationships that have not been altered by the sexual revolution. Ever since Kinsey, the figure has remained stationary: approximately 50 per cent of all married men have had or are having them. Age and sociological factors play a significant part in patterns of extramarital adventures. This tends to support the assertion that unhappiness with marital sex is not the only reason for straying.

Among those who do have extramarital encounters, younger men (under thirty-five) have their first within one to three years of the wedding, while husbands of an older generation usually wait from six to seven years (that celebrated "seven-year itch"). It is easy to surmise some of the motivations of the younger men. They find themselves shackled with new responsibilities, while their single friends are still getting plenty of action. They long to be a part of that superficially carefree scene and eventually capitulate. The pleasures are often illusory and seldom compensate for the feelings of guilt. But they keep trying.

I'm still young and, if I say it myself, attractive. I have as many opportunities as any of the other men that I know. But I don't give in. That doesn't mean that I don't find lots of girls very sexy. But I love my wife and honor my marriage. If marriage isn't a sacrament, something holy in the eyes of God and not to be trifled with—then what is it?

•

When we got married I wouldn't have dreamt of infidelity. Marriage was a sharing, something we were building together. Ten years later, I discovered that we'd been building an illusion. At about the same time, or a little after, I also discovered another woman. She's made my life bearable. I don't suppose we'll ever be able to marry. With kids in private schools, a house in the country, two cars, a wife who's gone back to get her college degree, I can't afford a divorce. Besides, I'm not even sure I want one. None of this is my wife's fault alone. She's trying to change. I still love her. It's the life we've made together that I hate. If we could find a way of changing that—but how? It's too late. We're caught in a trap.

•

It didn't take me long to start playing around. There we were—stuck in three crumby rooms with a baby yet. After working hard all day, who the hell wanted to go home to that? Shit, man, I was still young. Now it's different. We own a nice house. The kids are just about grown up. My wife's really on the ball. Keeping herself young-looking, making a real swell home. We entertain other couples, go over to their places, play cards. It's a life.

Because of moral scruples, rather than lack of desire or opportunity, religious men as a group show less interest in extramarital sex than those who are not so devout.

College graduates are likely to remain true to their wife in the early years of their marriage and wait until later on for their infidelities. On a lower educational level the reverse is true, with adultery commoner at the beginning of marriage and tending to diminish with the passing years. Let's look a little more closely at these education-infidelity ratios.

The lower-education men are far more likely to experience socioeconomic frustrations during those early years. They usually have occupations or jobs rather than careers or professions. Even those who start in relatively good economic positions at the time of marriage, have little chance of progressing much farther along the way. They are in a kind of rut, and their homes are a part of it. They often think of their wives as responsibilities rather than partners. It seems to be a kind of end of the road, a finish to youthful dreams, and the futility can bring on a sense of psychological emasculation. Counseling or therapy would be very helpful, but few think of themselves as candidates for it. Instead, they displace their discontent into infidelity. It's a way of adding adventure and variety to their lives.

Later, they realize that the sexual conquests have changed nothing and may, indeed, have added the extra onus of guilt. The encounters wane. For many, their own frustrations and failures are put aside as they live more and more in hope of better lives for their children. Fidelity is re-established as the home becomes the focal point of existence.

The college graduate enters marriage at a point when the future seems limitless. He usually has great ambitions, hopes, plans for his career and future. It is only later in life that fear of age, professional frustration, or conversely, the omnipotence seemingly bestowed by success, turn him toward acts of infidelity. He is likely to be the man who thinks that his wife does not understand him, or that she has not kept up with him as he's made his way in the world.

THE DOUBLE STANDARD

What I do is my business. I make certain she never finds out. It doesn't hurt if I play around a little. But if I discovered that she'd been to bed with another man, I'd throw her out so fast her head would spin.

Although the double standard on extramarital sex is not as pronounced as it used to be, the majority of married men still feel that infidelity is a man's game. Naturally, many wives do not agree. They subscribe to a theory that what's sauce for the gander is definitely sauce for the goose, and they're beginning to act upon it in larger and larger numbers.

As we've already observed, the percentage of males committing adultery has remained more or less stationary. But there has been a marked increase of instances among wives. Kinsey reported that only one third as many wives were unfaithful as husbands. The most recent figures indicate that 75 per cent as many wives as husbands commit adultery.

SWINGING, VOYEURISM, AND GROUP SEX

Our marriage was going nowhere until we got into "swinging." I mean, I couldn't even get it off with my wife most of the time. Then we got into this thing, and it's changed our lives. We communicate better on every level. It's as if a great burden was lifted.

•

It's not difficult to meet other "swingers." There are certain bars, advertisements in underground papers and even the *Village Voice*. We've never done the group bit. We go off to separate rooms. I don't think I'd like to see my wife doing it with another man. Sometimes we see the same couples a few times. There's one we sort of have a regular date with—like, every six months. But if we become real friends with any of them, we stop doing it together. It becomes too complicated.

A great deal has been written portraying wife-swapping and "swinging" as a cool or in thing to do. From the amount of space they get in magazines and newspapers, it seems as if they are almost becoming commonplace in modern marriage.

The publicity is misleading. Only about 2 per cent of all the married men in this country have tried them and the majority of these are under thirty-five. However, it must be added, that most of this small minority have only done it once.

We don't do it often, but occasionally my wife and I enjoy going to an orgy. They're fun. There's usually some pot. Everybody's doing it with everybody else, never knowing who's doing what to whom. Nobody gets hurt. Nobody gets involved. And a good time is had by all. Where's the harm in it?

•

We tried group sex once. I thought it was groovy, but my wife thought it was disgusting, so that was the end of that. Now I'm trying to get her into swinging. So far, no luck.

Group sex is actually far more popular than wife-swapping. As in swinging, the greatest number are in the under-thirty-five group, and most have only tried it once.

The least popular of all communal extramarital activities is voyeurism, in which a man watches his wife have sex with another man or she watches him have it with another woman. The overwhelming majority of people feel that sex is not a spectator sport.

There is nothing really wrong with indulging in swinging, voyeurism, or group sex, but *only* if the couple involved can maintain the depth of commitment and emotional response necessary to a good marriage. It is doubtful that they can. These activities are usually symptomatic of deep problems in the marital relationship.

The male is having many of his former prerogatives taken away from him, especially in the marital partnership. Often he is volunteering to give up some of his former rights. He is allowing himself to play a passive role in situations in which he was formerly the activist. He is being supportive of most of his wife's demands for greater freedom of action. But this support seldom extends to complicity in her extramarital activities without some accompanying destruction of his former feelings for her.

The virtues of extramarital relations, group sex, and swinging form the repertoire of the sexual chic group. We've seen it performed in films and on television, heard it on radio, read reviews of it in countless magazines. Yet, it has changed little for the majority of us. In our society, man is basically a monogamous animal dedicated to the long-term commitment of marriage.

The penis is an appendage of the male body connected by an intricate nervous system to the loftiest parts of the intellect and emotions, to those things that separate men from the beasts in the fields. Down through the ages, the needs that brought about the custom of marriage still have validity for us. And adultery remains a pursuit possessed of more negative than positive qualities.

Infidelity is kept secret not primarily out of fear of the consequences—though, of course, that does play some part. More important is the fact that the man committing this act feels that it is wrong. Four surveys, conducted between 1958 and 1968, found that the majority of both men and women believed that extramarital activities were wrong even under extenuating circumstances. Those who had tried it had disapproved of themselves. A minority did claim that it provided a growth experience and enlarged their sexual enjoyment. A few even said that it helped their marriages.

Leaving aside the question of guilt and pain, the surveys found that the amount of sexual pleasure in adultery was generally considerably less than the respondents experienced in their marriages. Women simply did not enjoy it as much as they did with their husbands, and consequently achieved orgasm far fewer times. For both sexes, the number of foreplay variations and coital positions was much more limited than with their spouses.

On the point of the value of fidelity, the institution of marriage would seem to be adhering to traditional attitudes. Marital sex has become more open, pleasure-oriented, and experimental, but it is still strongly attached to the conventional romantic-emotional commitments.

18

THE DIVORCED MALE

I should've known something was wrong with the marriage when I began to cheat six weeks after the wedding. Sure, I eventually got caught. And sure, we got a divorce. But I think we'd have separated even if I'd been true-blue. It might've taken longer, but we'd have ended up in the same place. I think what was wrong was *why* I cheated, and not what was wrong was *that* I cheated—if you get my point.

Compared to men who remain married, divorced men have had a somewhat higher rate of extramarital coitus and waited a shorter time before beginning—usually a year or less after the wedding. Divorced men and their former wives both feel that the adulteries played a part in the breakup of their marriages, but neither feel that it was the basic motivation. Indeed, it would seem that in most cases, the problems of incompatibility that broke up the marriages were the reasons for the infidelities and not the reverse.

SEX AND THE DIVORCED MAN

I don't remember it being this way when I was single. But now that I'm divorced, it's like a big ever-lovin' candy store out there, and I just have to walk up and pick out the sweet thing I want.

•

My divorce has made me a much sexier guy. I don't know what it is, but if I'm not in the kip with a dame two or three times a week, I chalk that week up as a dead loss.

•

My ex taught me one thing. Love 'em and leave 'em. Don't get involved. There's plenty more where the last one came from. One goddam ride to the alimony cleaners is enough for me. From now on, love is a prenuptial agreement.

The divorced (or separated) man has been hurt and made insecure by the failure of his marriage even when he instigated the breakup. He feels a need to reaffirm his masculinity through sexual activity. When this drive comes in contact with the high degree of availability in contemporary society, the results can be formidable.

The men in this group have intercourse with a median frequency of twice a week, which is slightly higher than the married man. In addition to that, they have many more sexual partners than the single man who has never been married before and often seeks some degree of emotional involvement. For the divorced man, macho is the name of the game, and it's won by the number of different scores you make. Their sexual partners often remain forgettable and anonymous vaginas, which is ultimately sadder for the man than it is for the woman.

The things I'm capable of in bed surprise even me. If I'd ever pulled some of my new tricks on my ex, she'd never have let me go.

•

Man, since my divorce I've become fucking good at good fucking.

Probably because of the lingering need to prove themselves as sexually potent individuals, divorced men use more sexual techniques and variations than any other group. They have the highest percentage of oral-genital sex, heterosexual anal sex, and numbers of coital positions. You name it, and they'll probably be much more likely to try it than even the most sex-obsessed adolescent.

For a long time I couldn't even bring myself to ask a woman out on a date, let alone think of going to bed with her. I wanted to crawl into the wall and nurse my bruises. Eventually, I began to meet some very nice and understanding women. Thanks to them, I'm having sex regularly and enjoying it very much.

Nine out of ten divorced men find their new sex lives highly enjoyable. Some have been so hurt that they may abstain for a while after the breakup, but within a year, almost all of them are once again actively engaged in the pleasurable pursuit of sexual intercourse.

When I left my wife, she got the membership in our old country club, and I had to join a new one. I don't know if it's me or the ambience of the place, but in the dining room, on the golf course, on the tennis courts, there always seem to be available and attractive women around. I get invited to dinner parties about two or three times a week, and there are more women. Now, I don't fool myself into thinking I'm a Robert Redford, but I'm doing fantastically. And I don't even have to shop around.

There was a time when a divorced man was looked upon as something of a libertine. He had difficulty finding sexual partners within his own circle. He often kept whatever sex life he had a secret from his friends and family.

The sexual revolution has changed that for him. The divorced man has been more influenced and changed by it than any other group. He is usually having such a good time that it takes an extended period before he is again ready for commitment and monogamy, although the majority do reach that point eventually, whether or not they have the courage to do something about it. Generally, they are great bed partners but initially poor risks for anything more permanent than a casual, for-laughs-only affair.

WIDOWERS

I suppose I'll want to marry again eventually. I can't think of that now. It's as if I just lost my wife. I look around, but I can't find anyone to compare with her. She was the best, the sweetest, the dearest woman in the world. I know that was young love. I'll never have it again. I shouldn't make comparisons. I know all that. My children tell me. But how can I help it? How can I settle for less?

There are a minority of widowers for whom the loss of a wife is the same sort of conscious ending of a bad relationship as a divorce. They may be more motivated by guilt than by feelings of inadequacy, but they will probably react to their new aloneness in a manner not too dissimilar from the divorced man.

The majority of widowers will react in a manner diametrically opposed to the divorced man, at least at the beginning. The widower is generally an older man who has to work through guilt and anger at being deserted, before he is again ready to contemplate sex as an important part of his life. Any new woman usually has to fight a formidable rival in the memory of his dead wife, which often grows more irreplaceable with each passing day. Some widowers shy away from any relationships, fearful of a repetition of the pain they experienced over the loss of their wives.

Most of them will always have the feeling that they lost somethng very precious. When they begin to have sex again, they are usually not very inventive but seek to reawaken the same pleasures they knew with their wives. As they come out of their grief, they tend to want long-term relationships rather than variety, especially if they were happy in their marriages.

It may take them a long time to choose, but there is an old adage about them: the once happily married man will eventually want to marry again. Their women friends may not find them the most exciting or experimental bedmates, but they are excellent potentials for extended relationships or marriage.

19

THE HOMOSEXUAL MALE

The conservative position (on homosexuality) has its roots in the stable stuff of religious beliefs, social traditions and the quieting reassurances of a uniform standard of behavior. The liberal position, on the other hand, is always short on these particular reinforcements. Whether its adherents come across as rebellious iconoclasts or as gentle peacemakers in search of a larger commonality, it has little backing from any of the classical traditions. But what it does have to an almost embarrassing degree is the ever increasing validation from the natural sciences. In the liberal column lands most of the fallout from biology, zoology, sociology and a dozen other disciplines. Most (though not quite all) of what is learned about man from a careful study of his nature and origins tends to underline his diversity, usually at the expense of his social traditions.

Dr. C. A. Tripp
The Homosexual Matrix

During the last thirty years, an increasingly enlightened recognition of facts about the male animal and his sexual capacities has brought an evolution in attitude toward "the problem" of homosexuality.

In the late 1940s, Dr. Kinsey's findings led him to believe that homosexuality was not a disease. This was considered an extremely radical point of view at the time, for the majority of the behavioral and psychiatric communities then believed it to be a serious one.

In the 1960s, the Wolfenden Report was put before the English Parliament. This historic document dealt with homosexual offenses and prostitution in England. It found no evidence of the presence of pathologic conditions accompanying homosexuality and led to a liberalization of the laws governing what was permissible behavior between two consenting adults in the privacy of their own home.

In 1973, the American Psychiatric Association made a landmark decision eliminating homosexuality as an illness and classifying it as a disorder only if it caused distress.

Oscar Wilde described homosexuality as the love that dared not speak its name. These days, it is not only named but openly discussed, analyzed, and dissected in prime-time television shows. The gay activist movement has made it a political issue by declaring that homosexuals suffer the same forms of economic and political oppression as other minority groups. Children not only know and speak the name but also all of the sobriquets for it: "gay," "queer," "fag," "queen," and so forth.

The notoriety has not produced a single definition that embraces all of its dimensions, degrees, and ramifications, one that would be universally applicable to all cases as well as acceptable to all those who claim to be knowledgeable or experienced on the subject.

The two most common criteria used to define homosexuality are indulging in sexual acts with another person of the same gender and feeling desire for or being attracted to another person of the same sex. Within these confines, there are refinements:

1. Self-definition. "He is a homosexual because he considers himself one."
2. Social definition. "He is a homosexual because others think he is one."
3. Subculture participation. "He is a homosexual because he associates with homosexuals."
4. Enforced behaviorism (e.g. army and prison incidents). "He is a homosexual when there are no women available."

THE KINSEY HETEROSEXUAL—HOMOSEXUAL RATING SCALE

In 1948, Dr. Kinsey created a scale which took into account the continuum of sexual behavior and psychic responses. Based on psychological reactions and overt experiences, individuals rate as follows:

0. Exclusive heterosexual behavior with no homosexual reactions or experiences
1. Predominantly heterosexual, only incidentally homosexual
2. Predominantly heterosexual but more than incidentally homosexual
3. Equally heterosexual and homosexual

KINSEY HETEROSEXUAL-HOMOSEXUAL RATING SCALE

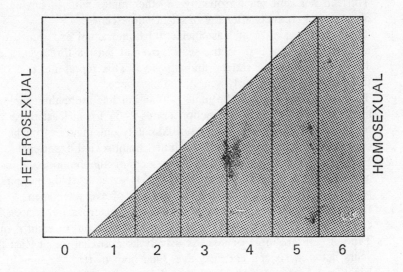

4. Predominantly homosexual but more than incidentally heterosexual
5. Predominantly homosexual, only incidentally heterosexual
6. Exclusive homosexual behavior with no heterosexual reactions or experiences

Kinsey's figures for all of these categories remain the most thorough available for publication. Some researchers feel that his percentages are too high in relation to homosexual frequencies and incidences, and that they should be lowered by about 5 per cent. On the other hand, there are those who might argue that, given the sexual permissiveness of our times, Kinsey's figures may be too modest. One might make adjustments in either direction, and the figures still remain staggering.

Dr. Kinsey interviewed over 4,000 white American males on their sexual behavior. One presumes that his findings would not be too different in a sampling from any other racial group. He found that:

a. Thirty-seven per cent of the total male population has had at least some overt homosexual experience to the point of orgasm between adolescence and old age. This accounts for almost two out of every five males

b. Fifty per cent of the males who remain single until age thirty-five have had overt homosexual experience to the point of orgasm since the onset of adolescence.

c. Sixty-three per cent of all men never have overt homosexual experience to the point of orgasm after the onset of adolescence.

d. Fifty per cent of all males have neither overt nor psychic homosexual experience after the onset of adolescence.

e. Thirteen per cent react erotically to other males without having overt homosexual contacts after the onset of adolescence.

f. Thirty per cent have at least incidental homosexual experience or reactions (i.e. rates 1–6 on the scale) over at least a three-year period between the ages of sixteen and fifty-five. This represents one out of three males past the early years of adolescence.

g. Twenty-five per cent of the male population has more than incidental homosexual experience or reaction (rates 2–6) for at least three years between sixteen and fifty-five. Approximately one male in four has had or will have such distinct and continued homosexual experience.

h. Eighteen per cent have at least as much of the homosexual as the heterosexual in their histories (rates 3–6) for at least three years between sixteen and fifty-five. This is one out of every ten men.

i. Thirteen per cent are more homosexual than heterosexual (rates 4–6) for three years between sixteen and fifty-five. One out of eight men.

j. Ten per cent are more or less exclusively homosexual for at least three years between sixteen and fifty-five. One man in ten.

k. Eight per cent are exclusively homosexual for three years between sixteen and fifty-five. One man out of every thirteen.

l. Four per cent are exclusively homosexual throughout their lives after the onset of adolescence.

Listen, baby, there are more closet queens around than you've got hairs on your head. The more the wild ones take to the streets, the more frightened the others are of coming out.

Depending upon their ages, 27 to 50 per cent of all single men have had some homosexual experience, with the figure increasing as they get older.

The percentages are in reverse order of age for homosexual experience among husbands during their marriages. The 21–25 age group report 10 per cent, with the encounters dropping off to 2 per cent for those over forty-five. The latter statistic is probably too low. In Kinsey's time, older men were more reticent about being interviewed on this subject than they would be today.

The factors that relate to the amount of homosexual activity (in a group) include religious feeling and education. As in all sexual activity, the devout of every religion have a low incidence of it.

The highest level of homosexual activity is among those with high-school-level educations. For example, 47 per cent of college men and 58 per cent of high school men have had homosexual experience to the point of orgasm, if they have remained single until the age of thirty-five. Those with grade-school educations have higher frequency than the college men, but lower than the high-school graduates.

THE HOMOSEXUAL PROFESSIONS

I don't have to take my wife to those big boring charity balls any more. I just buy the tickets and send her with her hairdresser or dress designer. They enjoy taking her out without ever wanting to go home with her. The fashionable faggot fills a definite need in most of the marriages in my set.

•

Being in the theater is none of the things you dream it's going to be when you're a kid. I mean, it's not glamor and parties, and witty people, and bright lights, and razzle-dazzle. It's goddam hard work, when there is work, and insecurity the rest of the time. But it does offer one thing to homosexuals. Acceptance. That means equal job opportunities *most* of the time. Not all. We have our butch types and closet queens who fear guilt by association and won't hire gay people. But generally speaking, it's good. And you can be yourself. You don't have to hide from anybody. Unless, of course, you're a star. The public's not ready for a gay Warren Beatty or Jack Nicholson. But there'll come a time when all the closet doors will open, and you never know who might come walking out.

There are certain professions in which homosexuals have played notable parts such as theater, films, television, music, ballet, fine arts, dress design and interior decoration. Some claim that homosexuals are in these more or less creative fields because they are more sensitive and talented than heterosexual men. An equally strong, if not stronger, argument is made for the theory that they are in these fields because the other people in them are more permissive, bohemian, or liberal in their attitudes toward the right to sexual choice. The truth is probably somewhere between the two points of view.

Homosexuals are not more talented or sensitive as a group, just as blacks are not better natural athletes or dancers, or Jews not better businessmen. It's more a question of selectivity, of developing those skills or aptitudes that will earn them places in fields in which they will be accepted.

The WASP heterosexual, equally skilled or talented, has many more options. He can make his choice based upon economics, aptitude, personal interest, or sheer lassitude.

HOMOSEXUALS AND THE "STRAIGHT" WORLD

In the Bronfman kidnaping case, one of the most convincing pieces of evidence was when that fireman admitted he was gay. For a fireman to do that, you felt he had to be telling the truth. Another thing, I don't know about the jury. In their eyes, was the kid more guilty of conspiracy or homosexuality? In the straight world, that's a question without an answer.

Many little boys want to be firemen, policemen, or soldiers when they grow up. This includes boys who will be homosexuals, despite the largely untrue stereotype that they prefer to play with dolls. If a heterosexual still has that ambition when he reaches his late teens or early twenties, he can fulfill it. A homosexual cannot do that unless he is willing to lie about his private life and sexual needs.

In the last few years, there has been a significant change in the attitude of the homosexual toward himself. This has largely been the result of both sexual liberalism and the coming into existence of groups like the National Gay Task Force, which concentrates on civil liberties and the political and legal problems confronting homosexuals.

It is not too surprising that artists, writers, and performers openly admit their homo- and bisexual lifestyles: it is more or less expected of them. But the admissions suddenly are also coming from other areas, from the bastions of stereotyped macho—from the "jocks." It is easy to handle the confessions of an esthetic sissy or nance, but the establishment panics when the same confessions come from its heroes.

A man saves the President of the United States from being assassinated. It is discovered that he is an admitted homosexual, and the man whose life he saved lacks the courage and courtesy to call him and thank him for it. Which of them is the bigger "sissy"?

A much-decorated military hero tells the world that he is homosexual, but that it has never nor will it ever influence his behavior as a professional soldier. The system is threatened, and the military authorities feel that they must discharge him despite a flawless record of outstanding service to his country.

The star National Football League running end, Dave Kopay, not only emerges from the closet but also writes a best-selling autobiography about it. In the book he contends that physical-contact sports are a form of sexual release, and that there is much more homosexuality in professional athletics than anybody suspects. The boys in the grandstand are as shaken as the boys in the locker room.

There are so many unisex hairdressing establishments and clothing stores that one wonders to what extent we are becoming an androgynous society. Many of the most butch-looking male models and actors, who establish our heterosexual male image, are flagrant queens. On the other hand, many limp-wristed ninety-eight-pound weaklings are great heterosexual Don Juans.

I'm beginning to feel good about myself. I even think I'm going to tell my parents that I'm gay, introduce them to my friend as my lover. Then along comes Anita Bryant and blows the whole thing. How can I tell them now? My parents live in Miami. Jesus, do you think they voted for that orange fruitcake and against me? Maybe I should have told them years ago, and then we might've won. I mean—if all the gay guys leveled with their parents. But you don't want to hurt them. By not hurting them, you may be hurting yourself. How do you know? I mean—if they love us. Love? My sister married out of our faith. My old man hasn't spoken to her since. And he loved her too.

Anita Bryant spearheaded a campaign that successfully rallied Miami voters to overthrow a ruling that would have given homosexuals equal rights in housing and employment. One of her prime arguments was that it was dangerous to have homosexuals teaching school, because homosexuals cannot have children and must recruit new members of their group from among young boys. The speciousness of the reasoning is mind-boggling, and yet she won.

HOMOSEXUALITY AND CHILDREN

What do you do about your homosexual friends and your sons? It's all right when they're still kids. That's Uncle Bruce, and no questions asked. But what about when they're adolescents? We all look at our fifteen- and sixteen-year-olds and wonder about their equipment, and if they're using it. We admire, maybe even envy, their youthful good looks. We're always looking at them appraisingly. But if a homosexual does the same thing, no matter how close we are, we're uneasy. We instinctively move to protect the kid. And what about protecting our friends from our sons? At that age they're cruel. They can say all kinds of hurting things. Their own male identity is not that strong. They strike out. And a homosexual's an awful big target.

A child in our culture would have to be deaf, dumb, and blind not to be aware of homosexuality. In the final analysis, we are our children's most significant male image. If we demonstrate the masculine virtues with love and understanding, they are not likely to be endangered by outside influences, and hopefully, that includes Ms. Bryant. The real threat is not the homosexual in the school system, or on the police force, or in the fire department, or on the football team; it is the home in which the father is too unassertive, too inhibited, or too rigid in the masculine stereotype that causes the child's confusion.

We begin to speculate about how the sons of Women's Lib mothers will turn out. We certainly wonder about the children of that new breed of television celebrity, the lesbian mother and homosexual father. It may well be that these will make the straightest and best generation of the lot, for their parents will have been freed of enslavement to roles that they found frustrating and from sexually unfulfilling marriages. Then again, they may be the most forlorn, inheriting, in their own adolescence, the residue of the frustrations that their parents relinquished in their move for independence. It is a very dangerous thing to be the child of a minority group, revolutionizing traditional emotional patterns, while still associating with contemporaries sired by the more conservative majority.

The fathers of the late twentieth century must take extreme care of the male models they present to their sons, or the twenty-first century may see a generation of males very different from the ones heretofore known. Some will loudly proclaim that any change is for the better. In view of the accomplishments of civilization to date, in which positive achievements far outweigh negative values, one must challenge their point of view.

Mankind (or personkind) has come a very long way from caves, where it was natural for the male to play the part for which he was naturally endowed by dint of physique, intuitive intelligence, and genetic structure. That proven strength should enable us to make room in our society (for it is *our* creation) for sexual diversity and new roles for those of both sexes discontented with the traditional ones.

THE HOMOSEXUAL SEX LIFE

Images of wild depravity often come to the minds of heterosexuals when they think of homosexual acts. Actually, homosexuals are probably a good deal less sexually adventurous than their "straight" counterparts. The most common form of reaching orgasm is through mutual masturbation.

In the last quarter of a century, oral-genital sex has become much more prevalent in heterosexual behavior; it follows that this is also true among homosexuals. It is estimated that over 60 per cent of all homosexual behavior now includes fellatio, but not always to the point of orgasm.

Like heterosexuals, homosexuals practice anal intercourse far less frequently than other ways of achieving orgasm. There are some who practice it almost exclusively, and others who never do it. Obviously, they have the choice of either active or passive roles. Some are always one or the other, and others interchange.

Being active in anal intercourse does not equate with being physically more masculine, nor does being passive equate with feminine traits. There is no telling by the appearance or social behavior of a homosexual which part he may be playing. Sometimes, the most overtly masculine homosexual is exclusively passive in bed, and the reverse is true of the seemingly most effeminate one.

My lover and I have been together for fifteen years. I'm not saying that we were completely faithful each day of every one of those years. But I'll stack our record of fidelity against that of any straight man who's been married the same length of time.

.

The worst part about it is the cruising, the one-night stands, the bar scene. The lack of commitment. I long to meet a fellow I can depend on and have a real relationship. But where do you find him? You meet the same Mr. Good-bars on the gay circuit as you do in the straight singles joints.

Homosexual relationships do not differ markedly from heterosexual ones. They form long-term unions or "marriages" in which many of the same principles of interrelatedness form a necessary part. The unattached homosexual might once have seemed a bit more promiscuous, spending a lot of time "cruising" or prowling around in search of sex, but that has changed in recent years. The need has been diminished by the openness with which men can live together and form long-term relationships. Ironically, while this has been happening to the homosexual, the availability of compliant females has brought into existence hundreds of singles bars and notably increased heterosexual cruising.

ATTITUDES TOWARD HOMOSEXUALITY

Despite the similarities, the professed heterosexual still feels threatened by homosexuality. This is more true of the male than of the female, possibly because so many of the former have experienced homosexual activity at least once and are frightened of another exposure of that part of their natures.

In 1965, a Harris poll found that 82 per cent of the male and 58 per cent of the female respondents thought that homosexuals were the third most harmful group to the nation behind communists and atheists. If that 82 per cent represented a cross-section, a comparison with Kinsey's findings indicates the distinct possibility of the fear of exposure as a motivation for the opinion in many instances.

In a CBS poll taken at about the same time, 71 per cent considered homosexuality an illness; 10 per cent thought it was a crime; 9 per cent called it a sin; only 8 per cent said that it was a sexual preference.

In 1970, a pair of behaviorists, Klassen and Levitt, made a survey of over 3,000 adults and found that:

> Two thirds of our respondents regard homosexuality as "very obscene and vulgar"; about two thirds state that they never liked homosexuals; and over 80 per cent express a reluctance to associate with them. . . . Substantial majorities of the respondents agree that homosexual men should be allowed to work as artists, beauticians, florists, and musicians, but almost equally substantial majorities do not believe that they should be permitted to engage in occupations of influence and authority. Three quarters would deny to a homosexual the right to be a minister, a school teacher, or a judge, and two thirds would bar the homosexual from medical practice and government service.

It sounds painfully like pre-twentieth-century European attitudes toward Jews and unreconstructed American attitudes toward blacks. Unfortunately, the laws in this country do much to reinforce this unsubstantiated and inane prejudice. In the majority of states, homosexuality is still a crime.*

With the Wolfenden Report as a model, changes are slowly being made in these archaic laws. In 1962, Illinois became the first state to legalize consentual homosexuality between adults in the privacy of their own homes. Similar changes have been made, during the early 1970s, in the laws of another sixteen states. A number of the larger cities have also acted to change the legal status of homosexuality.

The homosexual is beginning to feel much better about himself. Society has generally become more permissive. Yet, there is still a stronger negative feeling about homosexuality than about any other sexual activity, with the possible exception of bisexuality.

---

* Most forms of sex other than conventional intercourse are equally culpable before the law. A man performing cunnilingus on his wife or a woman performing fellatio on her husband is also breaking the law.

THE HOMOSEXUAL DOUBLE LIFE

I've led two lives for so long that I've forgotten what it's like not to be a sexual schizophrenic. For every social event—every public function that includes people I know professionally—I've got to have a date. If I meet a girl whose company I really enjoy and begin to see her steadily, she wonders why I don't make a pass. And I've got to terminate the relationship. I'm the target of all my friends' wives who want to fix me up with their single girlfriends. Finding different girls for every date is exhausting. I spend more time lining up girls than most straights do. The best thing is to find a discreet lesbian in the same boat that I'm in. That way, we play beard for each other. I sometimes wonder if the job is worth it. Or am I fooling myself? Does anybody care but me? There are guys in my line who we all know are gay. But the others shun them. You know they're not going to go far. I sometimes think that they don't give a damn, that they like things just the way they are. They don't want to play my game. God knows it's hard. Some of my straight pals bore the shit out of me.

Many homosexuals are still forced to live two lives. For professional, social, or family reasons, the closet remains the only alternative for them. One often finds this type in the big power fields such as banking, investment, heavy industry, labor, and government. At the very least, overt homosexuality is considered a security risk. Of course, it's a vicious circle: homosexuality is a security risk only so long as people think of it as one and the homosexual remains vulnerable to exposure. The moment it becomes an acceptable private pursuit, the homosexual becomes a smaller risk than the married man who is fearful that his wife will find out about an infidelity. That moment has not yet arrived.

The secret homosexual generally does not make his views known when the subject comes up in straight surroundings. He may even be so insecure that he feels impelled to convince people that he is antihomosexual on every level. His heterosexual friends usually know nothing about that part of his life. He often goes out of his way to avoid those homosexuals who are courageous enough to make their sexual natures known in the straight world.

The secret homosexual may have some gay friends, but they are usually as uptight as he is and in sympathy with his way of life, because they share it. He seldom makes any emotional commitments and prefers to cruise the gay bars and baths in search of the "one-night stand" for sexual release. He sometimes does not even know the name of the man with whom he had sex the night before.

It's a lonely life. Is society to blame for forcing it upon him, or is this inability to have an adult emotional life a part of his homosexuality? Each case is different. No definitive answers can be found until homosexuals are free to indulge their sexual choices without fear of reprisal.

THE HOMOSEXUAL SUBCULTURE

I hate the whole Greenwich Village-Upper West Side scene. The totally gay world. I think it's unnatural. Closing your eyes to most of the world. Before you know it, you're thinking the transvestite freaks are normal. They take to the streets representing the homosexual world, scaring the hell out of the straights. And that's how the Anita Bryants of this world win.

.

I just don't go places that won't accept the fact that my lover and I may kiss, or hold hands, or dance. If that's going to threaten the straights too much, to hell with them. They don't want me as I am, and I sure as hell don't need them as they are. Just give me my own places with my own kind. Equal but separate. Far be it for me to make those tight asses even more constipated.

Homosexuals tend to cluster in or near big cities, where it is easier to find others like themselves, as well as in restaurants, bars, and clubs in which they can feel free to display affection for another man. A private vernacular and special point of view have emerged from this restricted atmosphere that is part of what is called the "homosexual subculture." It is actually more closely related to minority behavior than to sexuality. Linguistic analogies might be found in the Yiddish slang that have infiltrated show business and the clothing industry, and the black street language that has entered the vocabulary of jazz musicians of all colors and the radical hip discothèque set.

Things often begin in the gay substratum that become fads in the upper or straight world. It has contributed unisex clothes and haircuts, a passion for nostalgia and old movies, and a phenomenon known as "camp" in which the clichés of the straight world are set up and normal sexual behavior exaggerated beyond the point of being merely ridiculous.

Homosexuals participate in the subculture in varying degrees. Some avoid it completely, while others spend all of their time in it. In many big cities, the far-out chic and homosexual subcultures have meshed and frequent the same bars, discothèques, and restaurants. Some of the formerly exclusively gay baths have nightclubs open to members of both sexes. Bette Midler, an entertainer who capitalizes on both nostalgia and camp, was discovered in one of them and has gone on to become the most popular entertainer with homosexual audiences since Judy Garland.

The large homosexual "coming out" has also spawned many serious projects dedicated to self-help. A group of counseling services, political organizations, health clinics, and churches have started to cater to the specific needs of the homosexual community. That is probably the largest distinction of this transitional period in homosexuality. It has become more of a community and less of a subculture.

20

BISEXUALITY*

Philosophically, I see bisexuality as the best of all possible worlds in terms of freedom and humanism. Personally, I am bisexual, and I feel I have always been and cannot be any other way. I will have my preferences but will not deny myself the pleasure of feeling arousal toward men and women. I feel badly for people who have shut this fact out of their lives, much less those who have not even the slightest notion of its existence.

The above statement is certainly a testimony of creed and lifestyle by the bisexual who made it. The positive qualities would assuredly be echoed by all bisexuals, were this the best of all possible worlds. Unfortunately, it is not for any of us, and especially not for the majority of bisexuals.

Heterosexuality, homosexuality, and bisexuality are the three major categories of sexual activity. All forms of specialized behavior are but subheadings under them. A man might be a sadist or masochist, but it would be within the framework of one of the aforementioned three. He might prefer cunnilingus, fellatio, or anal sex, but it would be practiced within that framework.

Of these three, the bisexual is the most isolated within his culture. Both heterosexuals and homosexuals are equally disdainful of him. Unlike the latter, he does not even have a subculture into which he can retreat. He cannot find a microcosm in which he can be comfortable, away from the menace of the larger world that will not accept him for what he is.

* The quotations come from interviews conducted by Dr. Klein for his book, *The Bisexual Option* (New York: Arbor House, 1978).

WHAT IS BISEXUALITY?

Nobody is quite certain of what constitutes bisexuality. Is it only an ability to switch-hit—that is, enjoy sexual relations with both sexes? Those who have accepted their bisexuality as an integral part of their lives would answer in the affirmative.

Since recognizing and then accepting my bisexuality, I need no longer take the stance that I am repulsed by my own sex.

•

I'm no longer afraid to touch men. I dig men and women. I think there are different sexual feelings one can have about each sex. I can enjoy without being disgusted a cock and balls, which obviously a woman does not have.

•

It's a good feeling to me not having to attach a strict label to myself sexually.

•

I'm not limited in choice. I don't like unnecessary limits and labels placed on me.

•

I feel complete in relationships with other human beings.

•

I find myself exploring closeness with people in different ways.

•

It's a learning process—to enjoy the uniqueness of both sexes.

•

You get to experience a lot of people from many different backgrounds. Different types. Everyone is unique, and that brings out different things in me.

These are bold and positive statements made by people who are able to accept their bisexual behavior. Among the experts, things are not so clearly defined, and there is little agreement on a definition of bisexuality. One group feels that only a man who is equally attracted to both sexes is truly bisexual (rating 3 on the Kinsey scale. See page 181). Others define it with specific reference to the number of bisexual experiences within a specified period of time or by the degree of attraction to both sexes (ratings

1–5). There are those who believe that if a man has had only one homo-sexual experience, he is bisexual.

I was only seventeen when I left Ohio and came to New York. I was a kid. On my own in the big city. It was goddam lonely. Jerking off was my only sexual outlet. One day I was walking in Central Park. This older guy started to talk to me. Right away I knew what was on his mind. But I didn't tell him to get lost. I sort of stayed with the situation. Maybe I was curious. Maybe I was just plain horny. Whatever it was, he saw that I wasn't discouraging him, so he made his pitch. He asked if he could suck my cock. He looked like a clean enough guy. I figured—what the hell—why not? It sure was better than all that jerking off. For the next two years I would meet him every now and then, whenever I was feeling hot. He always went down on me. And he en-joyed doing it. It was a great way for me to get my rocks off. And I never did anything to him.

This was obviously not a case of a single-experience molestation of an "innocent" adolescent by a "depraved" degenerate. The young man, John, C., knew exactly what he was doing and why. It was his single homosexual experience, and John never considered himself "gay" or even bisexual. It apparently gave him no psychological problems during the course of the affair. It was only "a great way for me to get my rocks off."

When he related the incident, he was a happily married, thirty-four-year-old automobile mechanic, the essence of everything that would super-ficially be considered "butch." The only other person who knew about the affair was his best friend, his "buddy." They both agreed that John was "straight." The crucial point was that he had never done anything to the older man. The delineation was in terms of "having been done" in contrast to "doing." There was no regard given to the ability to have an erection and satisfying orgasm.

Despite the bravura dismissal of the incident, John must have experi-enced some uneasiness. He never told his wife, because he feared that she would not understand, might consider him "a faggot" and question his masculinity.

Some experts would include John in homosexual statistics, others would consider him bisexual, while a third group would exclude him from either category and call him heterosexual with a negligible adolescent homosex-ual experience that would never have occurred had there been females available to him.

There are those who would question John's close, tell-all relationship with his buddy. He had no qualms about sharing an intimacy with him that he would not share with his wife. Referring specifically to this very close friendship, they would point out that sexual responsiveness can exist on an emotional level that has nothing to do with physical acts.

Most of us are completely heterosexual in our behavior. Physically, our bodies respond only to members of the opposite sex. Nevertheless, on an emotional level, we are able to relate closely to other men and even love them. The same is true of the complete physical homosexual. He can love women on an emotional level and sometimes displace that love into feminine services such as hairdressing, designing women's clothes, or interior decoration. The bisexual, however, is able to be completely intimate with both sexes on all levels.

"BUDDYISM"

Let us examine the phenomenon of "buddyism" as exemplified by John C.'s intimacy with his best friend. Is this a displaced form of homosexuality or bisexuality? Is there a subconscious sexuality to the need for a night out with the boys or, for that matter, an afternoon coffee klatch with the girls?

There are those who consider buddyism the latest manifestation of subliminal bisexuality in our popular culture. In the past, a Tom Mix or William S. Hart performed their deeds of derring-do and then rode off into the sunset alone. In contemporary films, a Paul Newman is much more likely to ride off into the sunset with a Robert Redford or Steve McQueen. There are always carefully planted heterosexual encounters between the two heroes and a series of women, but they amount to intercourse without involvement, or at least without deep emotional commitment: the latter exists only between the two men.†

Some even see a disguised bisexuality in the films of Humphrey Bogart, who has been called "the first truly modern mythic hero of the cinema." They see examples of sexual ambiguity in his best films. In *The Treasure of the Sierra Madre* there is the complex love-hate relationship among three men. In *Casablanca* he gives up the very feminine Ingrid Bergman and walks off into the misty night with the dandified Claude Rains, commenting that it looks like the beginning of a beautiful friendship. In *The Maltese Falcon* he turns the exotic Mary Astor over to the law, because his primary commitment is to avenging the murder of a partner of dubious character and morality rather than the defense of a woman he loves (albeit of equally dubious character and morality).

† Recently, there has been a reversal in which "buddyism" has been depicted in films as the strongest relationship experienced by women; i.e., *Julia* and *The Turning Point,* which are really little more than *The Sting* in drag.

Are we unconsciously drifting toward a recognition of duality in our sexual natures? There seems to be some evidence of it, and we find it threatening. The heterosexual often has more negative feelings about bisexuality than he does about homosexuality. After all, the bisexual also has heterosexual relationships with which he can identify. How can a man be a father and a faggot at the same time? If it can happen to the guy down the street, perhaps it can happen to him or his best friend. For some men, it's a terrifying thought.

ATTITUDES TOWARD BISEXUALS

Most homosexuals view bisexuals with disdain. They feel that they are basically homosexuals but are too cowardly to make the commitment. Bisexuality is a way station, another closet in which to hide their true feelings. In a recent television interview, Truman Capote stated that he did not believe there was any such thing as a bisexual. They were only homosexuals who had found extremely sympathetic women with whom they'd formed such close relationships that they were able to overcome their basic inclinations.

Until recently, many bisexuals would have agreed with Capote. They had great problems trying to resolve the conflict between heterosexual activity and homosexual feelings. When asked if he felt any shame, one bisexual replied: "Yes. I feel shame, anxiety, and guilt about homosexual pleasure, so I guess that applies to my bisexuality."

Many bisexuals have sought counseling or therapy for help in resolving their sexual conflicts. Considering the low esteem in which they are generally held, this is not surprising. What is astounding is that so many of them have such positive feelings about themselves.

It's not a question of pride. It's a question of *being*.

•

Pride may be the wrong word. Lucky is more like it.

•

I feel special, like being able to experience something others cannot.

Still, an ambivalence persists. Many feel an uncertainty about themselves and about other bisexuals with whom they become involved.

I accept my own bisexuality, but I'm not sure about other peoples'.

•

I'm ambivalent about it. Part of it is good and fulfilling, some of it is dehumanizing and demoralizing.

•

I'm still thinking about my feeling. I don't think I've been involved long enough to offer an opinion.

•

Part of me feels it's the only way to be, and part of me feels it's no way to be. I don't know.

The pressures of society and cultural patterns are certainly the greatest problems confronting bisexuals. Like the rest of us, they have been brought up in a culture that believes in monogamy as a positive value. Fidelity is inimical to a bisexual lifestyle. The moment one attempts it, he ceases to be a practicing bisexual and becomes homo- or heterosexual. The tensions of attempting to maintain a monogamous relationship can be unbearable.

I'm a jealous person by nature, and if the person I'm involved with is having other people, male or female, it can drive me right up the wall; as a bisexual, I understand. But understanding doesn't make the pain go away.

•

I have sex with other people of both sexes, and I feel guilty because it makes my lover jealous. What's happened is that in order to survive, I've become a really creative liar.

The need to lie and to conceal their true natures creates a major problem for many bisexuals.

I'm constantly aware, no matter where I am or who I'm with, that I must be careful with my secret. I sometimes long to blow it. Just to let it out and hang the cost. I never do, and the tension builds.

•

I want to be respected at work and with friends, but my bisexual secret increases my fear of being rejected.

•

There is just no way my mother and father would understand. I have thought of moving across the country, away from my family, so that they would never have to know.

•

It's difficult to choose a lifestyle. I can't be open to everyone, and sometimes I'm not able to decide what I want or conform to what is expected of me.

Once the bisexual has made his sexual commitment, society's disapproval remains the largest obstacle to finding happiness. Even when he wants to be open and frank, the almost inevitable rejection can be extremely embittering.

The most difficult thing is explaining to other people what I am. They just don't understand. It's funny, they understand variety in relationship to other things in life—like, say, if you go to a big city library, you have more books to choose from than in a small town library. But when it comes to sex, the most intelligent straight or gay person will just turn off on you. I really have kind of given up trying.

Although there are more bisexuals than homosexuals, there exists no bisexual subculture. The contacts are generally made either in hetero- or homosexual gathering places. The recent emergence of a few bisexual organizations, such as the Bisexual Forum in New York City, provide the only places where bisexuals can feel at ease among their own kind. Unfortunately, their combined membership is no more than from two or three thousand men and women. The reason for this low number may be inaccessibility. It may be lack of information. There are no bisexual equivalents of the homosexual magazines and newspapers which advertise bars and baths and announce homosexual community activities. It could also be that the bisexual's fear of public exposure extends even to other bisexuals.

Despite the negative feelings about them and despite their own fears and guilts, the position of the bisexual is improving. It has been helped by the generally more liberal sexual atmosphere and by the openness with which a number of famous figures in the entertainment world have not only candidly admitted their bisexuality but publicly paraded it. Their behavior has cast a light in which the bisexual can begin to view himself more affirmatively.

The formation of a bisexual movement, similar to Gay Lib, Women's Lib, and Black Power, would certainly help to change both society's negative image and the bisexual's own self-image. The situation, as it now exists, can be summed up in the words of one young male bisexual:

"It should be no big deal. But it is."

21

MASTURBATION

Masturbation serves a useful purpose, so useful, in fact, that if society did not have it, there would be serious dislocations and a substitute for it would have to be invented or discovered.

R. E. L. Masters
Sexual Self-Stimulation

All other types of sexual activity involve a man's body with the bodies of others; masturbation is his sexual involvement with his own body. It could be called "unisexuality" but is most often referred to as autoeroticism or onanism. The latter is a misnomer. The word derives from the biblical character Onan, who did not masturbate but instead practiced coitus interruptus, which is also known as onanism. The term's secondary meaning as masturbation probably stems from the fact that both acts are a wasting of the male seed in self-gratification and equally frowned upon in the Bible.

Autoeroticism is a word coined by the English psychologist Henry Havelock Ellis, who defined it as "the phenomena of spontaneous sexual emotion generated in the absence of an external stimulus." Masturbation is only one form of it. Others are the "wet dream" in which the ejaculation takes place in one's sleep, usually as the result of an erotic dream, and the unintended orgasm, which can be stimulated by pornography or even from the rhythmic movement of a train ride.

Masturbation seems to be a natural instinct in all animals. It has been observed in both the male and female of many species, in their natural habitat as well as in captivity, in wild as well as trained, domesticated, or tame animals. From childhood to old age, the majority of human males masturbate at least occasionally and often habitually.

METHODS OF MASTURBATING

Sometimes I masturbate just because it's the specific thing I want to do. It has nothing to do with being alone or not being able to find a woman. Beating my own meat is what I want to do most—what will give me the best feeling—the orgasm I desire at that moment.

Masturbation is the conscious manipulation of an erotic part of one's body for the purpose of sexual gratification. Most often, for men, it's "jerking off," milking the penis to bring on orgasm. The majority use their hands to masturbate, either the whole hand or only two or three fingers, establishing their own rhythm, touch, and speed.

The glans (head of the penis) is a highly erogenous zone for some men, and they get an extra charge out of manipulating it, partially or exclusively, in pursuit of the climax, while others work only on the shaft. There are those who derive the most satisfaction from beating down with some degree of force against the scrotum. There are others who love to lubricate the penis with spit, vaseline, oils, creams, or lotions.

Some men with sufficient dimensions use both hands, while others use no hands and get their kicks from sticking their penises between their thighs and rubbing them together. One group like to mattress- or pillow-fuck, while another enjoys making love to themselves, using the second hand to caress abdomen and thighs, to manipulate erogenous areas such as testicles, nipples, anus.

An assortment of mechanical aids are available, including vibrators (although these are more frequently used by women in masturbation), plastic vaginas, and rubber dolls. These, plus dozens of others, are on sale in "sex" shops and sometimes by mail order from companies specializing in distributing or manufacturing them.

In the novel *Portnoy's Complaint*, Philip Roth made a national joke out of masturbating with a piece of raw liver wrapped around the penis. Like all humor, it had its roots in reality. There are men who use liver to simulate the feeling of flesh in flesh.

When I first started masturbating, I did it while looking at that famous pinup of Betty Grable's rear. It was wild. From there, I graduated to Marilyn Monroe's calendar and *Playboy* centerfolds. In my fantasies I was a real tits-and-ass man. I still like to masturbate two or three times a month. Now I use some real pornography. I keep it hidden away from my wife and, when I feel the urge, sneak it into the bathroom with me. I love pictures of girls masturbating, even two girls doing it together. What I don't really dig is using one of a man and woman doing it together. Seeing another prick doing what I'm fantasizing mine is doing breaks my whole concentration.

Pornography is one of the most commonly used aids to masturbation. It often begins in adolescence, when a boy becomes so excited by the relatively innocent photograph of an actress or *Playboy* centerfold that he has to masturbate while looking at it. He may continue to resort to the same photograph, or another like it, or move on to hard-core material whenever he wants to induce orgasm. A pattern has been initiated that will probably persist for the rest of his life. How one masturbates is largely a matter of conditioning and habit.

ATTITUDES ABOUT MASTURBATION

I went to a parochial school. When we reached—oh, I guess it was about fourteen—one of the good fathers took us boys aside to preach a sermon on the evils of what he called "self-abuse." It was filled with fire and brimstone. At the very least, our hands would drop off. More likely, we'd spend eternity roasting in Hell. I don't know that it stopped one of us from masturbating. But it gave a lot of us a most unnecessary trauma.

For thousands of years, masturbation has been one of the most disdained and denounced sexual activities. It is a sin, an abomination before God, in the Judeo-Christian religions, with their emphasis on sex only for procreation. This attitude has been the source of some of the most patently absurd myths ever promulgated. Among them are the beliefs that it leads to baldness, feeble-mindedness, or blindness.

Many generations grew up believing that their genitals would be harmed by excessive masturbation. Actually, it is impossible to use the word "excessive" in the context of masturbation. What is too much for one man may not be enough for another. Some do it several thousand times more than others, and both may be the right rate for the specific men. They vary from those who've never done it to those who jerk off more than twenty-five times a week. With age, the frequency naturaly diminishes, but there are men who are still enjoying daily masturbation at the age of seventy-five.

But the guilts have persisted down through the years, and it was the rare exception for whom the act was not followed by some degree of regret. It is only in our own times that the situation is beginning to change. The re-evaluation of all of our attitudes toward sex is producing a more positive self-image for the masturbator. The new message is that there is a great deal of pleasure in store for all of us who open ourselves to the infinite varieties of sexual activity.

Masturbation should not be discouraged by parents. It is part of the child's process of self-exploration, a positive force in the development of body image, individuality, and in establishing object relatedness. A lack of any sex can be harmful to the creative process of growth. Masturbation, with its accompanying fantasies, is a great help in the development of the mature male. It helps to train his imagination in a way that can sustain creativity throughout a lifetime. The orgasmic release unlocks the joy of deep physical excitement.

To become responsible for our own orgasms is the beginning of individual liberty. This starts with masturbation. In one sense, it is a metaphor for independence.

Masturbation is not without dangers to a man. These should be balanced against its positive attributes. A man must not allow himself to become accustomed to the *easy* excitement inherent in the act. If he practices it to the exclusion of other sexual experiences, he can become trapped in his own controlled fantasy. The element of control is the negative side of masturbation.

Coping with another *real* body in sexual union is a merging of two control factors so that the act of building to orgasm contains elements of surprise that are often wildly exhilarating. The unhealthy masturbator is marked by a rejection of the unknown and uncontrollable. He often does not attempt intercourse, because he is secretly afraid that his body will only react to the self-induced fantasies that accompany his autoeroticism.

The healthy masturbator has no trouble releasing himself from private fantasy in the act of copulation. This man may masturbate every single day of his life without any ill effects, for he has the ability to see it as a separate and very distinct experience, quite different in psychic quality from intercourse.

All physiological studies prove that the same bodily changes take place during orgasms induced by masturbation as in those that occur in intercourse—thus, the objective pleasure or sense of release is as intense no matter what means of achieving it is practiced. To that extent, we can paraphrase Gertrude Stein and say that an orgasm is an orgasm is an orgasm.

There are many myths circulated about things that enhance the pleasure of masturbation. Some think that circumcised men enjoy it more, while others are positive that the balance of pleasure is weighted on the side of the uncircumcised. The presence or absence of a foreskin has no more effect on it than on any other form of sexual activity. The same is true of taking or abstaining from drugs during or just before masturbation. Those that enhance or inhibit other sex acts do the same for this one.

WHO MASTURBATES?

Certain personality traits are usually associated with the frequency of masturbation. A very inhibited or repressed man may not masturbate at all. Instead, he will displace the need into other activities such as excessive talking, addictive gambling, compulsive quarreling.

There is no universally applicable rule, but those who masturbate the most tend to be more introverted. They have a higher sexual drive when measured against all other forms of outlet.

I began to masturbate again when my wife got pregnant. I really got a charge out of it and didn't stop even after the kid was born. Sometimes I come into the bedroom when she's in it alone and start to jerk off in front of her. It's kicky when that gets her all sexy and she begins to go at it. And the two of us are pumping away. Looking at each other, getting hotter and hotter, until we come. It's a crazy scene, but sometimes I really dig it as much as anything we do.

Although men masturbate less often after marriage, it is generally not considered pathological for a husband to do it with some degree of frequency. Sometimes it is justified by abstinence during pregnancy or a wife's illness or by absence from her. However, there are married men who find it a pleasure in and for itself and do it even when their wives are available to them. There is nothing wrong with this so long as the man has a pattern of lovemaking with his wife that is satisfying to both of them. As a supplement, masturbation can be good. As a way of avoiding communication, it is suspect and can do real harm to a marriage.

If a husband fears rejection or feels angry, he should find a way of communicating this to his wife that does not entail his sexual absence from her. More arguments are made up in bed than by taking things in your own hands in the bathroom.

FANTASIZING

Ninety per cent of all men fantasize during masturbation. The married man should investigate these fantasies to see how they relate to his feelings about his wife. The following are cases in which the men were sufficiently disturbed to discuss their fantasies with a therapist.

While I was masturbating I could see my wife having continual sex with fifteen or twenty guys. It goes on for a long time, but she never gets off. She's begging for more for hours, begging to come, so more men are brought in. And finally she's on her knees with one man's cock up her rectum, another man's in her vagina, and a third in her mouth. That's when she comes bloody murder. And that's when I experience orgasm.

Further investigation indicated to the therapist that this fantasy represented the man's deep-rooted fear of his wife's sexuality.

In another case, a married man had the following fantasy while masturbating in a motel room during a business trip.

I am on an airliner crossing the country on a business trip. By chance, I'm seated next to a woman. She's on the inside near the window. We smile initially, but that's all. No conversation. About an hour later, it turns dark. The plane is quiet with most everyone asleep. The woman's about thirty, good-looking in a middle-class way, with a marriage band on her finger. She has large breasts with extended nipples showing through her nylon blouse. I notice that she's pulled her skirt up to her hips and her legs are open. I let my hand fall beside me on the seat. She looks at me invitingly, running her tongue over her upper lip. I lightly touch her thigh, and she turns in the seat toward me. We kiss. I feel her breasts and then slip her panties down to her knees, putting my finger in her vagina. She moans and reaches for my cock. I open my pants and she takes it out. It's hard and hot. She leans over and begins to suck it. Really suck it. Then she stops before I come, pulls down her skirt and buttons her blouse. She tells me she's going to the restroom and that I should follow in about a minute. She'll leave the door unlocked. When I get to the restroom, the door is open. She's inside sitting on the edge of a small sink, naked except for a pair of stylish high-heel shoes. There's not much room in there. She has parted the lips of her vagina with her fingers. It's very wet—so is her mouth when I kiss her. Then I put my cock in her standing up, and we fuck. In the fantasy, we come together. In reality, I come at that moment masturbating.

When everything in the fantasy is analyzed, it is a healthy fantasy for a man momentarily cut off from the possibility of marital intimacy. In this instance, it would have been healthy even had he experienced it in the bathroom at home with his wife asleep in the next room, because this man usually has an ongoing sexual relationship with his wife. The guilt factor was negligible and, in his words: "It was good. It was really good. I slept like a baby that night."

Men often fantasize during intercourse as well as during masturbation. There is a quantitative difference. These fantasies are effected by his sharing the experience with another human being. If the woman should groan, then one fantasy can be coupled with another because of her influence on the situation.

When a man uses fantasy to eliminate the woman as well as other external stimuli, intercourse approaches masturbation. He is using her as an object rather than a partner. Some men consider an alliance with a prostitute as the equivalent of masturbation. Some women consciously or unconsciously remove themselves from involvement and remain unresponsive objects being used by men, and this too can be considered a form of masturbation.

As a rule, the dangers of masturbation are far less than the dangers engendered by its prohibition. Not allowing children to masturbate is interfering with play. It is play in which fantasy and reality are given infinite game possibilities that aid in the discovery of how gradually to master sexual tensions. It is practiced without pathological overtones. It acts as an affirmation of what is to come, of the future, of the hope for existence beyond the present.

Masturbation is not unhealthy for the adult man so long as it doesn't interfere with his normal sexual interactions with a partner. It is a way of giving shape to what may become reality in the future, a way of releasing ourselves from frustrations that may cause neurotic displacement in other areas of our lives. Masturbation can be a very positive thing for any man when it enhances sexuality rather than substituting for it.

22

IMPOTENCE

There is confusion in some people's minds about the difference between impotence and sterility. Impotence is the inability to achieve or maintain an erection. It has nothing to do with being able to have an orgasm. A man can ejaculate with a flaccid penis. Impotence only applies to a condition of the penis that renders it unable to enter a woman naturally for intercourse.

Most men have some degree of impotence during their lives. But total impotence is relatively rare. The dysfunction is divided into two categories: psychological and physical impotence. The latter is caused by a real injury or disease (e.g. diabetes, accidents to and diseases of the nervous system, a generally run-down condition). It is sometimes a temporary ailment that can be cured by rest or medication.

Although there are few cases of physical impotence, the possibility of it must be excluded by medical examination before the treatment can commence for the psychological variety. Some of the causes of psychological impotence are: anxiety, stress, ambivalence about one's partner and/or the situation. Its consequences are manifold: depression (which can also bring it on), irritability, general hostility, hostility toward the sexual partner with whom one has failed, avoidance of all sexual contact.

Even if a man is incapable of achieving erection in any of his sexual encounters, he cannot be considered physically impotent if he gets one at any other time (e.g. the so-called "peepee hard on" in the morning). The man is afflicted with one of the degrees of psychological impotence.

VARIETIES OF IMPOTENCE

A man is suffering from primary impotence if he has never had an erection or never had one leading to a successful sexual encounter. It can be exemplified by the ability to achieve an erection while masturbating but not with a partner. A man has secondary impotence if he once functioned sexually but later developed total or situational impotence.

> I may not be completely faithful to my wife, but I'm not a chaser either. I like one mistress at a time. My wife once found out and confronted me. From then on, I couldn't make it with the other woman. No matter what I did, my cock wouldn't get hard.

As the name implies, situational impotence occurs in one situation but not in another. It is often a question of trust. If a man is at ease in a sexual situation, he can generally perform; if he's uncomfortable, he might become impotent. There are numerous examples: the man who's fine with his wife but not with his mistress (or vice versa), the man who's great in the dark but hopeless with the lights on, etc.

The solution to the problem of situational impotence is often as fundamental as removing the sufferer from the threatening situation. In the rare instance when this is not possible, the relatively small problem can intensify, and help should be sought either through an enlightened partner or therapy. It is basically one of the milder forms of psychological impotence and a problem only so long as the situation causing it is a problem.

The degrees of hardness of a man's erection can vary from moment to moment during a single sexual encounter. This has nothing to do with impotence unless even a partial erection is never achieved. It is perfectly normal to be completely flaccid, have a partial erection, and a full one within the span of one sexual incident. Hardness depends upon the eroticism of the situation, the degree of desire at the moment, general physical condition, psychological orientation, and the excitement generated by internal or external stimuli.

Some men mistakenly think that an erection must endure for as long as the objects of their desire are present. They worry about impotence if they cannot achieve another erection almost immediately after orgasm in preparation for a second round. There is a refractory period during which time is required to rebuild the energy necessary to produce an erection. This varies with the man and the situation. Generally, younger men need less time than older men.

When I was still a kid, there was one girl who put out for almost all the boys. Coming from the homes and backgrounds we did, we'd gladly lay her, but none of us would respect her or be caught dead taking her on a date. Before I got a chance at her, I'd listen to my friends boast about how well they did with her. My turn finally did come. I was so nervous I couldn't get a hard on. Worse than failing with her was the fear that she'd tell the gang.

Fear of judgment or comparison of our performance to others can produce such anxiety that we may be rendered psychologically impotent. There may also be a certain amount of conscious or unconscious hostility toward our experienced partner. If she is understanding as well as experienced, she will realize that this may well be due to a highly sensitive and questioning nature. She will know that the problem is best overcome by an exchange of loving vocal and/or physical (touching) communication. Patience and tenderness often provide the solution. If she is incapable of that, the judgmental becomes situational, and the "cure" is to put on your pants and go home.

Fear of failure will often lead to failure, and fear of impotence can cause impotence. However, it is a very human failure. Masters and Johnson have demonstrated that the man who fears impotence is a "spectator." He is continually watching himself in the role of participant and preventing his reflexes from doing their job: the result is psychological impotence.

THE EFFECTS OF DRUGS AND DIET

A number of drugs impair psychological responsiveness directly or indirectly. Some of the more common ones are: the anticholinergics (Probanthine, atropine, etc.), which inhibit the erectile response; the antiadrenergics (ergot alkaloids, some of the antihypertensives), which directly diminish ejaculation and indirectly work on the sex drive and erection; barbiturates, narcotics, and antiandrogens—all impair sexuality to a greater or lesser extent. Small amounts of alcohol may stimulate sexuality by releasing inhibitions; large amounts interfere with performance.

Did I ever tell you the story about —————— ——————. Great director back in the days when I was still making pictures in Hollywood. What a boozer that guy was. One night we were all at a party together. His wife and him. Me and my wife. As usual, he was in his cups. We were standing around gassing, when this little starlet comes up who is stacked. But I mean stacked! In front of his wife, the great director turns to this bimbo and asks her to accompany him to the garden for a quick fuck. And the bitch goes. Me and the missus don't know what to say. The wife, who is a real lady, merely smiles at us and says: "Relax. I know something about John that he doesn't know about himself. He can't get a hard on when he's drunk."

Diet can also play an important part in sexual functioning. Eating too much or too soon before sex can result in passing impotence, because the body is so occupied with digestion that it may not be physically capable of erection. Food is often a substitute for sex but seldom a prelude to it. Conversely, strenuous dieting and rigorous exercise may produce a desirable body, but it can hamper the ability to perform with the partners it attracts. Sex is itself strenuous exercise, and men are not up to it after workouts that have used up the limited energy provided by the foods in dietary regimens.

No food or drug is an aphrodisiac. All the olives and oysters in the world will not help to maintain an erection or increase the number of orgasms that can be produced successively.

Certain drugs appear to enhance sexuality, but they act only on specific people in specific situations: generally, those who have prepared themselves psychologically for their beneficence. Marijuana is a good example. Some swear that it works wonderfully on muscle contractions and generally increases eroticism. Others are not stimulated at all and even find that it causes a diminution of sexual drive and functioning.

THE CAUSES OF IMPOTENCE

Obviously, there are many things that may cause psychological or temporary impotence in men whose bodies are organically capable of erection. None are irremediable; many are not even serious; most need no more than the simplest adjustments to reverse the situation.

A man's body is a magnificent organism containing many delicate and interrelated parts. If it is not functioning well sexually, it is a good indication that the body is not being looked after properly. Fatigue must be avoided, for when a man is exhausted, impotence can be a brake that halts additional body activity.

Neither too much nor too little is the best rule as far as sex is concerned. Intercourse is not a vehicle for proving either piety or prowess but one that finds its chief functions in procreation and pleasure. Too much sex can adversely affect the quality of sex. More than the body can handle can cause temporary impotence. The sex motor needs a period of idling. No matter what a man's fantasy may be, his penis is not made of steel, nor is it a toy erector set to be constructed and taken down at whim. It is flesh and blood linked to mind and heart. It must have rest and relaxation to perform at its peak of capacity.

The older a man gets, the more fearful he becomes of impotence. He should bear in mind that as he ages, he functions differently in almost every area of his life. It takes more effort and a longer time to climb a flight of stairs. It requires more physical manipulation of the penis to attain an erection. Older men are usually content with fewer orgasms, although this is an individual matter. There are men over sixty known to have intercourse two or three times in one day on a regular basis, and men in their twenties satisfied with two times a week.

If sexual expectation is not unrealistic, impotence will not occur. Older men should not expect an immediate erection and to have it automatically recharged two minutes after an orgasm. That is almost universally impossible, and the disappointment might lead to self-doubts which, in turn, could result in impotence. Sexual pleasure is not one of the privileges denied to age, but, alas, that does not mean that age has the agility to pursue it with youthful ardor and energy.

Every man of every age has a potential for impotency: temporary, permanent, physical, psychological. For example, any kind of pain can bring it on, for pain causes stress, and stress is the antagonist of erectile functioning (except in the case of masochism, a sexual disorder to be discussed later in the book).

The foreskin can only cause impotence when it causes pain. *Phimosis* is the condition in which the foreskin is too tight to be drawn back over the glans. Erection causes pain which continues through intercourse. Anticipation of this can be a direct cause of impotence. The sufferer should consult a doctor immediately about the possibility of circumcision. There are no instances in which the latter is a direct cause of impotence.

I feel a little foolish about it. But I order undies for my wife from that Frederick of Hollywood catalogue. It really turns me on when she wears that stuff. But it's okay, 'cause she thinks it's a gas, too. It's been fantastic for our sex. We do it much more now.

Role-playing can influence impotence only in the sense that it fills a man's special need, and when this is frustrated, he often cannot perform. Some men are never impotent so long as they assume either dominant or passive roles, depending upon their needs. Many men request that their sexual partners assume roles capable of eliciting erotic responses. Most of these are fairly subtle and can often be requested in indirect ways, but some are as blatant as the case of the man who can only get turned on if his partner wears a maid's uniform. There is nothing wrong with role-playing as a spur to heightened sexuality, if both participants agree to it and are mutually satisfied in the relationship.

> She was the most gorgeous thing I'd ever seen. I pursued her for weeks, took her to only the finest places. Treated her like a queen. I really was hot for this girl. Finally—finally, she agrees to having a little affair with me. I'm so excited my hands are trembling. I can barely unbutton my clothes. Then we're in bed together. Without clothes, she's even more divine. You know what happens? I strike out. I kid you not. All that buildup. And I can't make it!

A surplus of love, zeal, or passion can create the kind of inner conflict that leads to psychological impotence. The passion involved in the pursuit of a very desirable woman can sometimes produce enough anxiety to create impotence at the moment of conquest. The woman has become a goal and, once attained, the prospect of performance becomes overwhelming. What if he fails? What if he doesn't live up to her expectations? or she to his? A block is set up. If the woman is as tender and understanding as she is desirable, she will probably be able to help him. If she isn't, the trauma may cause problems of impotence that last much longer than the situation.

> She had turned our sex life into a contest. She was coming on so strong, so aggressively, that I lost all desire for her. Not only couldn't I go to bed with her, I didn't want to any more.

The contemporary man can be victimized by the liberated woman in her new role of sexual aggressor. If that aggression, and the sexual power implicit in it, threatens his self-esteem, situational impotence is a possibility. Women should not become so absorbed in their own needs that they forget that sex involves two people.

Although everybody is ultimately responsible for their own orgasms, sex can be most rewarding when the erection is a collaborative effort leading to mutual fulfillment. The man who feels too strongly that it is solely his responsibility can cause unhappiness for both of them. No man should feel that it is his duty to exhibit a full erection the moment he is naked with a woman. The lack of one can induce impotence for the entire period of the involvement.

> I'd been dating this gal for about a week before I made it to her bed. But I couldn't get a hard on. It was a new scene to me. I was really unstrung. For

two hours we tried everything. Zero. I gotta say—she was very nice about it. We finally decided to get some sleep and try again some other time. In the middle of the night, I woke up with such a hard on you wouldn't believe. I was so proud you'd think I never had one before. I woke her up immediately, crying—"Hey, baby, look at this fucker!" And we did it. It was so great we did it again a half hour later—and a third time in the morning. But how about that first failure? I'm telling you—I'm worried about that shit.

Too many men expect to be hard at all times with all women. The responsibility for this unnatural demand upon themselves becomes too much to bear and causes impotence. It may also bring forth a hostility toward the women whom they most desire.

I don't know what I feel about her any more. Half the time—I could cheerfully kill her. The other half—I think she's the most wonderful thing that's ever happened to me. It's made a shambles of our sex life.

Hostility toward a woman can sometimes create actions in a man designed to punish her. Impotence may become his unconscious means of withholding love. In other cases, hostility is simultaneously mixed with positive feelings about the woman. There is ambivalence and, in the sensitive male, any form of ambivalence can lead to psychological impotence.

Because of his own pain, the psychologically impotent man often does not realize that the woman with whom he is involved is also suffering. He should try to let go of his guilt and assume some responsibility in the situation. He must reassure his partner in a loving way so that he, in turn, will be reassured. If she is understanding, she can help to try to find a solution for both of them. A deep bond of trust evolves from this sharing. Once trust is part of their union, he is on his way back to his former potency.

If the woman is too cruel or too impatient to help, the man should review the entire relationship rather than only its sexual part. He should avoid provocative situations if the impotence persists, and have sex only when he is certain that there is no hostility involved. Our immediate and intimate environment affects all of our reactions and reticences.

If the feeling of hostility persists, a change of partners may be the only solution. The intrapsychic situation may be so out of control that the impotence will continue with a number of women. It is at this point that professional help *must* be sought. It is always available, and if the initial relationship is important enough, it should definitely be sought at the beginning.

In marital psychological impotence, the pattern of sexual relatedness between husband and wife must change if the condition is to improve. It may be that he has felt an obligation to please her at the expense of his own pleasure. Whether he has imposed this explicitly or implicitly, it has become a source of constant pressure. She must remove it by letting her husband know that she is making no demands beyond what he desires or feels is possible.

Many couples find enormous joy in the simple sensuality of touching, holding each other during this trying period. The tenderness is sometimes as transcendent as the sex act. They are redefining themselves through a return to innocence. A new closeness begins to blossom in the warmth generated by two people who care enough to defer coitus. This tender deferment of sex as the only goal often leads back to it in a natural and spontaneous way.

If a man follows his own inclinations in sexual activities, impotence will not be a major problem. He will surely be "turned on," unless those inclinations cause internal or external anxieties. In that case, the turn-on will not happen: our penises are the sensitive barometers of sexual storms.

Impotence happens to every man at one time or other during his life. The more sensitive he is, the more often he is likely to experience it. A man who is impotent in conditions that go against his basic nature may be right or wrong in what he values, but his impotence is reasonable.

There is nothing to recommend a man who can maintain an erection and perform sex acts under such horrendous conditions as rape or "gang-bangs." One might almost say that he suffers from an unreasonable potence.

CURES FOR IMPOTENCE

Physical impotence cannot be cured so long as the physical condition that causes it is not cured. Devices and mechanical implements are available for the physically impotent man to use as aids in pleasing his partner. One can use an artificial penis (dildo) or vibrator. There are also penile splints to help him achieve coitus. Recently, there has been some experimental surgery with a silicon rod implantation as a method of making the penis hard enough to have intercourse. Not all of these devices help the impotent man, but they may please his partner. There are also things that she can do to give him pleasure. At times, fellatio and masturbation will help him to achieve orgasm even with a flaccid penis.

In cases of psychological impotence, therapy has proven the most widely used and efficacious cure. It has also been known to improve the functioning of some victims of physical impotence (e.g. diabetics) by ameliorating those psychological components that might also be present.

Contemporary therapy has progressed to the point where most cases of impotence can be satisfactorily resolved in a short time. Therapy must be elastic enough to accommodate the specific problems encountered in handling the different causes of impotence.

Authorities in the field have used many methods of treatment. These include hormones, various medications, vitamins, behavioral modification, psychotherapy, psychoanalysis, the Masters and Johnson method, marital therapy, counseling, group therapy, or a combination of two or more of these approaches. All have been successful in certain cases. For secondary impotence, some therapists and clinics claim success in over 80 per cent of the cases.

Many recent clinical reviews have demonstrated that short-term symptom-focused forms of sex therapy are superior to their lengthy insight-focused counterparts. The Masters and Johnson method was the first systematized short-term sex therapy. It utilizes many behavioral techniques and procedures.

The therapy is conducted by a team of therapists: one male and one female. The couple is seen both separately and together. Coitus is prohibited at first, which takes the pressure of performance off the man and relieves him of the fear of failure.

Assignments are given to the couple. The first is "sensate focus" (focusing on the giving and receiving of sensory pleasure by massage). It enhances nonorgasmic eroticism.

It is necessary for the couple to come to the Masters and Johnson Institute for two weeks of therapy during which they are seen daily. At the end of this period, they will presumably be functioning normally.

Variations on this system have also worked well. Each therapist or clinic employs different amalgams of treatment procedures. One might use medication and another delve into inner conflicts. Some will tackle the basic relationship, while others take a more physical approach, insisting upon the educative technique of giving physical examinations of the couple in front of each other.

Whatever method is used, the goal of therapy is constant. It is to enable a man to return to successful functioning through the reduction of both internal and external anxieties.

23

PREMATURE AND RETARDED EJACULATION

PREMATURE EJACULATION

There is no universally accepted definition of premature ejaculation. Among those most frequently offered are:

1. Any ejaculation occuring before it is desired
2. Lack of control of the ejaculatory reflex
3. Ejaculation within 15–30 seconds of intromission
4. Ejaculation immediately or within 5–10 strokes
5. Not satisfying one's partner, no matter how long one delays ejaculation

Obviously, the last definition is the least valid. If you delay your ejaculation for at least five minutes of coitus, and your partner still hasn't come, the problem is her slower climb to climax and not one of premature orgasm. We'll be discussing some of the things you can do to achieve greater control of the ejaculatory reflex, so that you can hold back until most women are ready for orgasm, if they are not suffering from their own physical or psychological problems.

Premature ejaculation does not exist as a problem if both people "get off" and are satisfied within the condition, even if only thirty seconds elapse between intromission and orgasm. "I banged her" or "He banged me" are common expressions for this sort of jackrabbit sexual encounter.

We spent so much time before, getting all hot and bothered petting, and sucking, and kissing, and jerking, that by the time I climbed aboard, we were both like pistols, and we went off before we knew it. It was sensational.

•

I come too quickly. I know it. I've tried to control myself. But I can't. Some women don't seem to mind. Some even come as quickly as me. But most of the others—well, I guess it's pretty frustrating for them. They get very uptight with me. But there's nothing I can do about it.

•

Whether they want to admit it to you or not, most guys come too quickly to satisfy women. But it's abnormal—freaky—to hang in there poking away for ten or fifteen minutes.

As there is no acceptable definition, so there are no firm statistics on how often premature ejaculation does occur. Many specialists claim that it is the most common male sexual dysfunction. Whether or not one agrees with them, it does happen often enough for many sex therapists and clinics to report a large number of men seeking treatment for the condition.

There are rare instances of premature ejaculation caused by urethritis, prostatitis, multiple sclerosis, and other neurological disorders. If the onset is sudden and free of accompanying psychological factors, a medical examination is in order.

THE PSYCHOLOGICAL ROOTS OF PREMATURE EJACULATION

Unless a woman makes me feel good about being with her, I come quickly. I just want to get it the hell over with.

•

You don't mess around when you know a girl's father is right in the next room. It's got to be over and out as fast as possible.

Within a psychoanalytical framework, premature ejaculation is viewed as an unconscious ambivalence toward women, accompanied by a desire to deprive them of pleasure and simultaneously defile them.

The behaviorists see it as a conditioned and learned response. Masters and Johnson propose that the man's early sexual experiences usually included a pattern of rapid ejaculation (e.g. in the back seat of a car or hurriedly with a prostitute).

Other theorists postulate as causes: anxiety, relationship problems, too little sex, a rapid ejaculatory reflex, or a lack of control of that reflex. Whatever has caused it, premature ejaculation can lead to secondary impotence because of the anxiety engendered by it. The reverse is not true: impotence has little effect on the ejaculatory reflex.

There can be a reasonable manifestation of the problem. Reasonable premature ejaculation is when the circumstances warrant the condition. If a man is having sex with an extremely desirable woman for the first time, his passion may be so high that rapid ejaculation is quite reasonable. Anxiety also makes it reasonable to come quickly: sex in an automobile while fearing an interruption by the police, in a girl's home when her parents or roommate might arrive momentarily, or in one's own home where the children are likely to burst in unannounced.

> When my wife and I are on vacation, our sex life is terrific. It's relaxed. I take my time. We really enjoy each other. But once we get home and I'm back at the old grind, I know I'm too fast for her. I try to keep up the movement even after I come, but a lot of the time I go limp in her.

Situational premature ejaculation occurs when it happens in one time or place and not another (e.g. with one's mistress but not one's wife, or vice versa; in the woman's home but not the man's; with the first orgasm of the evening but not with subsequent ones; only on first dates, etc.).

Expectation of the condition can cause the problem. A change of internal expectation will cause a change in the ejaculatory reflex, but it's difficult without help. The relationship between a man and a woman can be the cause, but it can also be the cure. Many of the techniques prescribed require the co-operation of an understanding and patient woman.

CONTROLLING PREMATURE EJACULATION

Most of us have some degree of voluntary control over the ejaculatory reflex and can be highly stimulated for some minutes before orgasm. Any of us can train ourselves to add minutes to that time.

> When I feel it's about to happen, I squeeze very tight and try to name the states in alphabetical order. Not out loud, of course. Sometimes, I get as far as Georgia. More likely, I come right in the middle of Connecticut.

The various "common sense" tricks do nothing to lessen sexual excitement or lengthen the time before ejaculation. Thinking of mathematical equations solves nothing except, perhaps, the equation. Staying power is not to be found in clenching muscles or teeth or digging nails into palms. When a man reaches the height of erotic arousal, he will have little control over his orgasm, and those suffering from premature ejaculation will continue to suffer.

For the premature ejaculation that most of us experience at one time or another, there is a simple and pleasurable solution. Continue to make love, have sex again as soon as possible. The ensuing orgasms will probably be sufficiently under control to give sexual pleasure to both partners.

Some try drugs. Local anesthetics numb sensation in the penis, thereby slowing the ejaculatory reflex. But numbing sense is a dubious method of enhancing pleasure. Some take tranquilizers or antidepressants just before sex. When ingested, these work directly on the nervous system and ejaculatory center. Nevertheless, drugs are only a stopgap—all right at those times when one might reasonably expect to be too quick, but not a cure for those with chronic conditions. When the dysfunction is unreasonable, it is better to learn control by using some prescribed techniques.

The "Semans" and "squeeze" methods are the two best-known techniques for coping with premature ejaculation. Both work on the principle of becoming familiar with the sensations of sexual excitement and stopping stimulation just before the climax is reached. In this way, a man learns how to bring his ejaculatory reflex under greater control. Both techniques need co-operative sexmates.

The Semans technique begins with the partner manipulating the penis until the man feels that he is about to ejaculate. At this point, she stops the stimulation until he either partially loses his erection or feels that he can be stimulated again without ejaculation. This eventually leads to longer and longer periods of reflex control.

Step two has him lying on his back, while she gently lowers herself on him until penetration is accomplished. He remains still while she moves up and down on his penis, halting at any point that he feels he might ejaculate.

In step three, the man does the thrusting up into her. He stops whenever he feels that he is about to come.

In step four, he assumes the male-on-top position and continues to thrust into her until they have both achieved orgasm.

The man will not complete all steps of the Semans method the first time that his partner and he try it. It may take many times, but eventually he will be able to go all the way.

Masters and Johnson recommend the squeeze technique, which is very similar to the Semans method. Instead of stopping and waiting for a partial reduction of erection or lessening of ejaculatory inevitability, the woman squeezes the erect penis just behind the glans, using her thumb and second and third fingers. This helps to lower the ejaculatory threshold.

If used with patience and diligence, either method may clear up the condition within a few weeks. Professional help should be sought if they yield no results. These more complicated cases need sex therapy, psychoanalysis, or family counseling.

The good news for those suffering from premature ejaculation is that, of all sexual disorders, this one has responded to therapy with the greatest degree of success. Most therapists and clinics report close to 100 per cent results in a relatively short period of treatment.

RETARDED EJACULATION

Retarded ejaculation is much rarer than premature ejaculation or impotence. It is a condition in which a man's ejaculatory reflex is inhibited so that he has difficulty in achieving orgasm or is entirely unable to reach the climactic point. Everybody has experienced it to some degree at one time or another, but it is only momentarily troublesome. Starting with the least difficult to deal with, the degrees of severity are:

1. Transitory problems in ejaculation
    a. Situational—difficulty in one circumstance and not another (e.g. with one woman and not another, one intercourse position and not another, one place and not another)
    b. Reasonable—extreme fatigue, illness, a fight with one's mate, having had a number of orgasms shortly before
2. Never having been able to ejaculate in the vagina
3. Never having had an orgasm with a partner, although able to ejaculate alone by masturbating
4. Primary retarded ejaculation (never having had an orgasm under any circumstances)

There are rare instances of retarded ejaculation that are caused by physical problems such as any general illness, hormonal imbalance, a neurological problem, prostatitis. Most cases are psychological in origin and the causes can be multiple, unconscious, and deep-rooted, or they can be simple and easily explained.

Experts view the affliction according to their own orientation. Psychoanalysts hold that retarded ejaculation is a symptom of man's unconscious fear of being abandoned and of his inability to express hostility in other ways.

The systems theory claims that it is the result of problems in the relationship and a form of rebellion or fear of reprisal.

The behaviorists believe that it is a learned, conditioned response with individual causes sometimes motivated by a specific trauma (e.g. a married man caught in bed with another woman).

Other theorists contend that it is a symptom of anxiety and guilt.

Recently, several sex clinics have reported an increase in patients with retarded ejaculation as the main complaint. The patients report a variety of complaints stemming from it: irritability, depression, hostility, a necessity to masturbate after each encounter, avoidance of intercourse, complete abstinence from sex. At the extreme, it produces secondary impotence.

Taking a long time to have an orgasm (let's say more than five minutes) is not a sign of retarded ejaculation unless one wants to come and cannot. Even then, it is no cause for concern if a pattern is not established.

Those truly suffering from the affliction can be helped by a co-operative partner, provided there are no deep-seated conflicts or unconscious hostilities. She begins by exciting him outside the vagina by masturbating him or performing fellatio. After a period of arousal in this fashion, he gradually begins to ejaculate in the vagina. This method is based upon the principle of removing the pressure to perform.

Professional assistance should be sought if one fails in all of the attempts to help oneself. It is easily curable if the dysfunction is an independent problem. The more linked it is to deep psychological disturbances, the more difficult it is to remedy. However, sex clinics and therapists do report a large percentage of cures no matter what the cause for the retarded ejaculation. They usually employ behavior therapy for milder cases and in-depth psychotherapy for the more complicated ones.

24

SPECIALIZED SEXUAL BEHAVIOR

We don't make a habit of it—but there have been times when I've put on my wife's undies and just laid back on the bed. And she's undressed me and got on top of me and played the active role. It's exciting to both of us. A kind of erotic joke.

Specialized sexual behavior may be defined as any departure from the accepted norms during foreplay and coitus. It is concerned with those perverse things that turn some men on that are very largely defined by the accepted social mores of the society in which he lives. What is defined as a disorder in one time and place is considered permissible sexual activity in another. Thirty years ago, in our own society, masturbation, fellatio, and cunnilingus were considered specialized sexual behavior. Today, a majority of the population engages in these acts, and they are rated as forms of normal and healthy sexual functioning. Until recently, homosexuality and bisexuality would have ranked high among specialized behaviors. They now tend to be recognized as forms of sexuality that are, themselves, plagued by the same dysfunctions and specialized disorders that beset heterosexuality.

We consider incest and pedophilia specialized behaviors. In other ages and societies, men were often encouraged to marry their cousins, and the pharaohs of ancient Egypt married their sisters. In many cultures preadolescents are given in matrimony, and child prostitution is a fact of life.

Nobody has ever come up with a general theory of causation that will cover every instance of specialized sexual behavior. The postulations are as numerous as the individual groups doing research in the field. The psychoanalysts believe that the majority of specialized sexual behaviors are regressions or fixations at early psychosexual developmental stages, and that they are almost always symptomatic of a castration anxiety. From a behaviorist point of view, they are learned and conditioned responses that tie the specialized behavior to sexual gratification.

Psychoanalysts see an exhibitionist as a man who is trying to assuage his fear of castration by proving that he has the equipment to perform sexually. The behaviorists believe that he is deriving sexual excitement from the exposure of his genitalia to women, obtaining positive justification from their shocked responses. The analysts concentrate on motivations for the acts, while the behaviorists find that the acts themselves are the significant elements. Beyond theories, each individual has a specific history and equally specific motivations for his behavior. Two people committing the same act will probably do so from different motives.

When we're alone, I like to dress up in my wife's clothes and do a record act. You know—I put on a singer—say, Barbra Streisand—and mouth the words, kind of imitating her movements. Then I go into my strip, sometimes showing an enormous hard on under my skirt. We end up in bed having great sex.

.

I casually take out a leather jacket I bought for my wife. She knows what that means. I really dig her in it. It's our sex jacket. She doesn't wear it any other time. She doesn't have to wear it. I guess we could have sex without it. I just like it better when she wears it. It's my little eccentricity, and she doesn't mind indulging me in it.

There are no verified statistics of the frequencies of the numerous specialized sexual behaviors. (See the glossary at the end of this chapter.) Some writers in the field claim that these behaviors, in one form or another, are practiced at some point by at least 70 per cent of the population, with more than 60 per cent taking part in them on a fairly regular basis during a given period in their lives.

The consequences of indulging in specialized sexual behavior are dependent upon the degree of reason involved in that behavior. There are few negative consequences to the more reasonable activities. If a man is turned on by a leather jacket (*fetishism*) or dressing up in his wife's clothes (*transvestism*), and his wife enjoys her part in the activities, then no harm is done to either of them. If he *must* dress up or have leather for sex, whether the woman likes it or not, his behavior is unreasonable and a danger to both the man and his relationships.

Sometimes I like to sneak up on the woman in my life and overpower her. Throw her down and tear away at her clothes, and really plow her—you know—like I'm raping her. You'd be surprised how many women really dig this. I mean it. That is—at least that's been my experience.

Rape is the most heinous of all specialized sexual behavior. Almost no condition can be envisioned that will make it seem normal or civilized, and yet many men have masturbatory fantasies of committing it. If they should find a woman who would enjoy it and comply with role-playing rape, as disturbed as that might be, the only real danger would be in an extension of this into other areas of life.

Like any other compulsion, sexual compulsion limits action. It should be treated professionally if it interferes with functioning to any large extent or poses a danger to others.

When his specialized sexual behavior is neither compulsive nor irrational, there is no reason for a man not to enjoy it. It becomes unreasonable only when it is his only form of sexual release, and it must be indulged in no matter how distasteful it may be to his partner and harmful to their relatedness.

Changing the pattern of behavior can sometimes lead to a lessening of compulsiveness and ultimately open the man to greater freedom of action. A fetishistic need for a woman to wear red lace underwear can be changed if the man makes a conscious effort to have sex without the garments. At first, it won't be as enjoyable, and he might even have difficulty functioning. But with the use of fantasy and an understanding partner, it is possible to change his behavior pattern.

A man should seek help when he cannot overcome his compulsions. The available forms range from psychoanalysis to behavior therapy. The type of therapy utilized depends upon the man's history, the severity of the condition, and his personality traits. Psychoanalysis or psychotherapy would be required to cure a profound compulsion causing difficulties with other people and with relationships. Isolated instances of behavioral idiosyncrasies can be handled by self-help or through some form of behavior modification.

E. F. Torrey, author of *The Death of Psychiatry*, summarized how sexual behavior can and should be viewed in our times:

. . . Sexual "deviations" are, of course, not real diseases at all. They are ways that people choose to relate to other people sexually. As such, they are merely a part of a spectrum of choices open to us. Some are common choices, some uncommon choices, but none are diseases.

To say that people "choose" a certain form of sexual expression does not necessarily imply a conscious element in operation. Our choices of the way we will relate sexually are usually a product of many things, some of which may be biological and many of which are clearly related to our early experience. Looked at broadly, it is not a person's *choice* of sexual expression which determines whether or not he has a problem, but rather his ability to achieve a satisfactory relationship within that choice.

GLOSSARY

BESTIALITY: Sexual acts with animals (also *zoophilia*). Kinsey reported that 17 per cent of all men raised in rural areas have reached orgasm with animals, and many more have had sexual contact of some sort with animals.

COPROPHILIA: Sexual gratification associated with feces or defecation.

EXHIBITIONISM: Exposure of genitals to an unwitting person or persons. The purpose is usually to shock rather than make contact. It accounts for 35 per cent of all sexual violation arrests.

FETISHISM: Sexual interest in an object (fur, leather, undergarments, etc.) or in a part of the body (feet, hands, specific hair color, etc.). In its most compulsive form, men are unable to achieve orgasm or even erection unless the object of their desire is present.

FROTTAGE: Sexual gratification by touching females while in public places, such as in buses, elevators, or subways.

INCEST: Sexual relations between blood relations. Every culture has different, often legal limits. In some, it includes nonblood relatives such as stepfather and stepdaughter. Most frequent between father and daughter, less frequent between brother and sister, least frequent between mother and son. The latter has strongest taboo associated with it.

MASOCHISM: Sexual gratification through experiencing pain (mental or physical) before, during, or after sex act. Name derives from the nineteenth-century masochistic writer Leopold von Sacher-Masoch.

NECROPHILIA: Erotic attraction to dead people. In its extreme, sexual violation of corpses.

OBSCENE COMMUNICATION: Sexual gratification via obscene utterance or language (also *coprolalia*) or through obscene telephone calls or letter writing.

PEDOPHILIA: Sexual desire for children. Greatest incidence between relatives (the "friendly" uncle), friends, or neighbors. Only small percentage involves "the monster on the corner."

RAPE: Compelling sexual intercourse by means of force or brutality, a combination of aggressive and sexual impulse in a single act.

SADISM: Sexual gratification through physically or mentally hurting or harming another. Whips, leather, and bonds are often used. At times, sadism and masochism (*sadomasochism*) are combined with transvestism and fetishism. The name is from the eighteenth-century French writer the Marquis de Sade.

TRANSVESTISM: Related to fetishism. Erotic stimulation from wearing women's clothes. Most often, transvestites are married men and non-homosexual.

TROILISM: Sexual gratification from watching one's partner have sex with another. It often involves two couples having sex in the presence of each other. Related to group sex, threesomes, a form of wife-swapping.

VOYEURISM (the "Peeping Tom" syndrome): Erotic arousal from watching other people having sex, most often unbeknownst to those observed.

INDEX